"I love it! *Contemporary Humanistic Judaism* is comprehensive, engaging, and compelling. I plan to assign it to my students."
—PHIL ZUCKERMAN, associate dean of Pitzer College

"Magnificent! The clearest and most engaging volume on the history and meaning of Humanistic Judaism ever written."
—RABBI EVAN MOFFIC, author of *The Happiness Prayer: Ancient Jewish Wisdom for the Best Way to Live Today*

"This is an important anthology that ought to be widely read and studied. It is essential to any college or adult ed course addressing the complicated map of current liberal Judaisms."
—RABBI EDMOND WEISS, coauthor of *Making Arguments: Reason in Context*

"Humanistic Judaism's contributions to the broader landscape of Jewish life are too often overlooked. *Contemporary Humanistic Judaism* will expand and challenge many traditionalist readers' sense of what Judaism is and has been—while simultaneously offering much-needed affirmation to readers with less-traditionalist instincts."
—LEX ROFEBERG, senior Jewish educator of *Judaism Unbound*

"Finally—a book that speaks wisely and powerfully to the secular Jew who seeks Jewish connection and meaning without traditional God-worship. *Contemporary Humanistic Judaism* is *the* crucial primer for all those who want to understand the foundational ideas of Humanistic Judaism and find the path to a vibrant Jewish life expressed through liturgy, ritual, education, celebration, and yes, the transcendent."
—ABIGAIL POGREBIN, author of *My Jewish Year: 18 Holidays, One Wondering Jew*

"*Contemporary Humanistic Judaism* is a must-read, especially for anyone who ever felt like a 'bad Jew' for not believing in God, for intermarrying, or for otherwise not conforming to traditional movements' constructions of Jewish identity."

—KEREN R. MCGINITY, author of *Still Jewish: A History of Women and Intermarriage in America*

"Through essays, case studies, liturgy, cultural offerings, and more, this important collection evocatively makes the case for deeply engaged, deeply principled, deeply intentional Jewish living that does not center God. *Contemporary Humanistic Judaism* demonstrates that, as ever, Humanistic Judaism raises essential questions about contemporary Judaism and offers piquant responses."

—RABBI DEBORAH WAXMAN, president and CEO of Reconstructing Judaism

Contemporary
Humanistic Judaism

JPS ANTHOLOGIES
OF JEWISH THOUGHT

University of Nebraska Press | Lincoln

Contemporary Humanistic Judaism

Beliefs, Values, Practices

Edited by Adam Chalom and Jodi Kornfeld

The Jewish Publication Society | Philadelphia

© 2025 by Adam Chalom and Jodi Kornfeld

Acknowledgments for the use of copyrighted material appear on pages 223–27, which constitute an extension of the copyright page.

All rights reserved. Published by the University of Nebraska Press as a Jewish Publication Society book.

Library of Congress Cataloging-in-Publication Data
Names: Chalom, Adam, editor. | Kornfeld, Jodi, 1956– editor.
Title: Contemporary humanistic Judaism: beliefs, values, practices / edited by Adam Chalom and Jodi Kornfeld.
Description: Lincoln, Nebraska: University of Nebraska Press, 2025. | Series: JPS anthologies of Jewish thought | Includes bibliographical references and index.
Identifiers: LCCN 2024028333
ISBN 9780827615649 (paperback)
ISBN 9780827619289 (epub)
ISBN 9780827619296 (pdf)
Subjects: LCSH: Humanistic Judaism. | BISAC: RELIGION / Judaism / Rituals & Practice | SOCIAL SCIENCE / Jewish Studies
Classification: LCC BM197.8 .C66 2025 | DDC 296.8/34—dc23/eng/20240829
LC record available at https://lccn.loc.gov/2024028333

Set in Arno Pro by A. Shahan.

This volume is dedicated to Rabbi Sherwin Wine, z"l, whose vision launched a movement; to our colleagues, many of whom are included here, for leading this movement forward; and to our families, for their unconditional love and support.

Contents

Preface: Introducing This Volume   xi

Acknowledgments   xv

Introduction: Judaism beyond God, Torah, and Israel   xvii

PART 1. Beliefs and Ethics

Introduction   3

1. The Jewish Experience   7
   Sherwin Wine, "Jewish History—Our Humanist Perspective" (1985)   8

2. The God Question   10
   Sherwin Wine, "Judaism without God" (1983)   13
   Yaakov Malkin, "God as a Literary Figure" (2007)   18

3. Positive Humanism   22
   Sherwin Wine, "Believing Is Better Than Non-Believing" (1986)   23
   Greg Epstein, "What Is Humanism?" (2009)   27
   Peter Schweitzer, "Purpose" (2021)   28

4. Ethics   30
   Daniel Friedman, "After Halakha, What?" (1996)   33
   Adam Chalom, "Are There Jewish Values?" (2009)   37
   Amos Oz, "Jews Argue with God" (2017)   42
   Denise Handlarski, "Truth and Reconciliation on Race" (2016)   45

5. Spirituality   47

    Yaakov Malkin, "What Makes the Secular Need Spirituality" (2003)   49
    Judith Seid, "A Secular Spirituality" (2018)   53
    Terry Toll, "Lighting Candles" (1994)   56
    Humanistic Judaism Facebook Discussion on Ritual Practice (2020)   59

PART 2. Identity

Introduction   67

6. Jewish Self-Definition   71

    Sherwin Wine, "Kinship" (1985)   73
    International Federation of Secular Humanistic Jews, "Who Is a Jew?" (1988)   77
    Association of Humanistic Rabbis, "Statement on Conversion/Adoption" (2005)   79
    Karen Levy, "Changing Perceptions, Changing Realities" (2002)   82

7. Welcoming and Inclusion   86

    Tamara Kolton, "Healing the Jewish People through Pluralism" (2005)   89
    Jeffrey Falick, "Dancing at Two Weddings" (2014)   91
    Miriam Jerris, "Gate Openers: Reaching Out to the Next Generation of Children from Intermarriage" (2017)   94
    Society for Humanistic Judaism, "Radical Inclusion" (2021)   98

8. Israel/Zionism and Diaspora   99

    Sherwin Wine, "Being a Secular Humanistic Jew in the Diaspora" (1993)   102
    Shulamit Aloni, "One Hundred Years of Zionism, Fifty Years of Statehood" (2000)   106
    Tzemah Yoreh, "Constructive Conversations about Israel" (2019)   111

PART 3. Culture

Introduction 117

9. Cultural Judaism 121

   Amos Oz, "A Full Cart or an Empty One? Thoughts on Jewish Culture" (1983) 124
   Yehuda Bauer, "Judaism Is . . ." (1995) 126
   Daniel Friedman, "Recovering Our Stories" (1995) 127
   Sivan Malkin Maas, "Cultural Zionism: Reclaiming Convention" (2009) 130

10. A Cultural Jewish Canon 134

    Julian Levinson, "People of the (Secular) Book: Literary Anthologies and the Making of Jewish Identity in Postwar America" (2009) 137
    Jodi Kornfeld, "Of Course There's Jewish Art!" (2022) 141
    Jonathan L. Friedmann, "Music by, for, as Humanistic Jews" (2023) 145
    Nathan Englander, "What We Talk About When We Talk About Anne Frank" (2012) 148
    Etgar Keret, "My Lamented Sister" (2016) 150
    Nicole Krauss, "Adding to the Jewish Story" (2017) 152

PART 4. Jewish Life

Introduction 157

11. Living Humanistic Judaism 161

    Eva Goldfinger, "Is Judaism Worth Preserving?" (1995) 162
    Society for Humanistic Judaism, "Statement of Values" (2021) 164

12. Liturgy 166

    Marcia Falk, "Honoring Torah" (1996) 170
    Adam Chalom, "Our Quarterback, Our King: Two Problems with Liberal Theology" (2007) 172

Adam Chalom, Jodi Kornfeld, Jeremy Kridel, Peter Schweitzer,
  and Frank Tamburello, "Liturgical Readings" (2019)   176
Yehuda Amichai, "A Man Doesn't Have Time" (1986) and
  "The Waters Cannot Return in Repentance" (1986)   180
Peter Schweitzer, "The Passover Symbols" (2003)   182

13. Life Cycle   185

Leadership Conference of Secular and Humanistic Jews,
  "Circumcision and Jewish Identity" (2002)   189
Camila Grunberg, "The Meaning of Life" (2016)   190
Association of Humanistic Rabbis, "Wedding *Ketubah*
  Texts" (1999)   193
Sherwin Wine, "Sitting Shiva" (1992)   195

14. Education   197

Mitchell Silver, "Treasures of the Legacy" (1998)   199
Ruth Duskin Feldman, "Jewish Education and
  the Future" (1991)   202
Sherwin Wine, "The Torah" (1985)   205
Denise Handlarski, "The Torah, the Ten Commandments
  and Us" (2019)   209
Society for Humanistic Judaism, Curriculum for Children's
  Education, "Philosophy" (2013)   211

Afterword: Choosing to Live as a Secular Humanistic Jew:
  Declaration of Eighth Biennial Conference of the International
  Federation of Secular Humanistic Jews, 2000   213

Go Forth and Learn   215

Source Acknowledgments   223

Appendix: American Jews' Identity and Beliefs   229

Notes   233

Bibliography   245

Index   251

Preface

Introducing This Volume

We are both Humanistic Jewish congregational rabbis who have studied and taught Humanistic Judaism, have modeled its values, and serve as leaders in the movement. Our paths to Humanistic Judaism differ—one was raised in it, and the other evolved into it from another Jewish denomination—but ultimately Humanistic Judaism has offered each of us a Jewish and philosophical basis for both our professional and personal lives.

Humanistic Judaism offers integrity in that we can say what we mean and mean what we say (in any language); it offers deep meaning in our celebrations, commemorations, and communities as we focus on human beings and human experience; and it offers affirmation of a Jewish identity rooted in Jewish culture. Humanistic Judaism empowers us with agency and authority over our lives. It gives each of us a deep, rich, and thoughtful Jewish identity resonant with our beliefs and actions.

Our Judaism is broadly defined as the collective historical experience of the Jewish people—a widely and wildly diverse experience that has helped foster the extraordinary resilience of the Jewish people. We also embrace the interpersonal diversity of Jewishly connected individuals and families, including those born Jewish, those adopting Judaism, and those who find themselves "fellow travelers" or loving partners in a wider Jewish family. These strengths are all reasons for celebration and optimism.

So, too, we welcome you, the reader of this volume. Perhaps you are intrigued to learn more about Humanistic Judaism, like many of those we meet attending a life-cycle event or holiday celebration who regret not knowing about us sooner. Perhaps you want to explore how Humanistic Judaism is both similar to and different from other approaches to Jewish life. Perhaps you are seeking your own path to reconcile a perceived conflict between being unabashedly Jewish and being an atheist, agnostic, or simply "God-questioning." You are in the right place.

About This Volume

This volume is designed to serve both individual seekers and those who teach comparative or modern Judaism in academic or informal settings. It aims to fairly and comprehensively present the contemporary Humanistic Jewish experience and core issues addressed by the movement. It defines the movement and helps answer many challenging questions Humanistic Jews face from other Jews, among them, "How can you (or your movement) be Jewish and celebrate Judaism if you don't believe in God?"

The introduction provides a historical and thematic overview of Humanistic Judaism. From there, we present and contextualize selected readings exploring the philosophical underpinnings and foundational ideas of Humanistic Judaism and then how that philosophy turns into lived Humanistic Jewish practice and experience. You will discover four parts, organized topically, each beginning with a broader essay introducing the subject. Part 1, "Beliefs and Ethics," addresses key philosophical questions of God, positive humanism as an alternative to being a "nonbeliever," how to define ethics without supernatural authority, and how Humanistic Jews find inspiration through secular spirituality. Part 2, "Identity," explores how Humanistic Judaism empowers individuals to define themselves as Jews, respects people's decisions to marry whom they love by welcoming them into a Humanistic Jewish community, and helps them navigate their place in the wider Jewish community, including Israel. Part 3, "Culture," articulates how Humanistic Jewish identity is rooted in Jewish culture, especially Jewish literature, art, and music. Lastly, part 4, "Jewish Life," demonstrates how Humanistic Judaism is expressed and practiced in liturgy, ritual, holiday and life cycle celebration, and education.

Each of the fourteen chapters features up to six essay selections. Some of these essays appear in chronological order (by date of publication), but usually the chapter's contents are organized to move from general to specific examples, from theoretical explanations to practical applications, and/or from the "beginning" to the "ending" of the content being discussed. By way of example, the selections on life-cycle celebrations (chapter 13) follow the sequence of the human life cycle from birth to death.

The book's afterword, "Choosing to Live as a Secular Humanistic Jew," expresses ten commitments of living a Humanistic Jewish life and, in so doing, summarizes Humanistic Judaism's beliefs, values, and practices in action. "Go Forth and Learn" offers our recommendations for ongoing exploration of the topics covered here in all forms of media—songs, artwork, and films included. Finally, the appendix presents data from the Pew Research Center's 2020 survey of American Jews showing that Jews are increasingly secular; a majority of respondents do not believe in the God of the Bible, and a majority identify as cultural Jews. In other words, the beliefs and self-conceptions of Humanistic Judaism increasingly meet American Jews where they are.

This book, then, is your invitation to get to know or deepen your connection to contemporary Humanistic Judaism. We hope it will help you better understand Humanistic Judaism as a movement and Humanistic Jews as an important part of the American Jewish community. If you are new to the movement, we hope you discover that Humanistic Judaism expresses much of what you have felt and believed for many years. If you are a longtime member or leader of a Humanistic Jewish community, we anticipate you will deepen your knowledge of the history and growth of the movement through its most important texts and ideas, collected here for the first time. The creative approaches to holidays and life-cycle celebrations described here may enhance your community's or your personal practices, and the issues explored in these selections will likely provide new insights into your chosen identity. Those seeking to explore Humanistic Judaism in even greater depth or in group study settings are encouraged to download this volume's complimentary discussion guide on The Jewish Publication Society's webpage https://jps.org/study-guides/. Both the Society for Humanistic Judaism (www.shj.org) and the International Institute for Secular Humanistic Judaism (www.iishj.org) also offer many online resources on their websites and through their active YouTube channels. We hope you will be inspired and uplifted by what we find so meaningful in our lives.

Acknowledgments

The editors gratefully acknowledge the following institutions and individuals for their financial support in bringing this volume to fruition: the Association of Humanistic Rabbis, the International Institute for Secular Humanistic Judaism, the Ron and Esther Milan Foundation, and Michael Egren through the Rochlin Grant.

We greatly appreciate the staff at The Jewish Publication Society (JPS), especially Rabbi Barry Schwartz and Joy Weinberg, who shepherded this volume from proposal to publication. Rabbi Schwartz, the JPS director when this volume was first accepted for publication, saw the value in the creation of this book, and after his retirement, JPS director Dr. Elias Sacks enthusiastically encouraged us in its completion. Managing editor Joy Weinberg deserves special mention, as she made sure, in movement terminology, that we always said what we meant and meant what we said. Our work greatly benefited from her keen eye and exceptional editing. We also express our thanks to the University of Nebraska Press for copublishing this volume.

We are very grateful for the early efforts of our colleague Rabbi Jeremy Kridel, who was instrumental in envisioning this project, creating the book proposal, and helping to choose the selections to include.

All of our colleagues contributing to this volume—Cantor Jonathan Friedmann and Rabbis Greg Epstein, Jeffrey Falick, Daniel Friedman, Eva Goldfinger, Denise Handlarski, Miriam Jerris, Jeremy Kridel, Karen Levy, Sivan Malkin Maas, the late Peter Schweitzer, Judith Seid, Frank Tamburello, and Tzemah Yoreh—set valuable examples of what it means to be a Humanistic Jew. We are grateful for their generosity to learn from them through their essays, liturgical pieces, and other commentary to effectively convey the tenets and traditions of Humanistic Judaism. We are especially indebted to the founding thinkers and leaders who have been the bedrock of this movement: Shulamit Aloni, Yehuda Bauer, Ruth Feldman, Yaakov Malkin, and most significantly, Sherwin Wine. We are standing on the shoulders of giants.

We are likewise grateful to those teachers, mentors, and institutions that helped us become rabbis through learning and experience. The International Institute for Secular Humanistic Judaism, which ordained us, helped us to refine our own understandings of Humanistic Judaism with depth, complexity, and rigor and empowered us to determine how best to conduct our rabbinate. Our own academic journeys have given us the opportunity to learn with outstanding scholars at Spertus Institute, the University of Michigan, and Yale University. We work with congregations affiliated with the Society for Humanistic Judaism, which provides resources, guidance, and expertise on which we draw frequently to support our members and ourselves. We have served in leadership roles with the Association of Humanistic Rabbis, experiencing both collegiality and support through good times and bad. Finally, because being a rabbi means lifetime learning, we are grateful to our own students of all ages at Beth Chaverim Humanistic Jewish Community and Kol Hadash Humanistic Congregation, who have always taught us as they learned.

Introduction

Judaism beyond God, Torah, and Israel

Attempts to summarize Judaism often claim three concepts connect all Jews: God, Torah, and Israel. In fact, nothing *divides* Jews as much as what is meant by "God," whether the Torah is of divine or human authorship (or both) and its resulting authority, and what constitute the (ethnic and political) boundaries of Israel. Jews debate whether God is immanent or transcendent, a cosmic force or an intervening personality, a presence in life or a character in Jewish literature and imagination—whether God made humanity or humanity made God. Jews dispute whether the Torah is a binding, eternal, God-given covenant with mandatory rules or a collection of timeless wisdom created by people under divine influence or a human composition with both lasting insight and limited values for contemporary readers—whether the Torah created the Jewish people or the Jewish people created the Torah. Jews wrangle over whether God chose Israel (both people and land), to what degree Israel is distinct from other religious/ethnic nations, and more—whether Israel defines the Jewish people or the Jewish people define Israel.

Humanistic Jews emphasize human power and responsibility rather than divine authority. They view god not as a divine force but as a literary character in the Bible created by human imagination.[1] They read the Torah as the beginning of the wisdom created, rewritten, and refined by the Jewish people over the centuries. They define Israel as both a world people and a modern country with the promise and perils of nation-states. These answers are no less Jewish for being nontraditional, because they are rooted in a cultural Jewish identity. Humanistic Judaism articulates the values and beliefs of a growing population of secularized Jews who define Jewish belonging, behaving, and believing on their own terms.[2]

Many twenty-first-century Jews are secularized, however one explores their Jewishness. A 2020 Pew Research Center survey identified 27 percent of all American Jews—and 40 percent of those aged eighteen to twenty-nine—as being "Jews of no religion."[3] Over half of American Jews describe being Jewish as a matter of ancestry or culture rather than religion, over half say they seldom or never attend synagogue, and 22 percent do not believe in God or a universal spirit.[4] Similarly, a 2016 Pew study of Israeli Jews showed that one-third never attend synagogue and a similar percentage do not believe in God or do not know.[5]

These figures are not surprising. American non-Orthodox Jews are more college-educated, more affluent, more urban, and more politically liberal than the general population.[6] All these features strongly correlate to secularization. In the United States, the growing proportion of Pew's "Jews of no religion," as well as the substantial numbers of "Jews by religion" who do not believe in "the God of the Bible," parallels the general "rise of the nones" among all Americans.[7] It also affirms the aphorism that the Jews are like everyone else, only more so.

Secular Jewish Identity without Secular Jewish Community

While the existence of secularized Jews is undeniable, their involvement in an organized Secular Judaism does not necessarily follow. Secular Jews have interacted with their Jewish inheritance in diverse ways. Some have consciously rejected traditional Jewish theology or liturgy or rabbinic authority. Others have drifted away from religious Jewish practices, such as following dietary laws. Many formed distinct Jewish identities and communities around Yiddish language and culture while rejecting "religion": they provided education and not ritual, their Jewish content was secular and not God-focused, and they organized schools and not congregations. Others emphasized universal human identity rather than particularism, essentially humanism over Judaism, as in the communities and ideology of Ethical Culture founded by former Reform rabbi Felix Adler (1851–1933). Still others have chosen to participate in liberal religious congregations without addressing the inconsistency between their personal beliefs and the congregation's liturgy and ideology. And still others have left their Jewish identity entirely behind.

Many narratives of Jewish secularization from the Enlightenment through the internet era demonstrate a similar pattern: after the initial joy of liberation (an exodus) comes the challenge of making choices (one's own self-definition). In this, even secular Jews who delightedly discover that Jewish identity is both possible and personally meaningful without traditional or even liberal Jewish theology tend to make two assumptions that also define the challenges of organizing a Secular Judaism:

1. The assumption that *Jewishness* may be ethnic, but genuine *Judaism* is primarily religious. Thus, any Judaism has to be based on the requisite—but, to the now-secularized Jew, irrelevant or even alienating—religious concepts of God, Torah, and Israel.
2. The assumption that no Jewish community of like-minded contemporaries exists—or has ever existed—with whom secular Jews could experience a shared secular Judaism.[8] In some cases, they know so few other secular Jews that secular Jewish community seems impossible. In most cases, secular Jews are unaware of the many varieties of secular Jewish community that thrived just a few generations ago.

In 1934, 10 percent of the children receiving a Jewish education—approximately 20,000 Jewish children—were enrolled in some variety of secular Yiddish school. The politically nonpartisan Sholem Aleichem Folk Institute, established in 1918, served about 2,000 students in 1934; initially it taught only Yiddish language and culture, before adding Hebrew to its curriculum in 1940. The Labor Zionist Farband taught both Yiddish and Hebrew as well as Zionist ideology (including encouraging *aliyah* to pre-state Israel); it founded the first Yiddish schools in America in 1910 and by 1934 taught about 5,500 students. The socialist yet anti-Soviet Workmen's Circle/Arbeter Ring (the American parallel to the European Jewish Labor Bund), formed in 1918, focused its education on socialist ideology as well as Yiddish language and culture; it served 6,000 students in 1934. A number of secular Yiddish schools that split off from Workmen's Circle in 1926 eventually became part of the communist International Worker's Order; they instructed their 6,800 students in communist ideology and Yiddish language and culture. These secular Jewish schools of all varieties met three to six days each week for one to two hours per day, providing a substantive supplemental Jewish education.[9]

Pre–World War II secular Jewish community was also more than just youth education. As scholar and activist April Rosenblum described it:

> Just as religious Jewish society had social institutions such as religious schools for children, *yeshivas* for higher religious learning, burial societies, kosher food outlets, and synagogues, so did secular Jews build a world of institutions in which Jewish secularism was the norm. Secular Jewish schools provided children with an education in academic subjects as well as Jewish history, Yiddish language and literature, and social justice ideals. One could read a multitude of Yiddish newspapers, sing in choruses, join activist organizations, send children to summer camps, live in apartment buildings—all created by and for secular Jews.[10]

Like contemporary secularized Jews, many of the adults in these organizations had been raised religiously and left it behind, and they too grappled with how much of their religious Jewish heritage could harmonize with their secular approach to life. A 1920 listing of Jewish holidays to be observed in Workmen's Circle/Arbeter Ring communities included "Passover—as the Jewish holiday of freedom..., Hanukkah—as the holiday of emancipation from the Greek yoke..., [and] Purim—as a children's holiday (for costuming, exchange of gifts and other amusements)" but omitted Rosh Hashanah, Yom Kippur, Shavuot, and other holidays evidently deemed too religious.[11]

These schools and communities suffered steep declines in the 1950s and 1960s. Secular Jews' political attachments to socialism and Communism were liabilities during the McCarthy and Cold War eras. The perceived importance of Yiddish diminished with increasing assimilation, reduced immigration, a postwar crackdown on secular Yiddish culture in the USSR, the death of millions of Yiddish speakers during the Holocaust, and the success of the State of Israel (leading to increased emphasis on Modern Hebrew). The upward mobility of American Ashkenazic Jews undercut both ethnic neighborhoods and socialist sympathies. Finally, American culture encouraged Jewish identification through religion rather than ethnicity.[12]

Today, the surviving secular Jewish organizations from this era are considerably smaller than in their heyday. The structural changes in American Jewish life that accelerated after World War II—cultural integration, affluence, residential dispersion, increasingly distant memories of the immigrant experience—suggested that a new organizational model might better serve the needs of secularized Jews.[13]

Creation of Humanistic Judaism

One of the most creative examples of a modern Judaism composed of, and serving, secular Jews today is Humanistic Judaism, which blends an explicitly human-focused and naturalistic philosophy of life with cultural Jewish identity, celebrations, and community.

The first Humanistic Jewish congregation began in 1963, when eight families and Rabbi Sherwin Wine founded The Birmingham Temple in suburban Detroit.[14] At first this was a Reform temple. Rabbi Wine, who had grown up in the ethnic Jewish neighborhoods of Detroit and attended Congregation Shaarey Zedek (Conservative) as a youth, had served a Detroit Reform congregation, Temple Beth El, as a student, received ordination from the Reform movement, returned to Temple Beth El as assistant rabbi, and then helped found a Reform congregation with the same name, Temple Beth El in Windsor, Ontario. However, Wine was growing increasingly uncomfortable with Reform Jewish theology and practice—both before and after ordination he had considered leaving the rabbinate to complete a PhD in philosophy. Yet instead of changing his own life direction, Rabbi Wine and The Birmingham Temple community created Humanistic Judaism within the temple's first year.

Initially the temple leadership had accepted the use of God language in the liturgy and Sunday school curriculum while redefining "God" to mean "the best in people." But after several months, the rabbi and members agreed that if they did not believe in an omniscient personality who intervened in the world as described in the TANAKH and the prayer book—which, they jointly affirmed, *they did not*—then saying clearly what they *did* believe would have more integrity and be more inspirational. If people, rather than a divine entity, enact justice, help those in need, and create communities and values, then humanity should get the credit.

A generation earlier, Rabbi Mordecai Kaplan had laid out the intellectual groundwork for a Jewish movement known as Reconstructionist Judaism by defining Judaism as an evolving religious civilization built on communal identification and ritual continuity. Human-focused beliefs appeared in Reconstructionist liturgy through reinterpretations, side commentaries, and/or supplementary readings. Yet Reconstructionist (today Reconstructing) Judaism did not change the traditional Hebrew liturgy beyond editing some problematic concepts, such as Jewish chosenness. Kaplan's redefinitions of God as an impersonal force or an expression of human hopes and ideals were not reflected in revised Hebrew texts of blessings and prayers addressed to a personal God. By contrast, The Birmingham Temple's evolving Jewish community took the next, radical step to be fully Humanistic: expressing its positive beliefs in both Hebrew and English texts. During the first several months of 1964, a ritual committee discussed and debated the congregation's ideology and liturgy. Ritual Committee participant Judith Goren later described the process:

Within a number of months, a number of changes were made in the traditional Reform service, most of them relating to the word "God." The Kaddish—the mourner's prayer for the dead, which praises the glory of God—was eliminated. The Sh'ma, regarded by the three traditional branches of Judaism as the basic credal statement... was also eliminated. The *Union Prayer Book*, used by Reform congregations in America, was put in storage, replaced by creative meditation services written by Wine. Sunday school focused on Jewish history, with little or no mention of the word "God."[15]

Goren recalled that this was controversial within the community even before the controversy became public. Some members wanted more traditional liturgy even if they were intellectual humanists, and some "stood behind Wine in wanting total intellectual consistency."[16]

The first bound collection of ten of these services, *Sabbath Services in the spirit of a humanistic Judaism* (capitalization original), contained services organized around basic ideals like beauty, peace, individualism, and reason and did not include any traditional prayers or Humanistic prayer adaptations. Instead, contemplative English prose was interspersed with short Hebrew songs, either original compositions or passages from Proverbs or other traditional Jewish sources that did not mention God. The candlelighting blessing omitted the traditional formula praising God in favor of this original text:

> *Ba-rookh ha-or ba-o-lam.*
> *Ba-rookh ha-or ba-a-dam.*
> *Ba-rookh ha-or ba-shab-bat.*
> Radiant is the light in the world.
> Radiant is the light in man.
> Radiant is the light of the Sabbath.[17]

The Ritual Committee explained their goals in the volume's preface:

> In an empirical age, when the prayer forms of a theistic religion seem less than relevant, the members of [T]he Birmingham

Temple have sought to create a new and more meaningful expression of group commitment.... We hope that this book will promote the cause of a Judaism that enjoys both intellectual integrity and emotional sensitivity.[18]

A second volume of Jewish holiday-focused services was subsequently produced, with observances for Rosh Hashanah, Yom Kippur, Sukkot, Hanukkah, Purim, Passover, and Shavuot. This volume described the congregation's liturgical creativity as "expressions not only of Jewish loyalty but also of a sincere commitment to the values of a scientific humanism."[19] Such balancing of Jewish and universal, tradition and innovation, would define Humanistic Jewish liturgy even from the movement's early days.

More broadly, Rabbi Wine differentiated Humanistic Judaism from both Reconstructionist Judaism and other Secular Judaisms by starting with two positive propositions: first, that religion meets human needs; and second, that a secular Judaism that takes Humanism seriously needs to address human needs for community, inspiration, and leadership. If a modern rabbi serves as a teacher and pastoral counselor, and a congregation provides mutual support as well as opportunities for communal learning, celebration, and social action, then maintaining these forms does not betray one's secular Jewish commitment. As he asserted:

> Congregations, Shabbat meetings and holiday celebrations [a]re not the sole possession of theistic people. Bar mitsvas and confirmations [a]re not, of necessity, attached to prayers and Torah readings. Religion [is] more than the worship of God. It [i]s, in the broadest sense, a philosophy of life turned into the morality and celebrations of an organized community.[20]

Furthermore, Wine asserted not only the acceptability but the *necessity* of Judaism continuing to adapt to new circumstances. Judaism itself had changed throughout history, moving from animal sacrifice to verbal prayers and observance of religious law, and from territorial national identity to international ethno-religious culture. By the twentieth century, Reform Judaism had moved considerably beyond rabbinic halakhah, transforming the role of the rabbi (from an expert in Jewish law to a pastoral counselor and preacher), the meaning of the synagogue (from a temporal religious meeting place to a replacement for the Jerusalem Temple), and the content of Jewish liturgy (e.g., by eliminating prayers for a return to Zion or a personal Messiah), among other modifications.

Humanistic Judaism was continuing this progress—and expanding it. As Wine insisted, historical religious beliefs and practices should not be emphasized at the expense of modern values and creativity. Instead, a Humanistic Judaism needed to evaluate Jewish life past and present on equal footing. If Jewish tradition was not divinely given on Mount Sinai but rather evolved through human effort, then humans should be encouraged to innovate new Jewish traditions.[21]

So, too, if Judaism is a culture created by people, then it was created in response to specific circumstances. To fully understand its texts, Jews needed to also understand the possible agendas of biblical authors and composers of traditional prayers. Human creation also meant that Jewish culture learned from surrounding cultures, from language (e.g., Yiddish from Middle German written in Hebrew letters) to Jewish holiday traditions like the Passover *afikoman* (the last piece of unleavened bread at the seder, whose name derives from the Greek *epikomen*, meaning "dessert").

Likewise, Wine asserted, the beliefs and values of any human culture evolve over centuries of lived experience. If contemporary Jews do not believe what earlier generations did, it is entirely appropriate for them to express their Jewish values in bold new ways:

> Cautious, piecemeal reform does not serve consistency well. Life is too short to be the prisoner of foolish contradictions. We do not exist to fit the forms of the past. The forms of the past exist to serve our needs and the needs of future generations. Sometimes only bold action will enable us to make things right.[22]

The tangible results of Humanistic Judaism's departure from conventional God belief, language, and imagery were manifold. New Jewish holiday and life-cycle ceremonies needed to be developed. Jewish history needed to be reconceptualized as the result of human actions and social forces rather than divine providence or punishment, and its content reevaluated based on archaeological and scholarly evidence. The need to balance among a secular approach to life, integration into non-Jewish society, and a continued Jewish identity required new answers beyond covenant and the Chosen People.

Humanistic Judaism began experimenting and finding these novel ways. For example, in time the traditional b'nai mitzvah ceremony became a "b mitzvah" (gender-neutral terminology) emphasizing the b mitzvah's interests and values; in keeping with a Jewish coming-of-age celebration emphasizing maturity and self-responsibility, the b mitzvah chooses to discuss a personally meaningful passage from the Torah or other Hebrew literature or a topic from just about any aspect of the Jewish experience. Likewise, Yom Kippur was reoriented, both conceptually and liturgically, from the traditional fear of divine judgment to an emphasis on self-judgment and self-forgiveness, and Simchat Torah shifted from celebrating divine revelation to celebrating human wisdom and discovery.

Early on, Rabbi Wine and the congregation became infamous locally for refocusing their Judaism on humanity rather than God. A January 1965 *Time* profile of Wine as "the atheist rabbi" then brought the story to national attention.[23]

The first Humanistic community expanded substantially, despite Detroit Jewish establishment opposition. In 1970 The Birmingham Temple community, now numbering several hundred member families, opened its own building. The congregation installed a sculpture of the Hebrew word *adam* (humanity) in its ceremonial meeting room instead of an ark with a Torah scroll. Community members also gave their Torah scroll a prominent place of honor in the library, as befitting an important ancient book housed alongside other human-authored books.[24]

A Growing Movement

Despite the local and national controversy sparked by the first Humanistic Jewish congregation, many Jews and their families living beyond metropolitan Detroit found Humanistic Judaism compelling. The Association of Humanistic Rabbis started in 1968, and the Society for Humanistic Judaism (SHJ) was founded in 1969 to support three existing and multiple nascent Humanistic Jewish communities. In the 1980s, when seventeen communities were affiliated with the SHJ, connections with secular Jewish organizations generated the Leadership Conference of Secular and Humanistic Jews (1982), for interorganizational dialogue; the International Institute for Secular Humanistic Judaism, or IISHJ (1985), for new leadership training; and the International Federation of Secular Humanistic Jews (1986), for connecting with Secular Humanistic Jewish communities in Israel, Europe, and elsewhere. All three of these institutions partnered with the Congress of Secular Jewish Organizations, a coalition founded in 1967 to connect and support surviving leftist/Yiddishist Jewish schools (today the renamed Cultural and Secular Jewish Organization, comprising thirteen communities in the United States and Canada). This partnership is why the movement's ideology has sometimes been called "Secular Humanistic Judaism" rather than simply "Humanistic Judaism."

As of 2023, over forty Secular and Humanistic Jewish communities engaging thousands of Jews of all ages are affiliated with the broader North American movement. Most major metropolitan areas in the United States have a Secular or Humanistic Jewish community, from Boston to Sarasota, from New York City to San Francisco, from Washington DC to Los Angeles, from Chicago to Seattle, from Detroit to Boulder, from Phoenix to Minneapolis–Saint Paul. Canadian affiliates are active in Toronto, Winnipeg, Victoria, and Vancouver. The largest Humanistic Jewish community is still in the Detroit area and now is called the Congregation for Humanistic Judaism of Metropolitan Detroit. Dozens of Secular Humanistic Jewish leaders (*madrikh/madrikha*, or *vegvayzer* in Yiddish), life-cycle officiants, and, as of 2023, more than twenty Humanistic rabbis serve Humanistic Jewish communities in the United States and Canada. Most of these Humanistic rabbis received ordination from IISHJ in North America or from IISHJ's sister institution in Israel, Tmura-IISHJ, though some have been ordained by other seminaries and, like Wine, evolved to Humanistic Judaism after ordination. The Society for Humanistic Judaism's website www.shj.org links to all of its affiliated communities and also offers online-only independent memberships to individuals who want to feel connected to the movement.[25]

Humanistic Jewish Thought

Humanistic Judaism is a developed and well-established example of what a Judaism designed by and for secular, cultural, and "nonreligious" Jews can be. It combines a secular philosophy of humanism—namely, emphasizing human knowledge, power, and responsibility—with a particular Jewish identity (a distinct peoplehood rooted in Jewish culture) and congregational Jewish community. This synthesis is unique to Humanistic Judaism.

Unlike liberal Judaisms (such as Reform, Renewal, and Reconstructing Judaism), which may reject a transcendent, authoritarian God in favor of more immanent or psychological "god-ideas" (a presence, force, or feeling), Humanistic Judaism insists that addressing, petitioning, or praising a personal God is neither meaningful nor sustainable for those who genuinely do not believe "there is a there there." As Wine says in his essay "Judaism without God" (chapter 2), such a linguistic attempt to "rescue" God language in hopes of retaining select liturgy and concepts to which one feels emotionally attached is, nonetheless, ultimately futile. The contradiction between one's beliefs about the universe and humanity and what the old blessings and prayers say remains.

Still, as IISHJ provost Yaakov Malkin explains (chapter 2), even secularized Jews view "God" as an important literary character in Jewish culture, just as the characters of Hamlet or Odysseus provide insight into the human condition without actual existence. "God" only becomes problematic when this character is ritually invoked as real at important moments in one's life.

Once one concludes that one does not believe in a personal God who creates the world, reveals written commandments, chooses one people, and actively controls history by rewarding the righteous and punishing the wicked and, moreover, one does not want to address such a being/concept through praise and petition, then the more attractive alternative becomes clearly and consistently expressing one's positive beliefs. "Humanism" is a positive expression of belief in human power, human knowledge, and human responsibility. "Say what you believe and believe what you say" is an important touchstone in Humanistic Jewish thought. This applies to personal, liturgical, and ritual expression in both English and Hebrew, which requires adapting traditional blessings rather than only offering creative translations (chapter 12).

Humanistic Jews articulate positive yet secular beliefs, strive to be good people, and find inspiration and meaning separate from a god or the supernatural. These positive beliefs impact their Jewish identity and expression. For example, the philosophical emphasis on human self-determination supports an open and welcoming definition of Jewishness that includes complete acceptance of individuals with multiple identities in the context of interfaith marriage. The belief that the Jewish people created Jewish culture empowers Humanistic Jews to choose from that heritage, disagree with convention, and invent new Jewish culture; if yesterday's Jews made Judaism, today's Jews can be remake it as well.

In that spirit, Humanistic Judaism also rejects that being a good person requires belief in God and that divine mitzvot (commandments) simply must be followed. For Humanistic Jews, obeying commands is not considered ethical in and of itself; rather, each of us should evaluate and choose how to act through our own moral reasoning. Ritual behavior, too, is a matter of personal choice rather than worthy of moral judgment on par with interpersonal actions. All the more, the historical Jewish acceptance of slavery and the inferior treatment of women, the LGBTQ+ community, and non-Jews contradict contemporary Humanistic Jewish values such as individual dignity, human rights, and personal happiness. Even if a Humanistic Jew abides by "love your neighbor as yourself" (Lev. 19:18), the rejection of other rules from the same biblical source as immoral means the Humanistic Jewish reader is the true moral authority choosing from the tradition.

Rejecting traditional authority-based ethics does not result in nihilist amorality, but rather in renewed attention to the impact of one's actions for oneself and for one's community in this life and in this world. A core application of humanism in Humanistic Judaism is the human responsibility for *tikkun olam* (repair of the world). If streams of traditional Jewish thought consider Jewish history to be the result of divine judgment, with prosperity as faith's reward and disaster as punishment for religious failure, a Humanistic reading of the same events not only rejects blaming Jewish victims for their own suffering, but also champions crediting Jewish (and other people's) actions for Jewish survival and successes. If God does not create justice, humanity must do so. Rabbi Wine's evocative articulation of this mandate in the first selection of this volume is worth reiterating here:

> If Jewish history has any message, it is the demand for human self-reliance. In an indifferent universe there is no help from destiny. Either we assume responsibility for our fate or no one will. A world without divine guarantees and divine justice is a little bit frightening. But it is also the source of human freedom and human dignity.
>
> We stand alone, and yet together, to create the world we want.[26]

Another distinct aspect of Jewish thought is the willingness to challenge authority, even "argue with God," the title of Amos Oz's essay (chapter 4). In this sense, Humanistic Jews rejecting commandments see themselves as being just as Jewish as pious Jews keeping them.

Authentic engagement in this world is precisely where one may also find Humanistic "spirituality": nature, interpersonal connection through ethics or activism, and bonds with something greater than oneself, be it factual history or concepts like Jewish peoplehood. John Keats's supposition that being secular is incompatible with inspiration ("Do not all charms fly / At the mere touch of cold philosophy?"[27]) is misguided. Humanistic Jews view "inspiration" as an essential human need that must and can be met in non-supernatural ways.

Jewish ritual and tradition remain meaningful sources of a natural transcendence. Humanistic Jews freely choose heirlooms and practices from their cultural inheritance at the intersection of beauty and meaning. As longtime lay leader Terry Toll describes (chapter 5), once lighting candles no longer represents fulfilling commandments, the practice is opened to new ascribed meanings. Diverse Humanistic Jews also make different spiritual and inspirational choices, and sometimes individual beliefs evolve. For example, the movement's *Guide to Humanistic Judaism*, written in 1993 and revised in 2017, rejected the wearing of *kippot* (skullcaps), a practice generally understood to signify piety before God, as fundamentally inconsistent with Humanistic Judaism's desire to clearly express a nontheistic approach to Jewish life. However, a recent Facebook discussion on the issue (chapter 5) demonstrates that today's movement also welcomes the opposite conclusion. Wearing *kippot* may in fact be acceptable, because Humanistic Jews should have the freedom to meet their own human needs for inspiration, including in what other Humanistic Jews may consider "religious" ways.

Portrait of a Humanistic Jewish Community

A 2003–4 survey of The Birmingham Temple's four hundred member families at the end of its first forty years offers some insight into the kinds of Jews who choose Humanistic Judaism.[28]

- Fifty percent have left the Judaism in which they were raised (Conservative, 30 percent; Reform, 20 percent) for Humanistic Judaism. Divergences between personal beliefs and synagogue practice as well as ideological issues have led many such Jews to choose Humanistic Judaism as a better reflection of their Jewish identity.
- Seventeen percent are interfaith/intercultural families in which one partner was not born or does not identify as Jewish. Couples like these appreciated that Humanistic Judaism welcomes both partners as equal members and empowers families to explore both heritage cultures. In other Humanistic Jewish congrega-

tions, the percentage of interfaith/intercultural families may be higher.
- Fifteen percent have chosen a stronger Jewish affiliation than their upbringing as "unaffiliated" or "just Jewish" Jews with little formal Jewish education or synagogue experience. This group includes former Soviet Jews who could not observe Judaism in the USSR.
- Ten percent are heirs to secular Judaisms, having been raised as secular, cultural, or Humanistic Jews.
- A total of 7.5 percent are rebels, Jews raised Orthodox or ultra-Orthodox who reject the strict religious observance and intense devotion to God of their upbringing but remain attracted to Jewish ethnicity and culture separate from religious beliefs and practices.
- One percent are secular Israelis harboring a strong affinity for Jewish language, history, literature, and peoplehood.[29]

Choosing Humanistic Judaism Today

Both in its communities and in its approach to Jewish values, Humanistic Judaism represents an important addition to the North American Jewish landscape. As with Reconstructing Judaism, its ideas speak for many more Jews than its dues-paying members. A common comment made by new members in Humanistic Jewish congregations is "I've felt this way for years, but I never knew there was an organized Jewish option."

In the twenty-first century, the boundaries of Jewish identity are fluid. Thousands have joined the Jewish people through conversion, millions of Jews have intermarried and raised children, multiple dynamics propel Israel-world Jewry relations, and Jews are challenged in old and new ways to find the meaning of particular Jewish identity in open society.

For secularized Jews in the twenty-first century, the key question moving forward is, simply, *why bother* being Jewish at all? Why not just embrace all of humanity?

A Humanistic Judaism identity enables "both/and." It is explicitly open to the experiences and ideas of world culture. It dignifies determining one's own personal balance between universalism and an open particularism—what has been called a "rooted cosmopolitanism."[30] In this rubric, Jewishness is just one of an individual's many overlapping identities; being a citizen of the world and a Humanist are two others.

Humanistic Judaism's combination of universalism and particularism is unique among other liberal Jewish alternatives in its explicitly pluralistic, welcoming, and inclusive approach. From its earliest days, Humanistic Judaism has celebrated intermarriages, welcoming intermarried families into its communities and accepting the children of intermarriage as Jewish. The Society for Humanistic Judaism's statement "Radical Inclusion" (chapter 7) demands acceptance of diverse identities in an open Jewish community as the direct application of Humanistic Jewish values of equality and dignity.

Also singular is Humanistic Judaism's devotion to Jewish culture (e.g., Jewish art, music, food, language, clothing, heirlooms) as wide, deep, rich sources of Jewishness, even as Humanistic Jews themselves may diverge on what counts as Jewish culture (see chapter 10). It is a conceptual shift to understand contemporary Jews as *heirs* of evolving Jewish culture, Amos Oz observes (chapter 9). For Humanistic Jews, this legacy includes ownership and the right, even the responsibility, to choose from and adapt one's inheritance for one's own needs, values, and circumstances. One may inherit an attic full of heirlooms, but one's own house remains one's own. Each Humanistic Jew is entrusted to choose from that cultural inheritance and determine how to use it.

Humanistic Judaism is most clearly distinct from other liberal Judaisms where the philosophical rubber hits the Jewish communal road: celebrating Jewish life. Humanistic Jewish philosophy is always *applied* in order to find meaning and purpose and to live an authentically Jewish life that is "worth preserving," in Rabbi Eva Goldfinger's phrase (chapter 11). Humanistic Judaism didn't evolve in an intellectual bubble; it has been working in lived Jewish experience since it began. Humanistic

Jewish rabbis and communities have created their liturgies and holiday observances by writing their own meditations, songs, and poetry as well as adapting traditional sources and choosing from both general literature and music and from the growing library of Humanistic Jewish creativity. Humanistic Judaism's focus on the individual rather than on God and commandments has transformed life-cycle celebrations by empowering choice and personal relevance; for example, Humanistic b mitzvah (gender neutral term for bar/bat mitzvah) students who choose their Torah readings or presentation topics are living a new Jewish tradition.

A revealing aspect of any Jewish movement is how it educates its youth. Humanistic Jewish education aims for students to become confident in their Jewish cultural identity, their human-focused positive philosophy, and their secular lifestyle—to appreciate the "treasures of the legacy," as Mitchell Silver puts it (chapter 14)—and also to have the freedom to make up their own minds whether they agree with those pillars or not. Humanistic Jews may define themselves both in reference to and in honest distance from their full inheritance.

It is here, in the realm of education, that Torah, TANAKH, and rabbinic literature find positive roles in Humanistic Judaism. These are the stories, laws, and ideas written, rewritten, and interpreted by the Jewish people over centuries. As such, they need not be eternally true to be culturally significant, and contemporary readers will discover which elements resonate most. Humanistic Jews are encouraged to define themselves in relation to or even in opposition to those texts when discontinuity is more honest. Proverbs may be more meaningful than Leviticus, and the lived experiences of Jewish history may be more inspirational than legends of heavenly voices. Traditionally, it is said of the Torah that one should turn it and turn it, for all is inside it,[31] an allusion to the bottomless curriculum of Torah and talmudic commentaries. Analogously, for Humanistic Jews, the world of human experience and the many worlds of the Jewish experience enable endless exploration.

Near the end of his career, Sherwin Wine described the lifestyle of Humanistic Judaism as the "life of courage."[32] It is challenging to face life without divine guarantees, he said, and all the more to live and speak and sing one's true beliefs no matter the criticism and hostility from others. Yet, he affirmed—and we hope this volume does as well—personal dignity and Jewish dignity are their own rewards.

Contemporary Humanistic Judaism

PART 1

Beliefs and Ethics

Introduction

Throughout Jewish history, many Jews have questioned specific Jewish religious beliefs. In the nineteenth century, thousands of Jews became more secularized through the Haskalah (Enlightenment) and experiences of emancipation and integration in Europe and America. Sometimes ideological secularists—particularly early twentieth-century Zionists working for a secular, Hebrew-speaking Jewish state and socialists creating new expressions of secular Jewishness in Yiddish—also adapted traditional Jewish forms to their political agendas.

What marked Humanistic Judaism as important and distinctive from these expressions at its birth in the 1960s was its fusion of secular philosophical beliefs with Jewish religious structure: liturgy, services, synagogues, and rabbis.

In suburban Detroit in November 1963, Reform-trained Rabbi Sherwin Wine and the founding families of The Birmingham Temple did something extraordinary as they began questioning the beliefs and practices of conventional Reform Judaism. Trying to further reform Reform Judaism was not viable if they did not believe in a personal god; they felt hypocritical praising and thanking one in their services. If they personally connected with being Jewish more through history, culture, humor, and language than theology and ritual, could they make *those* the focus of Jewish holidays and life-cycle celebrations? Could they center people and the natural world in a new, Humanistic Judaism? Could they say what they mean and mean what they said, as a popular movement phrase has it, with integrity? Under Rabbi Wine's leadership, the answers to all these questions were a resounding yes. In short, Humanistic Judaism would become a Judaism focused on people rather than prayer. Wine put it this way: "Laughing has always seemed to me more Jewish than praying."[1]

Publicity around the congregation's changes, both positive and negative (see "Introduction: Judaism beyond God, Torah, and Israel"), led to the growth of The Birmingham Temple and interest elsewhere in creating new Humanistic Jewish congregations. In suburban Chicago, for example, another previously Reform synagogue was undergoing a similar transformation under Rabbi Daniel Friedman (see chapter 4). In 1969 the Society for Humanistic Judaism (SHJ) was established as a national umbrella organization, with communities in suburban Detroit, suburban Chicago, and Connecticut; over the next decades SHJ would grow to some thirty congregations in the United States and Canada, ranging in size from *havurot* of a couple dozen households to full-service congregations with buildings and rabbis. The perceived need for educational resources and new leadership led to the 1985 establishment (in cooperation with the Congress of Secular Jewish Organizations, a similar community support network) of the International Institute for Secular Humanistic Judaism (IISHJ). Partnerships with like-minded Israeli and European organizations led to conferences, publications, and ultimately the establishment of a parallel institute in Jerusalem, Tmura-IISHJ, in 2003. These institutions have provided education and training to subsequent generations of Humanistic Jewish leaders and support for affiliate communities. After sixty years of community building, celebration, and education, thousands of Jews in North America and Israel have experienced Humanistic Judaism, from single events to lifetime affiliations and a generation raised in the movement.

Through all of this organizational building, Humanistic Judaism has always shaped its expressions of cultural Jewish identity through its humanist philosophy. Humanistic Jewish philosophy meets universal human needs and questions for those Jews for whom the answers do not lie in Torah or conventional religious observance. What is the meaning of human experience? How does the universe work? What is my purpose in life? How should I be a good person? And is what I see, touch, and analyze all there is to life?

In Humanistic Judaism, Jewish and human experiences are read as lessons in positive humanism: the importance of self-reliance, the value of human creativity, and the reality of human freedom. A Humanistic Jewish understanding of the universe makes the God of Jewish tradition a literary character created by human authors, reflecting their context and values. Given the literary biography of this character in the TANAKH and rabbinic literature, this character is vital to understanding historical Jewish thought and literature, but is not a conscious being who acts—or ever acted—in the world, reveals scripture, issues commandments, rewards the righteous and punishes the wicked, or should be beseeched or honored through devotional prayer. Attempts to redefine "God"—say, for example, as "love"—to salvage traditional liturgy must be rejected. "Love" is worth praising and beautiful enough without calling it "God."

For Humanistic Jews, a sense of purpose in life comes from positive affirmations of human dignity, reinforced by Humanistic Judaism's emphasis on human knowledge, power, and responsibility. The collective human achievement of understanding the natural world and applying that knowledge to improve and lengthen life has replaced reliance on revelation, miraculous intervention, and divine power both conceptually and liturgically. If human beings are the only conscious and active force that can do good, then it is a human responsibility to do so.

The question of how to define and do good (i.e., ethics) likewise reflects a human-centered approach. In the absence of binding divine or rabbinic commandments, Humanistic Jews are free to make their own choices. Our social nature and interdependence, as well as the historical Jewish experience, suggest that wise and ethical choices consider the welfare of others as well as the individual. Rather than ask whether a particular action is permitted or prohibited by traditional authority, Humanistic Jewish ethics evaluate the possible results of action or inaction as best as these can be predicted, an ethical system often called consequentialism. Traditional Jewish obligations *bein adam la-havero* (between people) are certainly worthy of consideration, even if obligations *bein adam la-Makom* (between a person and God) are mostly irrelevant. What ultimately makes an action right or wrong is not who or what commanded it; it is how it affects other people and oneself.

A full human life, whether religious or secular, is more than knowing and doing; it is also experiencing, feeling, being inspired. A Humanistic Jewish spirituality finds inspiration in natural transcendence. Scientific connections to each other and the world, from evolution to astronomy, expand our feelings of connectedness. Beauty—both natural phenomena, from mountains to molecules, and human creations like art and music—creates a sense of awe and wonder. Experiences of cultural heritage, like lighting a family menorah used for generations, spark emotional bonds. So, too, meaningful relationships with other people are life-affirming and create family and community. Going beyond the individual and the rational to experience psychological and emotional uplift without a supernatural being is one more way Humanistic Judaism meets religious needs through secular means.

These beliefs are the foundation of Humanistic Jewish community, practice, and values. In these first five chapters, we will take a closer look at them through five lenses: the Jewish experience, the God question, positive humanism, ethics, and spirituality.

1

The Jewish Experience

Sherwin Wine (1928–2007), the founder of Humanistic Judaism, was raised by Yiddish-speaking immigrant parents in Conservative Judaism in the Jewish neighborhoods of Detroit, but his study of history and philosophy led him to seek rabbinic ordination in Reform Judaism in 1956. After Army chaplain service and pulpits at Reform temples in Detroit and Windsor, Ontario, Wine was considering completing a PhD in philosophy when a small group of families in suburban Detroit contacted him about starting a new Jewish congregation. The Birmingham Temple (1963) would become the first Humanistic Jewish synagogue. As we've seen in the introduction to this volume, Wine later helped found the Society for Humanistic Judaism (1969), the Leadership Conference of Secular and Humanistic Jews (1982), and the International Institute for Secular Humanistic Judaism (1985), leading them all at various times.

Synthesizing universal humanist philosophy and particular Jewish identity, Wine argues that the Jewish experience also demonstrates the absence (or, at best, unreliability) of the caring, intervening divinity of traditional Jewish belief. As a result, a Humanistic Judaism that emphasizes human power, freedom, and responsibility in both its messaging and liturgy is not only plausible; it is *required* for Jewish identity to remain relevant and meaningful. Wine stresses this at the outset of this Shabbat service meditation: "The Jewish experience is the experience of humanism."

Written as a liturgical reading for a Shabbat service at The Birmingham Temple, which was published in full in 1985 in the movement's journal *Humanistic Judaism*, this meditation served as information and inspiration, exposition and liturgy. It expressed the core philosophical belief of Humanistic Judaism that people are in charge of their lives, it derived that lesson from Jewish roots, and it demonstrated that conclusion by itself serving as new Shabbat liturgy consistent with that belief.

Other Humanistic Jewish lessons can and have been derived from the Jewish historical experience, by Wine and others. The evolution of Jewish belief and practice over centuries and in response to new ideas and circumstances is precedent for contemporary Humanistic Jewish innovation. A diasporic minority experience encourages sympathy for other minorities and advocacy for human rights. The problems of authoritarian rule by patriarchal kings and clergy—both biblical priests and postbiblical rabbis—argue for democratic Jewish community decision-making and egalitarian practice. While it is true that these conclusions could also be justified by philosophical argument, rooting them in Jewish history and culture gives them added force and emotional resonance.

This seminal liturgical passage, however, best exemplifies two key points: the humanism of Humanistic Judaism is natively rooted in its Jewish cultural context rather than grafted on from outside philosophy; and what makes Humanistic Judaism distinctive is its willingness to apply historical and philosophical conclusions boldly and explicitly to theology, liturgy, and communal self-definition.

Sherwin Wine, "Jewish History—Our Humanist Perspective" (1985)

The Jewish experience is the experience of humanism.

Through the eyes of tradition, through the vision of priests, prophets, and rabbis, Jewish history is a testimony to the power and justice of a loving God. The Jewish people is a chosen people, chosen for special duties, special suffering, and special rewards. All that happens to the Jewish nation is part of a noble divine plan, even though we humans, like poor Job, have difficulty understanding its nobility.

But the real history of the Jews has a meaning different from that which the authors of its tradition—the priests, prophets, and rabbis—wanted it to be. No historic belief system can hide the undeserved suffering of the Jewish past. No age-old ideology can hide the cruelty of the Fates. In the century of the Holocaust the illusions of the past insult the memories of our martyrs.

If Jewish history has any message, it is the demand for human self-reliance. In an indifferent universe, there is no help from destiny. Either we assume responsibility for our fate or no one will. A world without divine guarantees and divine justice is a little bit frightening. But it is also the source of human freedom and human dignity.

We stand alone, and yet together, to create the world we want.[1]

2

The God Question

One of the most common questions Humanistic Jews are asked is "How can you be Jewish if you don't believe in God?" A growing majority of American Jews seem to accept that both can be true: only 26 percent of all self-identified Jewish Americans believe in the God of the Bible, meaning that the vast majority do not. (Twenty-two percent believe in neither the God of the Bible nor a "higher power/spiritual force.")[1] Indeed, Jewish religious thought today generally accepts the existence of *Jews* who do not believe in God, yet some find a *Judaism* without an active god concept inconceivable.

In truth, Jewish concepts of divinity have evolved significantly over time, through the Bible, rabbinic theology, medieval mysticism, and modern Jewish denominations. Even within liberal movements, Jews hold diverse theological views. For its part, Humanistic Judaism encompasses a range of secularized perspectives on God—from atheism to agnosticism to deism—even as Humanistic Jews agree on what they do *not* believe in: the personal, interventionist God found in the Bible and rabbinic literature. They find it implausible to believe in a god of the entire universe who chooses one particular people, who reveals ultimate truths only to them, who hears and acts on their petitions, who cares what they eat or whom they love, who desires their liturgical praise, and who rewards the righteous and punishes the wicked (in this life or a world to come).

Other liberal Jewish denominations may share some or many of these theological doubts, but leaders have chosen to redefine God in their liturgy rather than remove references to God or change the Hebrew texts. For example, the 1994 Reconstructionist *Kol Haneshamah* prayer book translates *melekh* as a softer "sovereign" rather than the hierarchical and male yet literal "king," as does the 2007 prayer book *Mishkan T'filah: A Reform Siddur*.[2]

By contrast, in early 1964 the first Humanistic congregation made a definitive break from conventional liberal Judaism by changing its liturgy to no longer address a god that members did not believe in (see introduction to this volume). The alternative to redefining god was to refocus from the supernatural to the natural, from the cosmic to the earthly, from the transcendent divine to the human. So, for example, today most Humanistic congregations sing the conventional "*oseh shalom*, may He make peace" from the *Kaddish* prayer as "*na'aseh shalom*, we will make peace." (For more on liturgy, see chapter 12.)

This shift has not left a void in the center of Humanistic Jewish identity, because Humanistic Jews share positive beliefs in human rights, human responsibility, and human power to understand and improve the human condition. A supernatural being is not needed when Judaism is less defined by a god concept than by a steadfast commitment to human welfare and empowerment.

Once one accepts "Judaism without God," as Sherwin Wine's selection below terms it, and bypasses the Jewish tradition of god-redefinition, Yahweh (a name for god) can be reconceived as a literary character in the Bible produced by Jewish culture rather than the source of revealed religion. This shift is emblematic of Humanistic Judaism overall: just as the Jewish god was created by people and changed over time in response to their needs and beliefs, so too does the Jewish people's evolving cultural heritage over thousands of years inform modern Jewish identity, community, holidays, and life-cycle celebrations (see parts 2–4).

This chapter sets forth essays by two of the leading original thinkers of Humanistic Judaism: American rabbi Sherwin Wine and Israeli professor Yaakov Malkin. Addressing the "God question" directly, they provide support for both the doubts and the positive beliefs of Humanistic

Jews. They also move beyond a simplistic rejection of any mention of god to understanding the god of the Bible as a literary character alone.

Jewish A-Theology

Can "God" mean anything one chooses, or is there a core, defined Jewish concept in which one may believe or disbelieve?

Reconstructionist rabbi Mordecai Kaplan (1881–1983) describes God as an impersonal force for good in the universe, while Conservative rabbi Harold Kushner (1935–2023) posits a limited being that offers emotional support without intervention. Feminist Judith Plaskow (b. 1947) articulates a decentralized and imminent experience rather than transcendent authority, while the Reform rabbinic body the Central Conference of American Rabbis speaks to a partnership between humanity and divinity.[3]

Sherwin Wine (see chapter 1) was skeptical of most contemporary Jewish theology. To him, it was a religious version of "The Emperor's New Clothes": people claiming to believe in a God for social acceptance or because declaring the alternative—that there *are* no clothes, or in this case no emperor—was unthinkable. The draft title of his major work on Humanistic Judaism, *Judaism beyond God* (1985), was "Judaism without God."

Wine's personal philosophy was more subtle than simple atheism. He is credited with coining the term "ignosticism": the belief that there is no way to prove whether or not a god exists because the very term "god" has no unambiguous definition, thus making the question meaningless. Nevertheless, both he and nascent Humanistic Judaism gained fame in 1965 when *Time* dubbed him "the atheist rabbi."[4]

Wine refused to redefine a god concept to save traditional liturgy and conventional pieties. His insistence on linguistic precision in the following essay excerpted from the movement's journal *Humanistic Judaism* reflects both his university training in philosophy and his practical experience of explaining Humanistic Judaism to ordinary people. Rather than maintain any personalized god language, Wine took the more direct approach of eliminating *any* god addressed in praise, petition, or gratitude in favor of the plain language of human freedom, self-determination, and happiness. This essay is a concise summary of the reasons behind this shift and therefore the need to create a new, Humanistic Judaism.

Sherwin Wine, "Judaism without God" (1983)

Judaism without God is a difficult concept for many people to grasp. If they are not outraged, they are puzzled.

For traditional Jews who see Jewish history as the evidence for the presence of God in the world, removing God is removing the reason for Jewish survival.

For people who view Jews as a religious denomination and who see religion as the worship of God, an atheistic secular Judaism is a contradiction in terms.

For religious naturalists who have rejected supernatural beliefs and who have redefined the word *God* to refer to nature or to some part of nature, the elimination of God is an unnecessary step.

For traditional moralists who derive their ethics from divine authority and who insist on clearly defined rules with absolute certainty, morality is not possible without God. And Judaism without morality is not much of a Judaism.

For atheists who agree that there is no God but who cannot imagine a religion without one, doing religion without God is like doing elections without candidates.

For people who may not be sure about God but who are sensitive to human needs, dispensing with God violates the requirements of human happiness. A Judaism without God cannot be emotionally satisfying.

To understand Humanistic Judaism is to understand why these ... responses are inappropriate.

1. *Finding a just God in Jewish history is like finding icebergs in Brazil*. If God has been the friend of the Jewish people, we do not need enemies. In the century of the Nazi Holocaust, the Jewish experience is a solemn testimony to the absence of God. If *Yahveh*

is indeed the lord of history, he cannot hide behind the excuse of Jewish sinfulness. Too many innocents perished in the slaughter.

Some theologians seek to rescue God in strange ways. The Lubavitcher *Rebbe* sees the Holocaust as a fitting punishment for the secular Jews of Eastern Europe. Richard Rubenstein [rabbi, author of *After Auschwitz*] views him as so high and mighty that the petty events on the surface of a small planet invite only his indifference and moral neutrality. Harold Kushner [rabbi, author of *When Bad Things Happen to Good People*] describes him as limited, a deity who means well but who does not possess the power to get what he wants. And his desperate defenders see him as the ingenious divinity who arranged the Holocaust so that the state of Israel could follow.

What can be said for such ludicrous defenses? Why would a just God slaughter the "innocent" religious together with the "wicked" secular? Why would anybody be interested in a God who did not care what happened to people and who viewed our suffering with the same indifference as he viewed our pleasure? Why would an incompetent and powerless God be more important to people than an incompetent and powerless human being? As for arranging a Holocaust to guarantee a Jewish state, that behavior is about as intelligent as burning down a house to get roast meat....

Practical humanism is the harsh awareness that the quality of human life is up to human beings. It does not depend on the kindness of destiny. No history teaches that lesson better than Jewish history....

3. *Saving the word* God *by redefining it is both evasive and immoral.* It is evasive because a word that can mean anything the definer wants it to mean is no longer intended for communication. Its purpose is either psychotherapy or social security. Either the definer "needs" the word for emotional reasons that have nothing at all to do with its historic meaning, or he finds it useful for social respectability. (Many people are afraid of being accused of atheism even if they are atheists.)

Redefining *God* is immoral because ordinary words are entitled to their ordinary meanings. *God* is not a new sophisticated scientific term unknown to the masses. It is a word as familiar as *man, child, house* and *storm*. It is an old word with an old historic denotation. Peasants are not confused about the meaning of the word in the way that liberal theologians seem to be. For the ordinary user, *God* refers to a supernatural father figure who made and runs the world and who consciously interferes with the operation of his creation. The vocabulary of prayer is directed to a personal power who can respond to praise and petition. Even after all the liberal theists redefine *God* to their personal satisfaction and social comfort, even after they insist that the term refers to some abstract non-anthropomorphic natural force of goodness or creative energy, they still end up talking to it as though it were a personal "papa figure." The historic meaning of the word makes that response inevitable....

The traditional God—if he is believed to be real—makes a difference. A personal God who watches our behavior and who judges it with rewards and punishments may be terrifying, yet he cannot be ignored. His presence is related to our survival and happiness.

But a god who is no more than the One, the Absolute, the potential for goodness and creativity, the ground of Being, Universal Love—or any of a dozen and one liberal redefinitions—is either too vague to be interesting or too familiar to be unique. If *God is Love*, how is that different from *Love is Love*? And if *God is Nature*, how is that different from *Nature is Nature*? Conservative theists need the word *God* because it refers to a being that no other word denotes. But liberal theists do not need the word. Perfectly ordinary words already exist for whatever they mean by God.

4. *As for morality, God is hardly indispensable.* It is quite obvious that the word *God* does not, of necessity, imply *good*. Gods can be wicked as well as benevolent. Otherwise, why all this insistence on demonstrating from human experience the "goodness" and "justice" of God?

If God's behavior can be evaluated, then the evaluator must already know what *good* means. He does not need God to tell him what is right or wrong. He is aware of what is right or wrong before he judges God.

Notions of right and wrong arise out of the social setting of parental discipline and are later attributed to a heavenly super-parent....

Even the Bible recognizes that divine endorsement is not enough to make commandments morally convincing. The system of rewards and punishments which the authors of the Torah so neatly articulated is evidence that divine authority is inadequate. The Hebrews are promised fertility and prosperity for their obedience, and drought and devastation for their resistance. The satisfaction—or frustration—of human needs becomes the selling argument. The implication is clear. Right behavior leads to pleasant consequences. Wrong behavior leads to unpleasant consequences.

In the reward and punishment system, the importance of God does not lie in his moral authority. It lies in his power to satisfy human needs and to provide for human pleasure—which, quite obviously, have their own intrinsic moral merit. A god that does not care about human welfare has no moral clout....

6. *Being nice to the masses because you think they need God even though you do not believe in God is an excuse for cowardice.* It provides people who are afraid of revealing their humanism with a reason for not doing so.

If human dignity is the strength to increase personal control over your own life and to encourage others to do the same for themselves; if human dignity is the primary goal of ethical living, enhancing survival and transcending pleasure; then therapeutic strategies which turn people into protected children undermine their rights. To be sheltered from the truth is to lose your dignity. If indeed there is no God, pretending that there is one neither enhances your self-esteem nor improves your ability to deal with reality. On the contrary, it may encourage you to have false expectations about the universe and what it can offer. It may also "train" you to be religiously passive and persuade you to prefer resignation to problem-solving. Yielding, without question, to an authoritarian super-parent is hardly the avenue to decent maturity. . . .

Judaism without God may be a surprising concept. But it is a perfectly appropriate one. It is a healthy non-theological religion which derives its morality from human need and which finds in Jewish history a reflection of the "absurdity" of the universe. Jews, as Jews and as individuals, are ultimately responsible for their own "fates."[5]

God as a Character Created by Human Authors

While Humanistic Judaism does not pray to, worship, praise, or invoke a personal god in its philosophy and liturgy, it has not eliminated the god character in Jewish stories. If one can read Greek mythology as literature reflecting human experiences and aspirations, so too the TANAKH. Once the Hebrew god is read as a character in a human-authored narrative, Yahweh may actually become more interesting and relatable. Yahweh also becomes "real" in the same sense that Hamlet and Job ring true to the human condition.

Yaakov Malkin (1926–2019) was born in Poland and moved to British Mandatory Palestine at age seven. Active in the secular Hashomer Hatzair youth movement, he helped run an underground radio station for the Haganah during Israel's War of Independence before moving into academia in Israel, the United States, and France. He ultimately settled at Tel Aviv University, where he taught rhetoric and drama criticism from 1969 to 1994. He also helped found the first community centers in Haifa, including the Beit HaGefen Jewish-Arab Center.

Over many decades, Malkin spoke, wrote, and taught on core themes of Humanistic Judaism: Judaism as culture, the Bible as literature, and the positive beliefs of secular people. He collaborated with Wine and others on international efforts to spark a global movement of Secular Humanistic Judaism (see introduction to this volume), and from 2003 until his death in 2019 he served as founding dean of Tmura-IISHJ in Jerusalem, which continues to educate and ordain Israeli Secular Humanistic rabbis.

In this selection from his book *Judaism without God? Judaism as Culture and Bible as Literature*, Malkin's emphasis on the Hebrew god as a literary character transforms its role from a judicial authority of the universe to a flawed being representative of imperfect human and moral reality.

Yaakov Malkin, "God as a Literary Figure" (2007)

In secular Jewish culture, the prevailing belief is that God—a character in biblical literature—was created by man. In Genesis, God was made in the image of man (male and female); in other works he is depicted as an incorporeal figure, omnipotent like nature and human in character, speech and temperament. Yahweh, god of Israel, created in the Israelite literature of the Bible, differs from the gods of other peoples, also created by man in the ancient myths of the Fertile Crescent and Greece. Contrary to the many gods created in the myths and literature of polytheistic peoples, Yahweh is alone in the world, without family and without a specific abode (like Olympus). Yahweh is portrayed in the Bible as a god who preceded the universe and nature, which he created out of the void and with which he continues to struggle.

In their belief that God created the world and man, the authors of the Bible ascribe to God all of the laws that govern individual and social human behaviour, thereby eliminating the difference between religious precepts (man's duties to God—e.g. cult and ritual) and civil laws (man's duty to his fellow man and to the society within which he lives). This kind of theistic belief makes it incumbent upon the individual to obey religious leaders, their laws and precepts, since they are perceived as representatives of God, creator of the universe and human society, king and overseer of all they do, who metes out rewards and punishments as he sees fit.

The belief of secular Jews that God and moral values are human constructs frees man from the authority of religious establishment leaders, the *Halakhah* they have created, the commandments they have spoken in God's name, and the system of rules called religion, which they impose upon those who believe in them and in the ability of human beings to speak on God's behalf. Such belief is essentially a-theistic, since it rejects the authority of religion and religious leaders to impose a specific set of beliefs or rules of conduct.

A-theism takes many different forms, e.g. various pantheistic approaches, which identify nature with the divinity, inasmuch as they (like Spinoza) view nature as divine; or conversely, identify the divinity with nature (God has no specific abode, because he is all-encompassing).

Agnostics reject the authority of religion, because they believe that it is impossible to know whether God exists independently of the literature that shaped him; and that consequently, religious leaders claiming to speak in God's name should not be believed, since he cannot be known, encountered or heard.

Deists (like Voltaire) have postulated that a supreme force one might call God could exist, but that such a force is far-removed from humanity and from individual human beings, so that those who purport to speak in its name should not be believed or obeyed.

An analogous approach is that of the religious philosophers (such as the author of the *Guide for the Perplexed*), who assert that the human mind is incapable of grasping God, to whom no characteristic—including existence—should be ascribed. Advocates of this approach believe God to be the supreme wisdom manifest in creation, accessible only to a select few scholars and scientists; or (as Einstein believed), "God" is what we call the enigma of the orderly harmony of all existence—microcosm and macrocosm—order that can be studied, but the source of which can never be known.

What all adherents of the aforementioned beliefs, pantheists, deists, agnostics and declared atheists, have in common [is] the following: A perception of the biblical God as a literary figure created by the authors of the various biblical works; given human form (mouth, arms, etc.) and human characteristics (speaking, commanding, striking) in order to provide unsophisticated readers with an allegory (as Maimonides claimed in *Guide of the Perplexed*), to which they could relate and in which they could believe. The literary figure God, fashioned by the works of the Bible, is anthropomorphic, and can therefore be said to speak words with a mouth, perform actions with an outstretched arm, express rage or disappointment when the Israelites are ungrateful and complain about the conditions of their liberation from slavery, etc. . . .

The distinction between God as creator of man, and God as literary figure created by man, is thus a decisive factor in determining one's approach to life within society, and to society's creations—the Bible included. Those who believe that man is sovereign, free to create laws, abolish or change them in keeping with moral values, adopt a critical approach to the biblical laws and precepts, as well as to the actions and statements of all the characters depicted in the Bible. Such a critical approach—whereby one may accept or reject any biblical precept, statement or action of God, Abraham or Moses—is part of the moral education served by acquaintance with the works of the Bible.

Even the biblical authors who truly believed in God as creator of the universe and supreme judicial authority, were extremely critical of Yahweh's morality. Abram asks whether it is right for the judge of all the earth to mete out collective punishment; readers of Job know that God and not Job was responsible for the latter's woes; the authors of Ecclesiastes and Jeremiah know that there is no justice in Yahweh's world, in which the wicked prosper and the righteous suffer. Like all literary figures in classical literature the world over, God sins in terms of the readers' moral values. . . . Plato was wrong about authors who depict sinful protagonists, when he suggested that they be garlanded with praise and expelled from the city. Characters in literary masterpieces—Yahweh included—are not paragons of virtue. They represent human, emotional, social, religious and moral reality.[6]

3

Positive Humanism

Historically the Jewish atheist has been considered a "nonbeliever" who rejects the consensus propositions of Jewish religion, including rabbinic authority and divine justice. Examples of such Jewish nonbelievers date back as far as the first few centuries CE, appearing in the Babylonian and Jerusalem Talmuds.[1] By the turn of the twentieth century, Jewish anarchists were hosting *Kol Nidrei* (Yom Kippur Eve service) banquets to flagrantly violate Yom Kippur fasting, and radical Zionists were proclaiming a "new Jew" unencumbered by rabbinic religious and spiritual limitations. These revolutionaries agreed that conventional pieties were obsolete and needed to be rejected, whether or not they themselves had a clear positive approach to Jewish culture and identity to replace what had to go.

By contrast, the Humanistic Jewish combination of religious Jewish structures with a secular approach to life resulted in something different: explicitly positive beliefs, affirmation rather than (or in addition to) negation. It was not enough to reach a nontheistic conclusion; one had to find new ways to solve problems, make meaning, and celebrate Jewish life. Moreover, the emphasis on negation was false: so-called nonbelievers do have definite beliefs and values concerning the world, humanity, and society. A major motivation to name the movement Humanistic Judaism rather than "secular" or "atheistic" was a preference for positive messaging and philosophy.

Humanistic Judaism was not the first attempt to create a humanistic religion. The original 1933 Humanist Manifesto (predominantly endorsed by leaders from Unitarian Universalism and Ethical Culture, as well some university professors and one campus rabbi), explicitly affirmed a religious Humanism in positive terms: "Religion consists of those actions, purposes, and experiences which are humanly significant."[2] The movement of Ethical Culture founded by former Reform rabbi Felix Adler (1851–1933) still self-defines "as a religious movement because for us the ethical quest has the depth of a religious commitment, and because we recognize the value of a community of support, celebration, and action."[3] For its part, Humanistic Judaism (1963)[4] did not become entirely universalist; instead, it has maintained an ethnic identity and particular Jewish cultural orientation (see Falick, "Dancing at Two Weddings," in chapter 7).

The three essays in this chapter describe how articulating positive beliefs contribute to self-esteem, comfort and support, and meaning. These beliefs also inform Humanistic Jewish self-definition, celebration of Jewish life, and ethical action, as we shall see throughout this book.

Focus on the Positive

Some secularized Jews define themselves only in relation to traditional Judaism, saying they do not follow its practices. By doing so, they put themselves in the reactive stance of being "bad Jews." Humanistic Judaism, by contrast, rejects such negative self-definition in favor of positive affirmations: to uphold one's own beliefs about the universe and the human condition and to choose to live fully as Jews consistently with one's values.

The following essay, one of Sherwin Wine's most appreciated within the movement, articulates both the need for positive self-definition and expressions of this positive approach. Wine (see chapter 1) emphatically denies that Humanistic Jews are "non-believers," since they have many positive values, truths, and commitments by which they lead their lives.

Sherwin Wine, "Believing Is Better Than Non-Believing" (1986)

> Humanistic Jews should be believers, enthusiastic messengers of a positive philosophy of life. . . .

["Religionists"] present themselves as "believers," as the messengers of a positive statement about the world and its future. Their opponents (namely, we "vicious" humanists) are labeled "unbelievers," deniers of the truth, and purveyors of negativism and nihilism. In fact, the religionists have been so successful with their propaganda that many humanists consent to their label and freely refer to themselves as "unbelievers."

Unbelief is a loser's style. It is a posture of inferiority, an acknowledgement that the message of your enemies is so powerful and so positive that you must define yourself by it. While the opposition has a compelling reason to speak about its beliefs, "unbelievers" have no really significant beliefs to share. Their style is a holding operation, a defensive stance. They only want to make sure that the religious world does not intrude on their lives. They have no urgent or important message for others.

So long as we present ourselves as unbelievers—whether in the Jewish community or in the broader world—we will be losers. We will be viewed as the deniers of other people's strong convictions, not the possessors of strong convictions of our own. Especially in a free society of competing ideas, unbelief is a disastrously negative strategy.

So what does it take to turn a Humanistic Jew into a "believer," an enthusiastic messenger of a positive philosophy of life?

Not very much. After all, we do have strong positive beliefs about nature, people, and morality. The problem is how we see ourselves and how we present our convictions to others. . . .

If you are a believer, you focus on the positive.

Believers tell people first what they believe, not what they do not believe. Effective humanists do not begin their presentation of personal conviction by announcing what they deny. They describe the things and the events in the universe that they think are really there. Agnosticism with regard to God may be the intellectual position of most humanists, but it is less important than our positive commitment to reason and scientific inquiry. Skepticism with regard to the divine origins of Jewish history may be the attitude of Humanistic Jews, but it is less important than our affirmation that Jewish culture is the creation of the Jewish people....

If you are a believer, you offer positive alternatives.

Too often, humanists and Humanistic Jews assault existing institutions and practices without providing adequate substitutes. Just because traditional Jewish communities were built around prayer and God does not mean that alternative Jewish communities cannot be built around a secular Jewish culture and ethical concerns. Just because the traditional Jewish puberty rite is male chauvinist and focused on Bible readings does not preclude an alternative growing-up ceremony that is discrimination-free and celebrates the child's connection to all of Jewish creativity....

If you are a believer, you choose to reverse roles.

Since unbelievers see themselves as outsiders in a community of believers, they make concessions more readily than do their opponents. If the Orthodox want to close down the Jewish Community Center on the Sabbath, if Conservatives want to keep humanistic literature out of the Jewish community library, unbelievers often will yield to the opposition out of a sense that their opponents feel more strongly about these issues than they, the unbelievers, do. But believers refuse to be second-class citizens. Humanistic Jews do not reject the Sabbath. They believe that the Sabbath should be a day for family celebration, personal recreation, and Jewish cultural stimulation. Humanistic Jews do not discard Jewish literature. They affirm the importance of seeing the Jewish experience through eyes that are not traditional. In most cases, their convictions are just as intense as those of their opponents. So, if the other side is always making demands, humanistic believers reverse roles. They have demands to make too.

If you are a believer, you seek out other believers for mutual support.

Unbelievers are notorious non-joiners. Because they often are refugees from authoritarian institutions, the idea of belonging to a group or community that supports congregations and fellowships—of developing a working network of philosophic brothers and sisters—is anathema to them. The very smell of organization terrifies them. They prefer the safety of isolation. Even though the opposition derives its strength, power, and effectiveness from the willingness of its members to express their solidarity through group effort, unbelievers resist measures that would enable them to be equally effective. But believers know that everything the other side does is not bad. Organization is not bad if the purpose of the organization is good. Believers also know that isolation is a self-destructive strategy. It reinforces helplessness and the sense of "outsiderness" and leads to ideological impotence. A voice that cannot be heard is no voice at all....

Believing is better than not believing. It is a strategy more conducive to self-esteem and effectiveness. If there have to be unbelievers, let those who do not believe in humanism play that role for a while.[5]

Life before Death

Religion strives to meet basic and universal human psychological needs, such as knowledge, meaning, control, and comfort. Therefore, a meaningful and positive Humanism has the challenging task of addressing those needs with non-supernatural answers. If one does not have faith in cosmic benevolence, divine intervention, or ultimate reward and punishment, then the importance of this world, this life, and human potential must counterbalance the fear that our existence is merely "nasty, brutish and short."[6]

Rabbi Greg Epstein (b. 1977) grew up in New York City and was studying religion and Chinese at the University of Michigan when he discovered Humanistic Judaism. Ordained by the International Institute for Secular Humanistic Judaism in 2005, he serves as Humanist chaplain at Harvard University and Massachusetts Institute of Technology. His book *Good without God: What a Billion Nonreligious People* Do *Believe* built on his training and experience with Humanistic Judaism to provide broader lessons in secular courage, dignity, and community.

Greg Epstein, "What Is Humanism?" (2009)

Humanism is a bold, resolute response to the fact that being a human being is lonely and frightening. We Humanists take one look at a world in which the lives of thousands of innocent children are ripped away every year by hurricanes, earthquakes, and other "acts of God," not to mention the thousand other fundamental injustices of life, and we conclude that if the universe we live in does not have competent moral management, then so be it: we must become the superintendents of our own lives. Humanism means taking charge of the often lousy world around us and working to shape it into a better place, though we know we cannot ever finish the task.

In short, Humanism is being good without God. It is above all an affirmation of the greatest common value we human beings have: the desire to live with dignity, to be "good." But Humanism is also a warning that we cannot afford to wait until tomorrow or until the next life to be good, because today—the short journey we get from birth to death, womb to tomb—is all we have. Humanism rejects dependence on faith, the supernatural, divine texts, resurrection, reincarnation, or anything else for which we have no evidence. To put it another way, Humanists believe in life *before* death....

At the most important times of our lives—when we or our loved ones are sick and dying; when a new baby is born; when we want to affirm our love in marriage; when we want to educate our children not only about facts and dates, but also important values—we need to be part of a group. We need what, at least potentially, can be found or created in a Humanist community: a place where family, memory, ethical values, and the uplifting of the human spirit can come together with intellectual honesty, and without a god.[7]

Self-Determined Purpose

How does a secular person, or a secular Judaism, answer the human need for meaning and purpose? Can there be meaning to a person's life in a meaningless universe?

Sometimes, incidental experiences can open doors to moments of deep importance. Without a cosmic "purposer" (i.e., God) determining the one goal of our lives, each of us is free to make our own choices and define our own purpose—or purposes, since there is no reason we may not choose more than one.

Rabbi Peter Schweitzer (1952–2023) was ordained as a Reform rabbi in 1979 and initially served a congregation in Indianapolis, but he found that his growing personal theological doubts and discomfort with traditional liturgy created too much cognitive dissonance.[8] Leaving the rabbinate, Schweitzer worked as a clinical social worker for the Jewish Board of Family and Children's Services in Brooklyn. During this time, he discovered Humanistic Judaism and joined The City Congregation for Humanistic Judaism in 1992 as a member, serving as a volunteer for many years before formally becoming the congregation's rabbi in 2005 and retiring as rabbi emeritus in 2018. Schweitzer was also a regular contributor to *Moment*'s "Ask the Rabbis" column and donated his collection of over ten thousand artifacts of Jewish Americana to the National Museum of American Jewish History in 2005. In this passage, an excerpt from a 2021 collection of congregational sermons, he reflects on the secular quest for meaning and purpose.

Peter Schweitzer, "Purpose" (2021)

> One of the messages that we deliver in Humanistic Judaism is that the universe is uncaring and amoral. Nature doesn't reward our good behavior with a good harvest; nor does it punish our bad behavior with flooding or a drought. It just is. Our task is not to make a causal connection or determine how we can placate the weather god to give us a break. Rather, our job is to figure out how to manage the world as it is and, in the face of cynicism, figure out how we can take steps to fix what is broken and improve it.

This is sometimes easier said than done, especially in the face of sadness and tragedy. Under these circumstances, life can lose its meaning and purpose and feel despairing and hopeless.

Of course, this also presumes that life has intrinsic value, that it is not a tale "full of sound and fury, signifying nothing."[9]

I was in the subway one day minding my own business, when I couldn't help looking at a woman standing above me a few feet away. She was holding onto a nearby pole. Along the inside of her arm there was a beautiful tattoo inscription that read, "What would love do now?"

I have since learned that that is a line from a song by singer-songwriter Jason Mraz.[10] At the moment, I thought how powerful it must be to carry around that constant reminder with you on how to lead your life. How every step of the way, every choice and action, would be mediated by that one ideal, giving this woman guidance and clarity. I also liked her tattoo because it seemed like a great secular riff on "What would Jesus do?"...

Other people have quite different mantras to get them through the day or the days of their lives. For example, did you ask a good question today? Were you sufficiently grateful today?

One website I saw catalogues a long list of possible purposes ranging from seeking pleasure or seeking power to survival and replication of the species, and my favorite, "Become the person you've always wanted to be."...

This is where the High Holidays come in, because they carve out time for us to engage in this kind of introspection. They allow us for at least a little while to be idle philosophers, who ponder the purposes of life generally and of our own lives more specifically.[11]

4

Ethics

In contemporary Jewish life, the Hebrew word *mitzvah* is understood as both "commandment" and "good deed." Traditional Jewish ethics is based on obeying divinely authored and rabbinically interpreted commandments; a Humanistic Judaism that instead emphasizes human autonomy and responsibility requires a different basis for doing good.

Being good without a god is not unique to Humanistic Judaism. Defining and prescribing ethics through reason rather than revelation has been a central focus of philosophy for two millennia. Philosophy has produced many schools of secular ethical thought, from Aristotle (384–322 BCE) and Epicurus (341–270 BCE) to Enlightenment idealist Immanuel Kant (1724–1804) and utilitarian John Stuart Mill (1806–73), and still more into the twenty-first century.

As Western culture has secularized, nonreligious ethics has become even more important. A 2014 global study showed that citizens in many developed countries accept that one can be moral without believing in God: 76 percent in Australia, 85 percent in France, even 59 percent in Israel, though in the United States a majority still connect morality with God belief.[1] The popular assumption one *cannot* be a good person—or at least a good president—without a god persists in the American popular mind: a 2020 Gallup poll shows 66 percent willing to vote for a Muslim for president and only 60 percent for an atheist.[2]

The positive ethics of Humanistic Judaism thus provide an alternative to traditional Jewish ethics, are based on a long tradition of ethical reasoning, and meet a key accusation against secularization. Like other secular ethical approaches, Humanistic Judaism measures actions as right or wrong based on their consequences and impact on central principles, such as human rights. However, a key detail distinguishes Humanistic Jewish ethics from general philosophy: Humanistic Jewish ethics respond specifically to the Jewish people's cultural heritage/historical experience. Unlike general philosophy, Humanistic Jewish ethics live in relationship with ethical sayings and traditions, and the balance of individual autonomy and group responsibility, expressed in Jewish culture. Humanistic Jews question the ethical authority of traditional prooftexts and the claim that the ethical values within such texts are uniquely Jewish. Bolstered by new values like freedom and self-determination, they apply values learned from Jewish culture and derived from general philosophy to important issues in the world.

What makes Humanistic Jewish ethics distinct from the ethics of other liberal Judaisms is its willingness to consider ethics in a world conceived without divine revelation, divine commandment, or divine justice. If there is to be justice and ethical action in this world, it must come from human minds and hands.

The ethical principles and actions upheld by Humanistic Jews may not necessarily be unique in and of themselves. Humanistic Jews and Jews affiliated with other liberal Judaisms may well agree on what ethical actions are recommended in a given situation, though they ground their actions differently. In fact, if one follows some Jewish values articulated in traditional Jewish sources like the Torah while rejecting others, then one's standard for obeying or challenging past commandments is one's own judgment. It is affirming for Humanistic Jews to find the ethics of caring for the stranger and not oppressing workers by withholding wages in earlier Jewish thought. However, since Humanistic Jews choose from their heritage how they live their own lives, any actions they may take in harmony with these traditional values are done because of the values' positive consequences today rather than because of their antiquity or purported authority.

Paradoxically, arguing with god and traditional Jewish authority is *itself* a Jewish tradition that Humanistic Judaism celebrates. When

Abraham bargains with God to save Sodom, he asks, "Shall not the judge of the universe deal justly?" (Gen. 18:25). For Humanistic Jews, the positive value of human dignity includes the right and duty to question authority—and challenging authority in the name of justice is impossible if that authority is assumed to define and embody justice. If that authority is itself a projection of human ideas and desires, then ethics demands that its commands be evaluated, debated, even denied if necessary.

This chapter presents four aspects of Humanistic Jewish ethics: the human-centered authority to make ethical decisions based on consequences; the source of values for ethical principles; the right to choose from, and indeed the obligation to argue with, tradition to make meaningful ethical choices; and the application of Humanistic Jewish ethics to our own times.

From Commandment to Autonomy

The revolution in liberal religious Jewish ethics and ritual practice of the last few centuries demonstrates a broad shift from ancestral authority to individual freedom and choice, from commandedness to consequentialist ethics and autonomy. Such a radical change in the basis of social behavior calls for new approaches to ethics.

Humanistic Jewish ethics strive to balance self-actualization and individualism with group responsibility and long-term communal consequences; so too with care for the self and care for others. Some Humanistic Jews approach ethics from a more communitarian perspective, shifting the balance toward group needs over individual choices, while others celebrate individual empowerment and freedom. Generally, however, Humanistic Jews agree that both require due consideration. Ultimately, the locus of authority for making ethical choices is with contemporary humanity rather than ancient tradition. The freedom to decide for oneself is itself a positive good.

Daniel Friedman (b. 1935) was raised in an Orthodox Jewish family in Denver, trained as a Reform rabbi at Hebrew Union College, and evolved into a Humanistic rabbi at Congregation Beth Or in suburban

Chicago, where he served from 1965 to 2000. A founding member of the Society for Humanistic Judaism, Friedman developed an individualist, libertarian approach to post-halakhic Humanistic Jewish ethics, as reflected in this 1996 article excerpted from the movement's journal *Humanistic Judaism*.

Daniel Friedman, "After Halakha, What?" (1996)

It is not difficult to understand why people prize freedom and why those who do not have it yearn for it. Freedom is a necessary condition for the flowering of humanness; for the fulfillment of talents, abilities, and dreams; for the realization of potential powers; for, in a word, happiness. To stifle freedom is to stifle humanity.

But freedom may under some circumstances be a frightening prospect. When taken to excess, it may undermine or destroy the very happiness that freedom itself makes possible. Too much freedom may lead to exploitation of the weak by the strong. It may allow indulgence in behavior that wastes one's talents and squanders one's very life. Absolute freedom may be as dangerous as no freedom at all.

Responsible living requires the development of moral self-authority.

Like water, freedom must be contained if it is to be useful and not wreak havoc. Freedom must be disciplined if it is to operate for the benefit of humanity. Is this not the essential task of civilization at its best—to create and uphold standards, laws, and institutions that promote the benefits of freedom while restraining excesses that would lead to chaos?

Freedom, in our contemporary sense of the word, is a modern value. There are few references to freedom in the Bible, for example, and these concern chiefly the release of a slave; none concern intellectual or spiritual liberty. The essential, bedrock doctrine of the Torah and of subsequent Judaisms until the eighteenth century—the obligation to obey without question the divine commandments as stated in the sacred writings—leaves little room for the autonomy that is essential to our meaning of freedom. "He that trusts in his own heart is a fool" (Psalms 28:26) is more typical of classical Judaism than is "Do your own thing."

Pre-modern Judaism may be viewed as an elaborate system of discipline wherein freedom is not recognized as desirable. Rabbinic Judaism cannot be understood apart from its complex regimen of prescribed and proscribed behavior. Every conceivable activity from dress to diet, from sexual relations to business practices, is meticulously and divinely mandated. It was believed to be God's will that a Jew discipline every act and thought in accordance with the demands of halakha. This is what it means to say that Judaism is a way of life.

With the coming of the Enlightenment and the Emancipation, Jews for the first time encountered and enjoyed the benefits of political and intellectual freedom. They became enamored of a new idea: the rights of the individual. Now, a new source of authority replaced halakha: the self. The self-legislating human being, free from physical coercion or interference by others, free to act on his or her own judgment on behalf of his or her own goals, replaced the servant of God as modernity's ideal man or woman.

In this new vision of humanity, freedom is the very basis of morality. Only a freely acting person can be a moral agent, held responsible for his or her behavior. Responsible living—that is, properly disciplined freedom—requires the development of moral self-authority. The great challenge of liberal, nonauthoritarian religions, such as Humanistic Judaism, is to develop the principles and standards whereby human beings, in the absence of theistic authority, may live responsibly. Lacking a revealed law whose authority is, by definition, beyond question, the method by which such standards and principles are created and evaluated in a humanistic context is the use of reason.

Responsible living—rationally disciplined freedom—is based on at least five principles or rules of behavior:

1. As self-owned, autonomous beings, we have the right to live and to use our minds and bodies without interference, but only so long as we acknowledge the equivalent right that inheres in every other person. We must, therefore, refrain from coercion—the initiation of force or fraud against others.
2. To maximize the length and the quality of our time on earth, it is necessary to care for our health by means of a wholesome diet, regular exercise, sufficient sleep, and moderation in pursuing our goals and our happiness....
3. To promote the healthiest environment for ourselves, our loved ones, and humanity in general, we should avoid behavior that pollutes or wastes the resources of nature.
4. To act responsibly, we must be mindful of both the immediate and long-range consequences of our freely chosen behavior upon ourselves and others.
5. To the extent that our happiness and enjoyment of life depend upon the development of our talents and abilities to the fullest, we will allocate the use of our time and resources intelligently so as not to squander those talents and abilities.

In number, this list falls short of the Ten Commandments, not to mention the hundreds of halakhic requirements that characterized Jewish life for almost two thousand years and still set the standards for Orthodox Jews. Prior to the modern age, tight restrictions were believed to be the necessary means to guarantee civilized behavior and to promote the survival of a community and its values. Once the significance of individual freedom became recognized as a primary good, and the primary source of authority over a person's life was seen as internal, the number of necessary moral restrictions diminished radically. This reduction does not signify that discipline is any less important. On the contrary, now that we enjoy freedom unimagined by previous generations, it is all the more urgent to identify and encourage the appropriate boundaries and limits that distinguish responsible freedom from destructive license. A life of rationally disciplined freedom enables us to express our powers fully in harmony with family and community.[3]

Ethics beyond Ethnicity

Many Jewish groups, from the ultra-Orthodox to secular Jews, claim to act by "Jewish values," yet there is no consensus as to what counts as a Jewish value. If insular isolation from modern society and universal concern to welcome and love the stranger both express "Jewish values," then more clarity is needed as to what different Jewish ideologies mean by the term and why they use it.

Humanistic Judaism celebrates both its continuity and its breaks with traditional Jewish beliefs, practices, and values. When the movement does claim "Jewish values," it explicitly acknowledges that historical Jewish values include both commendable and objectionable ones. Some Humanistic Jews, generally those who consider ethics as purely philosophical rather than cultural, decide what is right and wrong based on consequences and core principles independent of traditional Jewish thought and culture. Others claim a limited continuity—accepting Jewish precursors to some contemporary values when appropriate, along with the modern autonomy to reject other historical Jewish values when deemed necessary. Both sides agree that Humanistic Judaism defines ethical acts based on rational considerations of their consequences; where those conclusions agree with traditional Jewish values, there is a realistic ethical continuity of behavior, if not rationale.

Rabbi Adam Chalom (b. 1975) grew up as a Humanistic Jew at The Birmingham Temple, the founding congregation of the movement. His background reflects common paths to Humanistic Judaism: one parent raised in a secular Yiddish *shule* (school) and a Reform temple, the other a "refugee" from *Mizraḥi* (Middle Eastern) Orthodox Judaism. Ordained by the International Institute for Secular Humanistic Judaism (IISHJ) in 2001, Chalom serves as both rabbi of Kol Hadash Humanistic Congregation in suburban Chicago and dean for IISHJ in North America.

In this selection from a 2009 issue of the movement's journal *Humanistic Judaism* entitled "Ethics for Humanistic Jews," Chalom uses the movement debate between values as Jewish-specific or universal-philosophic to highlight both negative Jewish values rejected by Humanistic Judaism and positive Jewish values the movement celebrates.

Adam Chalom, "Are There Jewish Values?" (2009)

For all of his commitment to making Jewish identity relevant and meaningful for modern minds, Rabbi Sherwin Wine often criticized the idea that there are uniquely Jewish values:

> Good values are universal. They are to be found distributed among all cultures. Love, loyalty and compassion are very Jewish. But they can also be very Greek and very Chinese. Bad values are also universal. Hate, bigotry and greed have no single national home. They are welcomed by people of many cultures. They have even been welcomed by Jews.[4]

Education, family, community, even faith are trumpeted as "Jewish values." There are essentially two objections to claiming any value we admire as a "Jewish value":

1. other, less admirable, values in Jewish tradition are just as central; and
2. other cultures and peoples demonstrate the same good values.

Despite these objections, however, we will see that there is still a basis to claim certain admirable ethics as indeed Jewish values.

GOOD, BAD, AND IRRELEVANT JEWISH VALUES

If we are going to claim such positive values as education and family as "Jewish values," we need to distinguish among:

a. the beautiful ethics of Leviticus 19: for example, loving your neighbor as yourself, judging the poor and rich with equal justice, and not oppressing the stranger "because you were strangers in Egypt";

b. the ritual commandments of Leviticus 19: for example, "you shall not round off the hair on your temples or mar the edges of your beard" and "you shall not sow your field with two kinds of seed; nor shall you put on a garment made of two different materials," which seem ethically irrelevant or irrational commands testing obedience; and

c. the objectionable ethics of Leviticus 20:15: "If a man lies with a male as with a woman, both of them have committed an abomination; they shall be put to death; their blood is upon them." Or the acceptance of slavery, or the extermination of the Canaanites, and so on.

All three varieties of values appear in the middle of the same Torah and are even read in the same Torah portion, *Kedoshim*—"holy things." Which is the more Jewish value, the historic Jewish emphasis on education that created widespread male literacy, or the historic Jewish discrimination against women that denied them similar education and authority until modern times? It is too convenient (and not reasonable) to claim that what we like in our day are "really" Jewish values while what we have discarded were just "accidental."

The truth is that contemporary Jews have always been the arbiters of which values of their past were celebrated, and which were acknowledged and rejected or changed. Deuteronomy decrees that a stubborn and rebellious child should be stoned to death (Deut. 21:18–21). As anyone who has children knows, fully enforcing this law would bring a quick end to humanity. Several hundred years later, the *Mishnah* (200 BCE–200 CE) refined the definition of a "stubborn and rebellious child" to limit it to sons between the onset of puberty and the attainment of majority (*Bar Mitzvah*)—a very short period—and added many conditions required to activate this punishment....[5]

The United States Constitution (Art. 1, sec. 2) counted slaves as 3/5 of a person (with 0/5 of a vote!) for the first one-third of this nation's existence, but the presence of the "3/5 clause" does not ethically disqualify the entire founding document or the nation as a whole. Rather, it requires amendment, historical context, and a nuanced understanding of how culture and ideas develop. Slavery was a Jewish value; it is no longer. For most Jews today, separate seating of men and women in a synagogue would be a violation of their sense of Jewish values (especially with women rabbis), even though that was once a quintessentially Jewish tradition—and still is among the most Orthodox. Our sense of gender equality derives from the modern experience, not from traditional Jewish religious belief, practice, or teaching.

The most important lesson is that "our values" are not synonymous with "Jewish values." We don't accept *all* historical "Jewish values" as our own, so we must be making choices. We are pleased to find our choices prefigured in our cultural tradition, and we can find meaningful formulations that have emotional resonance and cultural importance in that past, but we don't agree or disagree with them simply because they're "Jewish"—we celebrate those values of Jewish culture that inspire us. Perhaps the best approach is to describe "our Jewish values," understanding that "THEIR Jewish values" may be different.

RESPECT FOR OTHER CULTURES

As Sherwin Wine wrote, "The attempt to equate Jewishness with a set of eminently respectable social values is an act of moral boorishness. It suggests, by implication, that these values (if they are defined as virtues) are absent from the behavior of non-Jews."[6] Our experience has shown us that family, education, and community are common to many civilizations, and it feels *chutzpadik* [audacious] to put our label on them as if they were ours, and exclusively ours.

Many traditions have some version of the "golden rule." Consider these familiar formulations:

Leviticus 19:18: "*v'ahavta l'rayakha kamokha*—love your neighbor as yourself."

Jesus in the New Testament: the proverbial "Do unto others as you would have them do unto you."[7]

Rabbi Hillel: "That which is hateful to you, do not do to your brother."[8]

Lao Tsu in the *Tao Te Ching*: "Love the world as your own self; then you can truly care for all things."[9]

Confucius in his *Analects*: "What you do not want done to yourself, do not do to others."[10]

And even the rationalist philosophy of Immanuel Kant: "Act only according to that maxim whereby you can at the same time will that it should become a universal law."[11]

Jewish civilization clearly does not hold the patent on inventing the golden rule; nor does it have a monopoly on its articulations. And thus for many other "Jewish values." . . .

Let us accept that we have neither the monopoly nor the patent on a particular value, such as education. That recognition does not change the historical reality that education is an integral part of Jewish civilization. In other words, education can be *both* a Jewish value *and* a value found in other cultures—its emphasis is distinctive of Jewish culture, even if not unique to Jews. My house has two entry doors, a garage and an open floor plan—a collection of features not unique to my house, but a truthful description of my house nonetheless.

FINDING OUR JEWISH VALUES

There are three legitimate routes to finding "our Jewish values." One can certainly read the traditional sources of Torah, Bible, Talmud, and commentary for conventional Jewish values celebrated in many Jewish circles, with which we may agree. One can also study the lived experience of the Jewish people. The *chutzpah* (audacity) of mocking authority in a satirical *purimspiel* (Purim play) or expressed in such proverbs as "Angels once walked on the earth; now they are not even in heaven" is not prescribed in religious law but is an important part of the Jewish experience for us.

The third route is to study Jewish history to see what lessons it can teach us; those, too, will be Jewish values, for they derive from the Jewish experience. In that same High Holiday passage in which Sherwin Wine objected to claiming good values as uniquely Jewish values, he affirmed...

> Humanistic values flow naturally from Jewish history and from the Jewish experience.... [We] who have suffered so much from hate cannot become the champions of hate.... If Jewish history could speak, it would proclaim a humanitarian ethic. If the Jewish experience could talk, it would guarantee the dignity of all men and women. To study Judaism is to hear these messages.[12]

Our values may or may not be "Jewish values"; but "our Jewish values" are clearly *ours*—values we find meaningful, inspirational, and motivational that are part of both our inherited tradition and our personal philosophy of life.[13]

Challenging Authority

While much of rabbinic Jewish ethics is based on obeying divine commandments, the Jewish tradition of argument, and even questioning the divine, goes back to Judaism's earliest sources.[14] The tradition includes both condemnation of Jewish argument as exemplary of being a "stiff-necked people" worthy of divine punishment and also celebrations of intellectual curiosity, the importance of human reason and debate, the collective nature of defining truth, and chutzpah. In our day, Humanistic Jews enthusiastically claim the tradition of arguing with religious authority as their own.

Born Amos Klausner in Jerusalem to immigrants from Eastern Europe, Amos Oz (1939–2018) was raised in a largely secular home that sent him to a religious school. At age fourteen, he left home to join the secular and socialist Kibbutz Hulda, studied philosophy and literature at the Hebrew University, and later became a professor of Hebrew literature at Ben-Gurion University of the Negev. A prolific and celebrated Israeli essayist, novelist, and public intellectual, Oz authored the novels *My Michael* (1968) and *A Perfect Peace* (1982), essay collections such as *In the Land of Israel* (1983) and *Jews and Words* (2012, with his daughter Fania Oz-Salzberger), and many other works exploring the human condition.

In this contribution to a 2017 volume of essays on secular Jewish culture edited by Yaakov Malkin, leader of the Humanistic Judaism movement in Israel (see chapter 2), Oz describes modern secular and Humanistic Jews as heirs to all of Jewish tradition, even those traditions with which they argue. Argument itself is a core feature of their Jewish inheritance.

Amos Oz, "Jews Argue with God" (2017)

There is no Jewish pope, but were one to be elected, we would all slap him on the back and say something like: "You don't know me from Adam, but your grandfather and my uncle once did business together in Zhitomir, or in Marakesh, so give me a couple of minutes, and I'll explain to you once and for all what God really wants from us."

Throughout Jewish history, there have been pretenders to the throne, some of whom may even have had a considerable following, but as a rule, the Jewish People does not like to be told what to do. Ask Moses. Ask the prophets. God himself complains constantly about how undisciplined and quarrelsome the Israelites are. They argue with Moses, Moses argues with God and even submits his resignation, which he eventually withdraws—but only after he has negotiated with and had his demands met by God (Ex 32). Abraham bargains with God, like a used car salesman, over the fate of Sodom—fifty righteous men, forty, thirty—and even reproaches the Master of the Universe, with his poignant "shall not the Judge of all the earth do justly?" (Gen 18:25). Nowhere does the Bible tell us that he was struck by lightning for his blasphemy. The people quarrelled with the prophets, the prophets quarrelled with God, the kings quarrelled with the people and with the prophets, Job cursed the heavens. The heavens refused to acknowledge that they had sinned against Job, although they did award him compensation, and in recent generations, there have been *hassidic* rabbis who have summoned God to appear before a rabbinical court.

Jewish culture is anarchistic at heart. We don't like discipline, and we don't simply obey orders. What we want is justice. A simple shepherd can become king of Israel or compose the Psalms, if he is moved by the holy spirit. A dresser of sycamore trees can become a prophet. A shepherd of the flocks of Kalba Savua, or a shoemaker, or a blacksmith, can teach and explain the Torah, leaving a lasting mark on the daily life of each and every Jew. Yet the challenge "who made you a ruler and a judge over us" or "how do we know that you are the one" is never, or almost never, far away. You may be a great scholar, but there is someone of equal stature just around the corner, who does not share your opinion, and often "both opinions are the word of the living God."

Questions of authority have generally been resolved by means of a partial consensus, never unanimously. The history of Jewish culture throughout the ages has been a succession of bitter and often tempestuous disputes, some of which have, nonetheless, been very fruitful. In the absence of an authoritative mechanism for the resolution of such disputes, the opinion of one rabbi was given greater weight than that of another, simply because the former was considered the greater scholar.

Jewish culture at its best is a culture of give and take, of negotiation and thorough examination of all aspects of a given issue, of keen persuasion and arguments for the sake of heaven, but also of strong passions merely masquerading as arguments for the sake of heaven. This spiritual foundation is quite compatible with polyphonic democracy—a choir of different voices, coordinated by a system of authoritative rules. Lights, not the light. Beliefs and opinions, not belief and opinion....

Bialik, Katznelson and Gordon never believed that we should "raze the old world to the ground." Even Brenner never said to the

Jews of Halakhah [Jewish law], "you can keep your holy scriptures and other antiquated baggage."[15] They said, "we too are heirs to Jewish culture—not sole heirs, but legitimate heirs." As legitimate heirs, we are not slaves to our inheritance, but may choose to highlight one aspect and downplay another. We may seek to develop a "dialectic" relationship between Jews and their culture—one in which an element of recurrence is also desirable. What flourished yesterday will fertilise that which will flourish tomorrow, and what will flourish tomorrow may in fact resemble that which flourished the day before yesterday. Cultures have seasons. For thousands of years, Jewish culture has been enriched by other cultures—on which it has, in turn, left its own mark.

All of this is encapsulated in the biblical phrase "renew our days as of old"; you cannot renew something without "of old," and "of old" has no future without renewal.[16]

Humanistic Ethics in the Real World

Jewish ethics encompasses not only abstract theories of ideal behavior or definitions of what it means to love one's neighbor, but also applications of Jewish law and philosophy to real-life complexities. Applying Jewish teachings to lived experience has long been a Jewish tradition, from the early rabbis debating biblical laws after the loss of Jewish sovereignty through medieval interpretations of talmudic law in new circumstances under Christianity and Islam to modern popular works invoking Jewish wisdom to address contemporary issues.[17]

Rabbi Denise Handlarski (b. 1979), ordained in 2013 by the International Institute for Secular Humanistic Judaism, is a professor of education at Trent University, community leader, and Jewish labor and birth doula in Toronto. In 2018, Handlarski founded Secular Synagogue, an online-only Jewish community dedicated to inclusion, creativity, and joyful Jewish experience.

Handlarski's approach to universal ethics and inclusivity is informed by her own experiences as an intermarried rabbi. In this contribution to the movement's journal *Humanistic Judaism* issue "Change, Fear and Hope in the 21st Century," she demonstrates the application of both Humanistic and Jewish values to the contemporary challenges of minority status, privilege, and equality.

Denise Handlarski, "Truth and Reconciliation on Race" (2016)

When I was studying for my PhD in South African literature, I became fascinated with South Africa's Truth and Reconciliation Commission (TRC)....

My work in South African literature eventually turned to the Jewish experience. At once part of the "white" majority, which had clear and obvious privilege, but also a targeted minority, on the receiving end of anti-semitic violence and discrimination, the double-edged position of South African Jews fascinates me. And in Canada, again, I see similarities. We as Jews are, generally speaking, both a tiny minority still exposed to anti-Semitism and, simultaneously, part of the privileged race/class groups of our society. Just as I could never understand Jews who could reconcile themselves to living in apartheid South Africa, knowing what we know about oppression, I could never understand anti-Aboriginal racism amongst Jews here. I see it as a Jewish imperative, for reasons coming from our history, our traditions of pursuing tzedaka (justice) and Tikkun Olam (repairing the world), and loving/living with/respecting the "strangers" we live among (never mind that from the Indigenous point of view, we are the stranger!) to understand and honor FNMI [First Nations, Metis, and Inuit] peoples....

What does any of this have to do with being a Jew? For many, there are commitments to Tikkun Olam. And we as Humanists have a particular desire to see and value all of humanity equally, so the trends described above should worry us. But for me, our insider/outsider status in North America of the minority group with social power, of the once stranger who is now largely assimilated, of the original wandering cosmopolitan subject in a world that is increasingly globalized and cosmopolitan, gives us a unique opportunity to build bridges. Our concerns as Jews: exile, diaspora, language, cultural separation and assimilation, nationhood and belonging, are largely the issues of the other minority groups among whom we live. We can really talk about what it means to be different. We can really talk about what it means to be excluded and persecuted. And we can make sure we are never part of a "majority" that silences those experiences, but only if we acknowledge that systemic racism exists, in our schools, in our systems of justice, in our workplaces, and beyond.

Much of Canadian and American society has been founded on the idea of "equality," that we are equal before the law, have equal opportunities in education and employment, and share equally in the resources of our respective nations. And yet, there is overwhelming evidence that suggests that equality remains a dream and not a reality. It can be difficult to acknowledge the fictions and frictions that surround us. But we as Humanistic Jews are in favor of reason and truth over mythology, and doing so is necessary for us to live full lives as Jews, as Humanists, and as human beings in a very complicated and still very unfair world.[18]

5

Spirituality

Can a Humanistic Jew be "spiritual"? Spirituality often evokes the supernatural: souls, angels, revelation, and divinity. Yet the etymological origin of "spiritual" is the Latin *spirare*—"to breathe," an essential act for human life in *this* world. If "inspiration," uplifting the human spirit, feeling part of something larger than oneself, is a basic human need reflected in every culture, then even a naturalistic approach to life like Humanistic Judaism must meet that need. As André Comte-Spoonville put it in *The Little Book of Atheist Spirituality*, "The human spirit is far too important a matter to be left up to priests, mullahs or spiritualists. It is our noblest part, or rather our highest function. . . . Renouncing religion by no means implies renouncing spiritual life."[1]

Humanistic Jews find their natural inspiration in many ways. Humanistic Jewish services and celebrations provide inspiration through emotional connection with community and Jewish civilization. Humanistic Jewish ties to family heritage and traditions, like using an heirloom *Kiddush* cup or lighting Shabbat candles, provide both emotional uplift and a natural transcendence of connecting with family and culture. Meditation and reflection create opportunities for calm, focus, and self-evaluation. Experiencing nature, from personal moments to contemplating the universe, creates moments of wonder, curiosity, and feeling connected beyond the individual self. Art, music, and the appreciation of beauty express and evoke deep human emotions. The study of history, from standing in an ancient synagogue to seeing a thirty-thousand-year-old human handprint, provides a temporal transcendence through common human experience. Ethical ties to other people, whether through helping an individual or working collectively for social change, can provide the kind of psychological oomph also found in religious experience.

It is a given that many of these sources of inspiration are also experienced by other Jews. For Humanistic Jews, however, these are means not to reach the divine, but to transcend the self, experience inter- and intrapersonal human connection, and imbue life with a sense of meaning and purpose.

Because Humanistic Judaism empowers people to make their own Jewish choices, Humanistic Jews develop their own inspirational practices. They may even disagree on whether a particular practice is or is not consistent with Humanistic Judaism or whether it is "spiritual" rather than psychological or emotional. Jewish and human, scientific and poetic, individual and communal, secular and spiritual, cultural and religious are some of the tensions inherent in Humanistic Judaism

This chapter will explore the phenomenon of Humanistic Jewish spirituality through four lenses: how Humanistic Jewish community can meet the human need for inspiration; the many paths to Humanistic Jewish inspiration members of the movement can choose; the reframing of traditional rituals from following commandments to celebrating culture and creating meaning; and the diversity of ritual practice among Humanistic Jews in the twenty-first century.

Meeting Human Needs

Secular spirituality could be a contradiction in terms—if one is secular and focused on this world and this life, one cannot conceivably also be spiritual and connected to the spirit world of the supernatural. Romantic poet John Keats (1795–1821) laments:

> Philosophy will clip an Angel's wings,
> Conquer all mysteries by rule and line,
> Empty the haunted air, and gnomed mine—
> Unweave a rainbow. . . .[2]

If there is no more mystery with a rational and scientific approach to life, there would seem to be no room for the supernaturally spiritual. Yet what is called "spirituality" also encompasses much that is compatible with a humanistic philosophy of life, such as art, music, and deeply felt connections to other human beings.

In 2001 the International Institute for Secular Humanistic Judaism hosted a colloquium titled "Secular Spirituality: Passionate Search for a Rational Judaism." An essay by Yaakov Malkin (see chapter 2), excerpted here from the published proceedings of that event, articulates the strong spiritual needs of secular Jews.

In particular, Malkin highlights interpersonal connection as a key element of Humanistic Jewish spirituality. Community membership is itself a spiritual matter. Moreover, that belongingness not only is present among one's contemporaries, but extends back through time to all those who have died but whose memory and legacy still remain a treasured part of that community. "Secular humanists can rise to the spiritual plane because they recognize and welcome the ability of men and women to devise new realities, physical, mental, or spiritual."

Yaakov Malkin, "What Makes the Secular Need Spirituality" (2003)

So many people in the West today, Jews and non-Jews, secular and religious, are looking for activities and lifestyles that can generate spiritual experience, that can lift them out of the day-to-day world and out of their image of themselves in that day-to-day world.

Large numbers of seculars have sought spirituality in journeys of exploration to the civilizations and religions of the Far East. Others seek the source in Kabbalist studies or in the new communities of faith to which Judaism has given birth (New Age, Jewish Renewal) and which—through new-old rituals, community singing, close interpersonal contact, and strong communal bonding—aspire to restore enthusiasm and emotionality to the faith, to emulate a Hasidic fervor.

While these seekers for spirituality, religious and secular, do not agree in their definition of what they seek, they are nonetheless of one mind that the level of spirituality possible in their current lives is no longer enough. The routine of their lives, religious or secular, lacks stimulation and challenge, something to lift them to a higher spiritual level, to generate moments of exhilaration beyond rationality.

Rational behavior engages only part of our mental and psychic abilities. Intellectual development and rational knowledge and judgment exhaust our capacity for experience but do nothing to spark that emotional connection to what lies beyond the rationally explicable—masterpieces of art and literature, the unique experience of standing before a vast natural panorama, the encounter with a rare and captivating personality, be it human or divine.

Men and women cannot have a spiritual life without engaging and developing these mental and spiritual capacities. These capacities enhance life, bring us face to face with the sublime that is there to be found in both the human and natural worlds. Letting these capacities lie inactive results in dissatisfaction and boredom—expressions of the soul in pain, no different from the pain felt in any limb kept inactive. The search for spirituality is the search for a way to rise above the tedium and mental boredom of life in the practical world. . . .

The mental-spiritual life that fuses sensation, experience, and reason gives us pleasure and excitement by using memory to give present meaning to pleasurable events from the past and by using our capacity for imagination to conjure into mental reality people and things we have never seen. This is the source of the contentment derived from time-honored rituals, ordered by custom but also expressing identity with our community. The certainty that self-evaluation must be imbued with a strong element of rationality stimulates us to vitalize our ritual activity with new customs and ceremonies, rich with the resonances of our own experience and time as secular Jews have been revitalizing Jewish festival and celebration for the past hundred years.

But none of this leads automatically to happiness. Happiness is not a realm of contentment we can find our way to and dwell in by spiritual means alone. Happiness does not visit our lives only in fleeting if recurrent moments of contentment, but also as the outcome of knowing that the way we are living our life is bringing real benefit to others. This sort of life is possible only when we pour the whole of our selfhood into it, mind and body. Mere devotion to the self, a life of exercises in "pure" spirituality designed to empty our consciousness, is no way to real happiness....

The desire for a spiritual dimension to life that takes the form of a longing for social contact and belonging often finds its satisfaction in joining a community—religious or secular—and participating in activity that lifts the individual over the walls of ego. Community membership is a spiritual matter, bonding an individual not only to a group of people, all of whom know and acknowledge each other as group members, but also to a historical community, generations old....

In a "community of culture," allegiance is to the nation, tribe, ethnic entity, people, or one of the many other terms applied to an amalgam of smaller communities united by a common cultural heritage, language, and territory. These "communities of culture"—in all religions and national civilizations—also acknowledge as members the dead of previous generations. (The head of a small Jewish community in the Atlas mountains explained to the documentary film director Arnon Tzafrir that his community numbered twenty-five thousand persons, of whom three hundred were still living.) Tombstones, pictures and photos, names, stories, songs, and ceremonies of remembrance keep the dead present in the community's spiritual environment.

A "community of culture" takes care that its education nurtures communal solidarity and an awareness of the community's history and traditions and of the key figures in its heritage. The community's story becomes central to its cultural heritage and is shaped and colored by written texts and works of art, by festival rituals and traditional customs. The degree to which community membership impinges on the individual depends on the degree of his or her involvement in and awareness of communal institutions and cultural life. . . .

Secular humanists can rise to the spiritual plane because they recognize and welcome the ability of men and women to devise new realities, physical, mental, or spiritual. . . . This confident conviction in humankind's spiritual and creative potential, in the moral heights men and women can reach—mirrored in the depths of murderousness and evil to which they can sink, for they have a sovereign power of choice—is an *empirical* conviction, based on knowing what humankind has already created and done.[3]

Diversity in Humanistic Jewish Spirituality

Humanistic Judaism's approach to spirituality exemplifies the contemporary movement's emphasis on positive humanism over negative secularism. Before World War II, Jewish secularists often rejected anything reminiscent of religious Judaism, including bar/bat mitzvah, God-focused holidays like Yom Kippur, and ritual actions like lighting Shabbat candles. Instead, the congregational structure of Humanistic Judaism transposed these religious elements to a secular key, opening possibilities for new meaning. In all likelihood Humanistic Judaism's beginnings a generation later in the 1960s contributed to this: what the intellectual parents of Humanistic Jews might have rejected to break away from traditional Judaism, they themselves could reconnect with, once they seized the creative freedom to make their cultural Jewish practices newly meaningful.

Rabbi Judith Seid (b. 1949) has roots in Jewish secularism and Humanistic Judaism, both of which influence her approach to spirituality. Raised in a secular Yiddishist *shule* (school) in California, Seid graduated from the leader, cantor, and rabbinic programs of the International Institute for Secular Humanistic Judaism and also holds an MA in Jewish communal studies from Hebrew Union College–Jewish Institute of Religion (Reform). She has led secular Jewish communities in Ann Arbor, Baltimore, and California's Castro Valley. Two of her books exemplify important paths to secular Jewish spirituality: *We Rejoice in Our Heritage: Home Rituals for Secular and Humanistic Jews* (i.e., the transcendence of Jewish cultural inheritance) and *Kumzits! A Festivity of Instant Jewish Songs* (i.e., the inspiration found in communal singing of shared heritage and values). This passage from a third book, *God-Optional Judaism: Alternatives for Cultural Jews Who Love Their History, Heritage and Community*, explores some of the pathways Humanistic Jews pursue for beautiful, self-congruent, and empowering secular Jewish inspiration.

Judith Seid, "A Secular Spirituality" (2018)

The great generational difference between the traditional Secularists and the present cultural Jews lies in the way they think about spirituality.

Because we recognize that we are more than our bodies, that we are different from the other animals in some qualitative way, and that we need rest and music and love, we have come to ask if we also need what is called a spiritual or even religious experience—a feeling of congruence, order, and harmony, the feeling of being part of something larger than our individual selves. This need may be hardwired into us, part of our human system, part of our need to make order out of a world of chaos. Secular and Humanistic Jews are beginning to embrace the notion of spirituality because we want to be able to access that experience which many Secularists enjoy in other-than-Jewish environments.

Given that we have this need, how do we fulfill it? Buddhist chants? Surrender to an all-powerful god? Why should we allow this basic part of our humanity to be separate from a basic part of our individual selves, our Jewishness? Rather, let us explore the meaning of a secular spirituality.

The late Max Rosenfeld, . . . a contributing editor to *Jewish Currents* magazine, and a teacher of Yiddish at Graetz College, talked about spirituality as "a state of mind that reinvigorates the spirits of Humanists," and said that spirituality serves to "acknowledge and express the connection between humans and the universe."

Sherwin Wine, rabbi of the Birmingham Temple and founder of the Society for Humanistic Judaism, described spirituality as "the experience of intense beauty" such as the majesty of nature. He quotes philosopher George Santayana that beauty gives meaning to our lives and is related to our survival and happiness. This feeling of overwhelming beauty, according to Wine, is the result of an interplay between the person and the object perceived as beautiful, and is thus an act of creation. (He gives the example of a concert of Yiddish music that moved him deeply but might have left an Irishman emotionally unaffected.)

Marilyn Rowens, former ceremonial director of the Birmingham Temple and a Certified Secular Humanistic Jewish Leader, describes spirituality as validating or touching a piece of the true self, a reaching inward.

These three conceptions of the religious or spiritual experience have one commonality, a feeling of congruence that can take place in three arenas: the self, the outside world, and the interface between the two.

The experience of congruence with self is that rare feeling of peace and self-knowledge at once. In the 1960s and '70s, my friends used to chant or meditate or take drugs to induce that state, but intense self-awareness can be attained in Jewish environments and practice as well. A Jewish spiritual home needs to provide the opportunity for people to reach that touching of the self, the congruence between what we seem to be and what we are.

Congruence with the un-self-aware universe is another sort of spiritual experience. The sense of being part of a wondrous universe, of awe at living in a world that has the Rocky Mountains or the Pacific Ocean or the perfect trillium flower can be overwhelming. The sense of identification with a painting or piece of music or a poem is, perhaps, the same sort of experience, one that swells the heart with the perception of beauty in the world.

The sense of being part of something greater than oneself is the third element in the triad of congruences that make up a secular spirituality. I grew up in a wonderful era of political struggle. With my parents, my kindershule [children's school], and my friends, I went on civil rights marches, peace marches, women's and gay rights marches. I sang with hundreds and with thousands and once with hundreds of thousands. Each time, I knew my voice was part of the chorus, and, though I couldn't hear its separate tones at all, I knew that without it, the sound would not be the same. It was a magnificent, joyful, and empowering feeling, a feeling of congruence with others that I cherish.

That same congruence with others exists in those rare moments of perfect oneness with a lover. It comes into being when we sing a song that was sung by our ancestors and we enter into the stream of our people's history and heritage.

This experience, universal as it seems, most clearly differentiates secular from religious spirituality. For the religious believer, the feeling of being part of something greater than the self means entering into the larger something that exists independent of the people who enter into it. For the Secular Humanist, it means entering into the larger something that is made up only of its participants and relies upon human beings for its existence.[4]

The Resonance of Ritual

Why do some Humanistic Jews light Shabbat candles? Their motivation is not simply to obey mitzvot (commandments), since many other ritual mitzvot, like following kosher dietary laws or immersing in a *mikveh* (ritual bath) at the end of a menstrual period, are not generally followed.

Rather, Humanistic Jews reframe elements of Jewish traditional ritual humanistically to embrace the natural transcendence of connecting to their heritage and global Jewish peoplehood and sometimes to universal human experience. They welcome interpreting ritual actions with new significance through contemporary symbolism, poetry, and aesthetics. Their choices reflect the movement's declaration that such rituals are human-created and thus eligible to be chosen or rejected, modified or preserved, or understood with new meanings. They select those symbolic expressions that meet their current human needs for meaning and a natural transcendence.

Terry Toll (b. 1950), raised a Conservative Jew in Philadelphia, connected with Humanistic Judaism in lay-led communities in New York City and New York's Westchester County. Professionally she worked with Jewish Women International and the American Jewish Committee, finding that her Humanistic Judaism both enriched and complicated mainstream Jewish communal work. In this essay excerpted from an issue of the movement journal *Humanistic Judaism* focused on Shabbat, she offers multiple meanings for lighting candles rather than limiting the experience to one prescribed *kavanah* (intention). "Lighting Candles" has since become both a meditation for communal reflection and personal inspiration for private practice.

Terry Toll, "Lighting Candles" (1994)

As we humans move through time and space, we assign different roles to the act of lighting candles. Sometimes candles serve the purpose of signaling the onset or passage of holy days and special occasions. At other times, we light candles to communicate our solidarity with people from whom we are separated, by time or space, or by other barriers. We light yahrzeit candles in memory of deceased loved ones. At still other times, we light candles to brighten dark corners and to improve vision and understanding. . . . Perhaps one reason for the universal appeal of candle lights is that candles are a reflection of the human spirit, Jewish and otherwise.

At its best and most glorious, the flame of a candle points high up, striving to move beyond its immediate reach. An active, burning candle emits a glowing, golden haze. Its flame communicates strength, vitality, triumph, vision, and warmth.

In the course of its lifespan, the flame of a candle is dynamic, not static. It surges up and falls down. It sways back and forth. It expands and contracts. The flame of a candle can brighten dark spots and expand our vision. That same flame can narrow our focus and blind us if we fail to note other sources of light in our environment.

The flame of most candles has two parts. The upper, outer layer is brilliant gold. The inner, lower layer is blue. This inner layer is like a shadow box, inviting us to explore the many images it suggests. These images, like the human spirit, are both creative and destructive. Shadows suggest negative visions of Jewish synagogues and homes set afire during pogroms and wars; of books, secular and religious, burned during cultural purges; of civilians' and soldiers' faces scarred by the flames of wartime bombs. Flickers of candles also conjure images of great moments in history, such as the victory of the Maccabees, or more mundane but equally pleasant memories of the past. The latter include flames that heated the savory meals of yesteryear and provided light to dark households and passageways, enabling people to better control their world and communicate with each other.

Candles have a finite existence and demonstrate the fragile nature of life on this earth. Candles begin to glow while in a solid state but eventually burn down to nothingness. From the first moment of burning, candles seem to shed tears of awareness as the wax drips down their sides.

In lighting candles, we seek connection with the past, with each other, and with ourselves. Burning lights give us a sense of our strength, vision, and dynamism. They reflect the complexity of our experience on earth and the delicacy of our coexistence, peaceful or otherwise, here and now.

May the lighting of candles always remind us of the dynamic, multifaceted, and fragile nature of our lives. And may the light of candles direct us to seek each other in peace.[5]

Evolution of Humanistic Jewish Practice

Humanistic Judaism contains a paradox: the movement celebrates individual choice, yet some of its communities employ Humanistic rabbis as communal authorities. The movement's leading rabbis from the 1960s to the 1990s were ordained by other movements (Humanistic Judaism ordained its first rabbi in 1999) and tended to be prescriptive, declaring definitively what Humanistic Jews should do or not do. Its second generation of rabbinic and lay leadership tends to be more descriptive without demanding uniformity, by explaining what most Humanistic Jews choose to do and why. As such, defining boundaries for Humanistic Jewish ideology and community practice becomes ever more challenging.

Adding to this complexity is how Humanistic Judaism approaches received tradition. Whereas in traditional Judaism the antiquity of an earlier generation's teachings generally gives its decisions greater authority, in Humanistic Judaism the argument "This is the way we've always done it" holds limited sway, since each generation is empowered to question what it has received. Like Jewish tradition as a whole, the movement's past practice and belief are respected—but it is a given that they can and should be challenged too. At the same time, this descriptive approach also means that rabbis and laypeople alike participate in the conversation.

A 2020 conversation in the Facebook Humanistic Judaism Discussion Group grappled with the Humanistic Jewish "tradition" of rejecting *kippot* (skullcaps) as set forth in the *Guide to Humanistic Judaism* (originally published in 1993) and the ritual practice's more positive reception by new voices in new circumstances twenty-five years later.

The original post that challenged the Society for Humanistic Judaism's *Guide to Humanistic Judaism* (1993, 2017) was penned by William Thompson, an independent member of the Society for Humanistic Judaism who helped found the online Spinoza Havurah, independently authored *The Jewish Humanist Siddur*, and majored in philosophy at Clemson in South Carolina. Other commentators included here are Courtney Harrison, an ESL teacher in Germany originally from Michigan who is engaged with the online community Secular Synagogue; Joshua Silberstein Bamford, an Australian academic who studied cognitive and evolutionary anthropology at Oxford University and was formerly active in the secular Jewish community Kehillat Kolenu in Melbourne; Jen Naparstek Klein, a New York City–based psychologist and longtime member and song leader at The City Congregation for Humanistic Judaism; and several Humanistic Judaism professionals: Rabbi Adam Chalom of the International Institute for Secular Humanistic Judaism (IISHJ) and Kol Hadash Humanistic Congregation in suburban Chicago, Executive Director Paul Golin of the Society for Humanistic Judaism, Rabbi Jeremy Kridel of Machar: The Secular Humanistic Jewish Congregation of Greater Washington in Washington DC, and Rabbi Sivan Maas of Tmura-IISHJ in Israel.

In particular, this passage in the *Guide* sparked this discussion:

> Every symbol stands for something—an idea, belief, value, or commitment that is being affirmed and communicated by its use. Only when the user sincerely accepts the meaning underlying the symbol is its use proper and significant. A Jew would not wear a cross or venerate the Koran without violating his or her own convictions and identity.... By the same token, Humanistic Jews would not display those symbols of theistic Judaism whose clear meaning conflicts with humanistic principles....
>
> As testimony to faith in the supposed supernatural author of the texts contained in the *tefillin* [phylacteries] and mezuzah, these symbols are inappropriate for use by Humanistic Jews. So, too, are all other symbols, such as the tallit [prayer shawl], whose inherent meaning and purpose is inextricably linked to theism.... To wear a *kippah* or yarmulke, a head-covering signifying awe before God, clearly would not be appropriate in a Humanistic gathering.[6]

Humanistic Judaism Facebook Discussion on Ritual Practice (2020)

William Thompson: I really disagree with what the author writes regarding the appropriateness or inappropriateness of some Jewish symbols for Humanist Jews. For example . . . that the mezuzah, tefillin [phylacteries], tallit [prayer shawl], and *kippah* [skullcap] are inappropriate because they are "inextricably linked" to theism. [This is] ... the case ... [for] everything but the *kippah* because the[se] are mandated by the Torah, and the *kippah* is supposed to signify "awe before God."

But they think that Sabbath candles and matzah are acceptable because they're not "inherently theistic." This, of course, completely ignores the rationale for these things. Sabbath candles were a work around to allow light on Erev Shabbat because the Torah forbids kindling a fire on Shabbat, and matzah is a direct commandment from the Torah!

The simple fact of the matter is, a lot of Jewish practices and symbols come either directly from the Torah or are an interpretation on how to do something commanded by the Torah, including a lot of the holidays. I don't think that we need to necessarily reject every symbol or tradition that might be perceived as theistic because that would be almost everything Jewish. Humanistic Judaism should be about finding ways to embrace traditions in a way authentic to ourselves as humanists, which might require a lot of reinterpretation. New readings for our mezuzahs (and tefillin if there's a desire for that), new interpretations for the meaning of tallit and *kippah*. Symbols of course represent things, but the meaning of symbols evolves over time, and I think we should be helping the meaning evolve rather than just rejecting well-established Jewish symbols outright on the basis of pretty flimsy reasoning. . . .

Courtney Harrison: I think wearing Jewish symbols is a way to be loudly and proudly Jewish, but not necessarily religious. I'm fine if people want to wear them, I'm fine if people don't want to. I just don't like being judged for wearing them. I've had some stares for wearing *kippot* from Orthodox men who were mad I was wearing one. I've also had some stares from Humanistic Jews for choosing to wear one. Both situations sucked equally. Personal choice of self-expression without judgment is what I hope to see in a movement.

Joshua Silberstein Bamford: Having these symbols of identity may be even more important now, with rising antisemitism in some parts of the world. When I wear a *kippah*, it's out of solidarity with other Jews and a marker of cultural identity.

Adam Chalom: I want to offer some explanation/defense of the *Guide*'s position, with the big caveat that I believe strongly that every person is in charge of their own head/clothing and can wear what they choose or find meaningful. Also, some of that rhetoric is held over from the classical Reform inheritance of our founding rabbis Dan Friedman and Sherwin Wine—if you read the 1885 Pittsburgh Platform, you'll find similar imperious "we don't do those primitive things any more" rhetoric. So maybe this is explaining MY choice to NOT wear these items, to not have a basket of *kippot* and tallises at our congregation, and so on.

The original distinction that was attempted was between explicit commandments (e.g., the traditional tallit design has the theistic blessing embroidered along the edge) and cultural elements that have either anthropological or more easily adaptable meanings. For example, matzah is an older technology of breadmaking and hearkens back to the farmer roots of *chag ha-matzot*; however the Torah and Rabbis took it differently. And the Shabbat described in the *Guide* is VERY different from the Torah or Rabbinic Shabbat. Of course, the *kippah* is NOT in the Torah, that is a rabbinic commandment, but that leads to the second rationale.

I believe that someone who wears a *kippah* all the time (i.e., not just in synagogue) is generally thought to be a more conventionally religious person. And a rabbi who wears a *kippah* and tallis when leading services or ceremonies is believed to be doing so for religious reasons. Yes, I know that for some it is cultural, but many do hearken back to the holiness/humble before the supernatural reasoning. And meaning is both individually and socially determined. The approach of interpreting anything and everything however we want is more Reconstructing Judaism than Humanistic Judaism, at least as HJ has been in the past.

In other words, and about words, our movement has accepted that... we do not just reinterpret [some words] differently [when] they don't work as metaphor: revelation, god, etc. Our current incarnation may be more open to reinterpreting some symbols—putting new texts in mezuzahs, thinking of the *kippah* as cultural. However, sometimes there IS a value in looking different, doing things differently, choosing rituals and language and symbols that clearly express what you believe and avoiding those that are more easily confused. If I were a secular Jew who walked into a "Humanistic" congregation where most or all people wore *kippot* and *tallitot*, would I believe them when they told me they didn't mean it religiously? We would be as foreign to them as a Reconstructing Judaism congregation would be. My congregation has a Torah scroll, and we stand when we take it out, but we do not parade it around and kiss it. Some (even in my congregation) think we are too "religious" to ask people to stand, and so they stay seated. But whatever the HJ rationale might be for a Torah parade and kissing, THAT symbolism would be too far for me to reinterpret.

My family tradition has been to NOT wear a *kippah* for many generations—my father didn't wear one in my lifetime other than when visiting an Orthodox synagogue as he would have taken off shoes entering a mosque, and on my mother's side it was my great-grandfather who became secular and without a *kippah*. And my congregations both growing up and working have never had that as a norm, though I have had to remind my current members that anyone is welcome to wear one if they bring their own and choose to. We are a movement of immigrants, some raised explicitly secular while others raised more religiously and still others adopting Judaism in their own life journey. We all have different needs and reactions to symbols, so while some will like the *kippah*, others will reject it as symbolizing a religious lifestyle and belief. The latter are allowed their perspective as much as are the former....

Paul Golin: I think what we're getting at is personal practice versus setting "communal norms." The entry may be the rationale for why those are rejected as communal norms, but it should also be accompanied by an explanation of how it is meaningful for some Humanistic Jews to incorporate them into their personal practice.

Jen Naparstek Klein: I agree with other posters that these symbols both give an impression to others about level of religiosity AND hold personal meaning to the less theistic among us. I like mezuzahs on my doorframes. I loved watching and participating in passing the Torah through the generations to my children at their bar/bat mitzvahs. The Torah functions as a symbol to me, even if I find many of its lessons and theism dated and sometimes even offensive. Honestly, I'm not a fan of hard lines when it comes to individual practice, so if it holds personal meaning, I say use it. We all have our own connection to things and memories and traditions. That feels the most humanistic.

Jeremy Kridel: We had this discussion at Machar [Washington DC affiliate of the Society for Humanistic Judaism]. It was really interesting. I gave some what-ifs: what if I responded to a request to wear "clerical garb" (a common request at rallies, etc., for clergy) by wearing a *kippah*? What about giving *tallitot* to b mitzvah [preferred gender-neutral term for bar/bat/b'nai mitzvah] students?

People had little difficulty with the latter. Most people had little difficulty with the former. However, one person stated outright that they would drop membership and leave Machar were I to wear a *kippah*. The lines were super-movable for us!

Adam Chalom: I have had this discussion with both Kol Hadash (Illinois) and Kahal Braira (Boston). We recommend our families who want to give Judaica gifts give their kids a seder plate or Shabbat candlesticks, items they will use no matter where on the Jewish spectrum they land. Especially if they never see their parents, rabbi, or community wear [a tallit or *kippah*], a more relevant gift is preferred even if it is different or less traditional. After all, we no longer give fountain pens either!

If it is an heirloom, that may be different. Or if the student themselves has a strong value connection to the item. But not just to make their kids look like their b mitzvah picture and then not wear it again.

Sivan Maas: Thanks for some great questions and answers. As we grow here in Israel as a movement with Secular Humanistic congregations we face similar challenges. I recall my father Prof. Yaakov Malkin, who as you know has been the provost of our IISHJ institute etc., used to say, "Being a Secular Humanistic Jew is for me tradition. Yes, I am a traditional Jew. My father and mother were SH, I am, so are my children and grandchildren." Well, for me being third-generation Secular Humanistic, I too am a traditional Jew. The fact that our traditions, customs, dress vary is part of the way we believe we have and should express our legitimate variations. . . . I like being a SH traditional Jew, and I also like my "Jewish cultural treasure box." I choose from it based on the fact that I am Secular (sovereign), Humanistic (have a moral compass), and Jewish (peoplehood and culture). This is how I choose. But hopefully there are many things that we can choose together as a movement, i.e., SH with our own philosophy and practice. If you will "SHT Secular Humanistic Tradition."[7]

PART 2

Identity

Introduction

What are the Jews?

Jewish identity began as the political and theological nationality of those living in the kingdom of Judah and worshiping at its shrine. After 600 BCE, Jewish identity grew into a diasporic ethno-religion incorporating ancestry, theology, ritual practice, and culture. Diverse experiences as a minority within non-Jewish majority cultures, from welcome to indifference to hostility, led to diverse definitions of Jewishness between extremes of rootedness and expulsion, religiosity and secularization, tradition and change.

In premodern times, the dominant approach to Jewish identity defined Jewishness as assigned at birth or conferred based on—or, in limited cases, granted after—specific rituals of formal religious conversion. Its foundation was an eternal covenant with God, established at Mount Sinai and defined by the fulfillment of mitzvot (commandments). During the nineteenth century, the prior ethno-religious consensus of Jewishness diversified to include movements that were primarily nationality (Zionism), primarily religion (early Reform Judaism), and primarily ethnicity (Yiddishism). The twentieth century then saw the evolution of Zionism from nationalism to political allegiance, and ethnicity broadened to include both genetic heritage and the problematic category of "race." The Israeli state's legal need to define Jewishness for immigration, personal status, and government religious functions intensified the debate beyond sociology and institutional membership policies; who can become a citizen is very different from who can join a synagogue. This has often put Israeli bureaucracy at odds with most Jews, since the Orthodox approach of the Israeli Ministry of Religious Affairs conflicts with the dominant non-Orthodoxy of both diaspora Judaism and Israeli Jews.

Today, when there is no consensus about Jewish identity, it becomes vital for any contemporary Judaism to determine its own normative answers to the essential question "Who is a Jew?" In Humanistic Judaism, to put it simply, a Jew is a person who self-identifies with the Jewish people and its culture, religion, ethnicity, and heritage. Because culture, ethnicity, and heritage, and not only religion, are the foundational elements of Humanistic Jewish identity, it necessarily follows that those who self-identify with them are accepted as Jews.

Today, too, when Jewish identity is no longer the exclusive "Jewish or"—Jewish or Italian, Jewish or Japanese—Humanistic Judaism prefers the positive stance of a multifaceted "Jewish and," which affirms multiple heritages, identities, and choices: Jewish and Italian, Jewish and Japanese, Jewish and LGBTQ+, Jewish and secularized. Humanistic Judaism officially recognizes more permeable boundaries of Jewish belonging, reflecting how many non-Orthodox Jews informally view Jewish identity today (see the Pew Research Center report "Jewish Americans in 2020" in the appendix).

Humanistic Judaism brings a new paradigm to the question "Who is a Jew?" It finds the old dogmatic and hierarchical approach to Jewish identity unacceptable. With no Sinai covenant or heavenly commander, the meaning of becoming Jewish—or being Jewish, for that matter—is to be found through identification with the historical experience and culture of the Jewish people.

Historically, whom one accepted as Jewish depended on what one considered Jewishness to be. The category of ancestry evolved from a patrilineal system in the Bible whereby non-Hebrew wives produced Hebrew children to the matrilineal system of Rabbinic law. Rabbinic conversion reflected a combination of ancestry and theology, since converts received a new spiritual pedigree as a *ben Avraham* (son of Abraham) or *bat Sarah* (daughter of Sarah). Those joining the traditional ethno-religion were interrogated about their motives and took on a new name after proof of sincere belief and practice.

Humanistic Judaism preserves the tradition of Jewish identity from Jewish descent, accepting either matrilineal or patrilineal descent. For those choosing Jewish identity, Humanistic Judaism's core values of the dignity of the individual and respect for individual choices require a more flexible and welcoming approach: accepting Jews who sincerely declare themselves to be Jewish. Self-definition, rather than an identity bestowed from any other authority, is the criterion. One adopts Judaism instead of being converted into it, and one is adopted by the Jewish people. This choice may stem from being the partner of a Jewish person, from Jewish family heritage, or from personally connecting with Jewish culture and community. For Humanistic Judaism, if you say you are Jewish, you are. The question of with whom and where you can create Jewish community follows.

Also core to Jewish identity in the modern period is the question of where Jews should be living to fulfill their lives as Jews. Humanistic Judaism is agnostic on the question of where its cultural identity is best expressed, in Israel or in the Diaspora. Some secular Israelis insist that the only possible setting for sustainable nonreligious Jewish community is in a Jewish state, through a secular Jewish popular culture created in a Jewish language and surrounded by other secularized Jews. As a diaspora creation, Humanistic Judaism is more optimistic about the future of secular Jewish identity outside of Israel, even as it recognizes the challenges involved. It also articulates the tension between the universal human rights commitments learned by liberal Judaism from its diaspora experience and the ethnic nationalism of the modern State of Israel. In this, Humanistic Judaism is not radically different from other liberal Jewish denominations. The movement's early pride in Israel as a creation of primarily secular Jews has tempered today into the complicated relationship of American Jews to an Israel that may not even accept them as Jewish. While Israel is part of a Humanistic Jewish identity, Israel is not its center.

Any definition of Jewish identity includes boundaries. A purely ethnic or biological definition would preclude both conversion (becoming Jewish) and apostasy (rejecting Jewish identity), while a purely ritual-theological definition would preclude Humanistic Judaism altogether. Humanistic Judaism is a voice in the chorus advocating for open borders and a welcoming Jewish family. Humanistic Judaism's concept of Jewish identity is grounded in the movement's combination of Jewish tradition with secular modernity, the particular and the universal. Its complicated relationship with the promise and reality of secular Zionism and Israel also reflects this polarity between diaspora humanity and Jewish peoplehood, with a foot in both worlds.

The essays and organizational statements in the next three chapters devoted to questions of Jewish identity—"Jewish Self-Definition," "Welcoming and Inclusion," and "Israel/Zionism and Diaspora"—set out a key appeal of Humanistic Judaism: it counts and welcomes many more Jews with meaningful connections to Jewish life. This is a strength inherent in Humanistic Judaism, reflecting its essential values of inclusion and integrity.

6

Jewish Self-Definition

Jewish civilization has seen many attempts to define Jewish identity. The national identity of the kingdom of Judah before the Babylonian exile (c. 586–515 BCE) gave way to a hybrid of biology and theology in the post-Exilic priest Ezra's "holy seed" (Ezra 9:2). Rabbinic Judaism limited biology to those born from Jewish mothers, yet also created a spiritual pedigree from Abraham and Sarah for converts. The Reform movement's 1885 Pittsburgh Platform declared, "We consider ourselves no longer a nation, but a religious community."[1] Theodor Herzl's 1896 pamphlet *The Jewish State* asserted, "We are a people—one people."[2] The Nazi Nuremberg Laws defined Jewish racial identity from one grandparent, while (both oddly and understandably) the Israeli Law of Return was written to accept immigrants with the same degree of Jewish ancestry. Colloquially, Jewish people are often comfortable with terminology like "member of the tribe"—a vague amalgam of history, culture, and biology.

Humanistic Judaism's definition of the Jewish people as "a world people with a pluralistic culture and civilization" and Judaism as "the culture of the Jews" (see below, "Who Is a Jew?") attempts to include all Jews, from the most Orthodox to the most secular and with any degree of meaningful ancestry, in its orbit. What counts as "meaningful ancestry"? That is up to the individual who chooses to self-identify as Jewish to decide. For Humanistic Judaism, there is no one prescribed way to declare oneself Jewish, both for those born Jewish and for those becoming Jewish. Continuing the Jewish culture and traditions with which one was raised, joining a Jewish community, studying Jewish history, a public ceremony of Jewish affirmation—all are possibilities for an implicit or explicit declaration of Jewishness. While this does mean that someone could choose to no longer identify as Jewish, it also means—and prioritizes—that those who want to be Jewish are accepted as Jews.

This chapter explores four integral elements of Humanistic Jewish self-definition: how Humanistic Jews understand Jewish identity generally, how they define Humanistic Jewish identity specifically, how Jews by Choice are welcomed into the Humanistic Jewish family as a result, and how to best define Humanistic Judaism itself—as religious, secular, or both.

Jewish Peoplehood as Jewish Family

Rabbi Sherwin Wine (see chapter 1) founded Humanistic Judaism on twin pillars: the philosophy of humanism and the ethnic and cultural Judaism he experienced in the Detroit Jewish neighborhoods in which he was raised. From the fusing of the two emerged a philosophical, humanistic approach to life framed by Judaism rather than abstract reason.

If Humanistic Judaism was to be rooted in Judaism, then the movement needed a clear definition/understanding of Jewish identity. "Religion" was not inclusive enough for many reasons. The wide range of theological beliefs, including outright atheism, held by Jews who self-identified and were accepted as Jewish demonstrated that Judaism is not simply a religion. In like vein, ethnic Jewish experiences of language, culture, community, and identity were often expressed by one's being a "member of the tribe," not a "member of the religion." So, too, the traditional definition of Jewishness from matrilineal descent applied regardless of individual religious belief or practice. Even the external antisemitic view that Jewishness is a matter of birth rather than belief, and thus inescapable by religious conversion, provided a social verdict.

Jews as well sometimes self-described themselves exclusively as a "nation," whether in Zionist terms or as a synonym for the global Jewish people, as in the popular song "Am Yisrael Chai"—"the Jewish nation lives." Yet for his part Wine felt strongly that Jewish dispersion and diversification over centuries of diaspora life had created such distinct Jewish languages and cultures that there were *many* Jewish cultural "nations." The State of Israel, for one, had created its own national Jewish identity through its distinct culture using Modern Hebrew—a nationality that did not encompass all Jews, particularly English-speaking Jews in North America. As for "culture" or "civilization," Wine observed that most liberal Jews primarily participate in Western culture, with Jewish culture as an episodic experience; as he quipped elsewhere in the chapter excerpted below, "American Jews can choose Passover and Hebrew classes. But they can also choose Chinese food, karate, and French lessons."[3] Thus, he concluded, their Jewishness must be something other than an all-encompassing identity in a "civilization."

Wine defined what today is often called "Jewish peoplehood" as "kinship." Jews throughout the world were Jews not because of a claimed biological or spiritual descent from a mythical Abraham, but because they were heirs to a diverse family heritage with many branches. A family can encompass many different cultures and lifestyles, most families continue to accept their members no matter what their relatives may believe, families can welcome new members through marriage and adoption, and one person may simultaneously feel part of multiple families on all sides of one's personal family tree. So, too, with Jewish theological and cultural diversity, joining the Jewish people, and children of intercultural and interfaith partnerships, as demonstrated by selections in this chapter and the next.

Defining Jewish identity as kinship, then, includes Jews regardless of theological beliefs or ritual practices, or marriage partners, or parentage. This passage from Wine's magnum opus on Humanistic Judaism, *Judaism beyond God*, puts this kinship definition of Jewish identity front and center.

Sherwin Wine, "Kinship" (1985)

It is quite obvious that Jewish identity includes religious, racial, national, and cultural behavior. But it cannot be adequately defined by any one of them. A broader and more inclusive concept is required.

What realities should this concept embrace? What are the parameters that surround *all* Jews, whether they choose to engage in uniquely Jewish activity or do not choose to do so, whether they value their Jewish identity or do not value it?

Jewish identity, first of all, means a sense of shared ancestry. The Jews began as a nation, an ethnic federation of tribes. Their epic literature, which has become part of the sacred scriptures of the Christian world, speaks of their common ancestors. Whether Abraham, Isaac, or Jacob were real personalities or personifications of tribal invasions is irrelevant to the issue. The Jews saw themselves (and their neighbors saw them) as a *true* nation, a people united by "blood" ties and family loyalty. Even in talmudic times, joining the Jews was never a mere religious conversion. It was an "adoption." New Jews severed all connections with their old families and adopted the ancestry of Abraham and Sarah.

The Jewish people was dispersed from its homeland and became a family of new nations. But Jews never lost their sense of kinship. No matter where they lived, no matter what language they spoke, no matter what culture they adopted, no matter what racial elements they incorporated—they believed (and their neighbors believed) that they were united by a bond of "blood." Nineteenth-century writers would not have hesitated to use the word *race* to describe this awareness—even the most pro-Semitic. But the dangers of that word in the twentieth century forbid its use. The more benign word *kinship* may be more discreet. Or the phrase *family sense*.

All Jews—even those who hate being Jewish—have this awareness of other Jews being their "relatives." New Jews, those who choose to become Jewish, also sense that they are joining a family fraternity where enthusiasm may confer fewer privileges than birth. Outsiders, too, both the pros and the antis, have this view of tribal connection. The phrase *member of the tribe*, although offensive to some, captures the awareness of a condition that is less than national but more than ideological.

The second parameter of Jewish identity is shared memories. Kinship means family roots and family history. The story of the Jews, whether positive or negative, fills the popular culture in the Western world. Christians give the Jews center stage in their drama. Muslims assign them a more peripheral role. But both traditions force Jews—even Jews who want to run away from their history or who are indifferent to or ignorant of it—to confront their past. The Jews have a secure place in the popular memory. Announcing that you are a Jew is different from announcing that you are a Swedenborgian. Receivers of the news can fit you into their cultural memory. Even the peasant folk who have "never met a Jew before" know that Jews are not novelties. Even Jews who claim that they "know nothing about Judaism" know that they have a secure place in the history of any Western culture.

The third parameter of Jewish identity is shared danger. Jews are a vulnerable family. For whatever historical reasons, we are surrounded by hostility. The potential of anti-Semitism is part of the self-awareness of all Jews. It is also part of the awareness of Gentiles who deal with Jews. The events of the twentieth century have reinforced this apprehension. The Holocaust has tied Jewish identity to such fundamental emotions as fear, anger, loyalty, and pride. Frequently, Jews and Jewish leaders complain about the overemphasis on the negative side of Jewish existence. But Jewish anxiety and Jewish behavior do not pay any attention to this warning. Most parents who seek a Jewish education for their children want their sons and daughters to feel "proud" of their Jewish connection. They are obviously afraid that someone will make them feel less than proud. Being defensive is part of the Jewish condition.

Vulnerable kinship is an imperfect classification of Jewish identity. But it is more accurate than the words *religion, race, nation,* or *culture*.[4]

Identifying with the Jewish People

As noted, there is a significant difference between Humanistic Jewish identity as a claimed family kinship expressed through Jewish culture and community and traditional understandings of Jewish identity (matrilineal descent or religious conversion by an approved authority). As an exceptionally anti-authoritarian Judaism, Humanistic Judaism puts the power of defining who is part of Jewish peoplehood in the hands of Jewish individuals themselves.

What differentiates Humanistic Jewish self-identification from what some might call cultural appropriation (that is, the improper adoption of elements of another's culture or identity, generally by a member of the dominant or majority culture) is the expectation of each individual's deep personal meaning and sincerity, as well as the understanding that this is not a costume one wears temporarily and then removes, but rather is who one is. Humanistic Judaism's acceptance of these newly self-identifying Jews completes the mutual adoption process and welcomes them into the Jewish people.

The International Federation of Secular Humanistic Jews (IFSHJ), established in 1986 with representatives from secular and Humanistic Jewish organizations in North America, Israel, Europe, and Latin America, focused through the mid-2000s on holding biennial conferences and issuing statements on key issues. The most important of these, "Who is a Jew?," was adopted in Brussels in October 1988 at the IFSHJ's second biennial conference and has been broadly accepted within the movement. The statement succinctly summarizes Humanistic Judaism's definition of what it means to be Jewish: to be part of the Jewish people. Accepting self-definition as Jewish reflects both the humanistic belief in individual self-determination and a Jewish identity based on an open family and cultural community.

International Federation of Secular Humanistic Jews, "Who Is a Jew?" (1988)

PREAMBLE

Who is a Jew? After more than thirty centuries Jews continue to debate this question.

At stake is the integrity of millions of Jews who do not find their Jewish identity in religious belief or religious practice, but who discover their Jewishness in the historic experience of the Jewish people. At stake also is the Jewish identity of thousands of men and women, in Israel and in other countries of the world, who want to be Jewish, but who are rejected by the narrow legalism of traditional religious authorities.

We, the members of the International Federation of Secular Humanistic Jews, believe that the survival of the Jewish people depends on a broad view of Jewish identity. We welcome into the Jewish people all men and women who sincerely desire to share the Jewish experience regardless of their ancestry. We challenge the assumption that the Jews are primarily or exclusively a religious community and that religious convictions or behavior are essential to full membership in the Jewish people.

The Jewish people is a world people with a pluralistic culture and civilization all its own. Judaism, as the culture of the Jews, is more than theological commitment. It encompasses many languages, a vast body of literature, historical memories, and ethical values. In our times the shadow of the Holocaust and the rebirth of the State of Israel are a central part of Jewish consciousness.

We Jews have a moral responsibility to welcome all people who seek to identify with our culture and destiny. The children and spouses of intermarriage who desire to be part of the Jewish people must not be cast aside because they do not have Jewish mothers and do not wish to undergo religious conversion. The authority to define "who is a Jew" belongs to all the Jewish people and cannot be usurped by any part of it.

RESOLUTION

In response to the destructive definition of a Jew now proclaimed by some Orthodox authorities, and in the name of the historic experience of the Jewish people, we, therefore, affirm that a Jew is a person of Jewish descent or any person who declares himself or herself to be a Jew and who identifies with the history, ethical values, culture, civilization, community, and fate of the Jewish people.[5]

Secular Jewish Conversion

Humanistic Judaism's acceptance of self-definition as sufficient to join the Jewish people forms the basis for the movement's approach to conversion/adoption. If being Jewish is more than religion or biology and includes elements of culture, ethnicity, and history, becoming Jewish is less a theological conversion than a kind of adoption/naturalization process. Since Humanistic Judaism considers Jewishness a family identity, "adoption" seems a more appropriate framework for welcoming Jews by Choice who feel part of the Jewish story and prefer a Humanistic approach to Jewish life. Like naturalized U.S. citizens who learn American customs, culture, and history to affirm their legal connection to and membership in the American people—inheriting the "Founding Fathers" and singing, "the land where my fathers died" in "My Country 'Tis of Thee"—Jews by Choice similarly adopt Jewish folkways, history, and culture in addition to practices and beliefs.

That said, unlike naturalized citizens, who undergo a rigorous process of forms, fees, and interviews and cannot simply declare themselves American citizens, for Humanistic Judaism there is no external authority that grants the status of "Jewish" to an individual; rather, it is up to that individual to claim it. In order to help the prospective adoptee make an informed decision to self-identify as a Jew, a welcoming community, or the movement itself, encourages and supports a period of study and learning that encompasses exploration of the collective historic and cultural experience with which the aspirant will be identifying—but without requiring courses or text materials or tests that need to be passed. Sometimes the adoption process is completed by the choice of a Hebrew name and, often, a Society for Humanistic Judaism certificate, which reads in part:

> [Individual's name] has been warmly adopted and welcomed as a member of the Jewish people, has linked their fate to the fate of the Jewish people, and taken the Hebrew name [name inserted] as a sign of membership in the Jewish people.... For wherever you go, I will go; wherever you lodge, I will lodge; your people shall be my people....⁶

Throughout a Humanistic Jewish conversion/adoption process, whatever it may be for each person, the authority of the individual to self-identify with the Jewish people is affirmed and celebrated.

The Association of Humanistic Rabbis (AHR), established in 1967, initially attracted progressive rabbis primarily from the Reform movement for the purposes of creating alternative perspectives on important issues of the day. This 2005 AHR "Statement on Conversion/Adoption" articulates both the movement's understanding of Judaism and its approach to welcoming new Jews. While the statement recommends both a learning process and ceremonial acknowledgment of the individual's adoption into the Jewish people, the minimum requirements are "personal choice and acceptance by a Jewish community." That community can be the movement of Humanistic Judaism itself.

Association of Humanistic Rabbis, "Statement on Conversion/Adoption" (2005)

PREAMBLE

The Jewish people began as a nation and evolved into an international family. Over three thousand years this nation/family has been the host to competing religious beliefs and diverse philosophies of life. The heart of Jewish identity has always been a strong sense of membership in the Jewish people, identification with its history and participation in its culture.

For most of Jewish history the Jewish people welcomed others to join the Jewish family. Jewish conversion is adoption into the culture and future of the Jewish people.

STATEMENT

We, the members of the Association of Humanistic Rabbis, welcome all individuals into the Jewish people who desire to link their lives with the experience of the Jewish nation/family, to identify with its historic memories and to participate in its culture and future. Both personal choice and acceptance by a Jewish community to which they belong are necessary to make their adoption significant and valid.

The act of adoption should be preceded by a period of preparation, when the prospective adoptee studies the fundamentals of Jewish history and Jewish culture. The welcoming community may offer a celebration and certificate of adoption.[7]

Is Humanistic Judaism a Religion?

Up until now, this chapter has focused on the identity of individual Jews. But how should the identity of the Humanistic Jewish movement itself be understood?

As explained above, Humanistic Judaism has a foot in two worlds: philosophically secular in beliefs and liturgy while structurally religious with Shabbat and holiday observances and rabbinic leadership. Thus, the question sometimes arises: is the movement a religion or something else?

Some movement institutions, created in coalition with the Congress of Secular Jewish Organizations (est. 1968), describe the broader movement as "Secular Humanistic Judaism." For example, the seminary training Humanistic Jewish rabbis and leaders is the International Institute for Secular Humanistic Judaism (IISHJ, est. 1985).

In this essay, from a seminal movement journal issue entitled "Is Humanistic Judaism a Religion?," Rabbi Karen Levy (b. 1948) explores the complexity of the "religion" label for Humanistic Judaism, a complexity born from the movement's dual foundations of Judaism and secularity.

Levy herself first joined a secular Jewish community in Toronto in 1982 when seeking a congregation for her family. In this choice, she was influenced by both her parents' commitment to Jewish community and her own values of dignity, compassion, and rationalism. Growing into leadership and professional roles, locally in Oraynu Congregation for Humanistic Judaism and in the wider movement, she was ordained by the IISHJ as *madrikha* (leader) in 1993 and then as rabbi in 2009. She served as rabbi of Oraynu from 2009 to 2015 and is currently rabbi emerita. Levy coauthored *Values and History Curriculum for Secular Humanistic Jewish Supplementary Schools* JK-7 and was the editor of *The Early Modern European Roots of Secular Humanistic Judaism* (IISHJ, 1998).

In Levy's view, shared by most Humanistic Jews, Humanistic Judaism is *both/and*: both religious and secular. As she expresses it, Humanistic Jewish services, communities, and rabbis, acting in a religious capacity, address human needs in philosophically secular ways. Humanistic Jews need Humanistic rabbis to meet their pastoral and spiritual needs, but without prayer; Humanistic Jewish children need to be educated about Jewish history and Jewish texts, but in human-centered, nontheistic ways; Humanistic Jews need pathways to meaningfully celebrate Jewish holidays, but without praising or petitioning a deity. The structure Humanistic Judaism uses to meet these needs lies in religion.

Levy notes that various dictionary definitions of "religion" could include Humanistic Judaism. For example, in her article Levy cites *Webster's New World College Dictionary* 1997 version: "any specific system of belief and worship, often involving a code of ethics and a philosophy." Levy also cites *Webster's Third New International Dictionary*, published by Encyclopedia Britannica, which recognizes "religious humanism" as "a modern American movement composed chiefly of non-theistic humanists and humanist churches and dedicated to achieving the ethical goals of religion without beliefs and rites resting upon supernaturalism."[8] Despite all the ways in which Humanistic Judaism fits these definitions, Levy goes on to clarify that one cannot stop there, because it is too simplistic to convey the nuances of Humanistic Judaism, which is, in different ways, both secular and religious.

Karen Levy, "Changing Perceptions, Changing Realities" (2002)

Does the word religion apply today to Secular Humanistic Judaism? . . .

There is no question that Secular Humanistic Judaism qualifies as a religion according to . . . [dictionary] definitions. However, words bear more significance than their definitions convey. Let's close the dictionaries and ask whether the meaning suggested by religion merits its use as a label for our movement. . . .

At all significant turning points in our lives, our emotional, psychological, and spiritual needs cry out loudly for attention. The events following September 11, 2001 demonstrated that in a time of crisis people will flock to religious ceremonies to express their fears, their grief, and their group loyalty in a spiritual experience with likeminded people. Whether we are suffering unexpected tragedy or joyful life cycle events, we long to affirm our goals and the meaning of our lives. We seek to know our place in the universe; we crave the support of our community and the love of our family and friends; we desire hope for the future. Religion provides the worldview, artistic expression, community, and ceremony that respond to these yearnings. In doing so, religion shapes the patterns of our memory, for by life's turning points we measure our days and frame our memories of the past.

Beliefs held with ardor and zeal can inspire us to create beauty and do great good. They also can motivate us to do terrible harm. Critics of religion blame it for causing the worst suffering that humans inflict upon one another. However, religion as a social structure is in itself neither good nor bad. Likewise, religious ideology as a way of expressing human thought, emotion, and spirituality is in itself neither good nor bad. Each religion and its ideology must be judged on its own merits and consequences. To say that religion causes war and violence is akin to saying that love causes jealousy and therefore we should not love. Avoiding religion will not put an end to violence and abuse committed in the name of ideology. It is a mistake for people of liberal and humanistic beliefs and values to think they can fight fanaticism and aggression by avoiding religious organization and structure. We can diminish the harm done by destructive religious ideas only by making available alternatives, by strengthening our own religious movements.

This is a very important issue for our movement. Without the structure of religion it is not likely that Secular Humanistic Judaism will survive as a meaningful force in the Jewish people and in the world. No religion can be sustained without some kind of structure, which includes bureaucracy and rules of operation. This structure depends upon knowledgeable experts: clergy, accountants, musicians and artists, administrators, scholars, teachers, publishers, cooks, and custodians. Clergy serve the spiritual needs of members and, with scholars and educators, ensure the development and continuity of the belief system. Without this structure members' needs are not met and the enterprise ceases to exist, no matter how valid and worthy its beliefs. The rational skepticism and democratic ideals upon which liberal ideologies are based make us distrust authority and bureaucracy. Creating a cadre of religious experts is difficult but necessary for us. Anti-authoritarianism requires us to distrust the abuse and misuse of authority. It does not mean that there is no authority. Skepticism requires that we not place our trust blindly. It does not require that there be no trust. . . .

As individuals and as a movement we have so much to gain by participating in a religious enterprise: a structure and organization that will perpetuate our cherished beliefs; being part of a cooperative endeavor that brings more peace and justice into the world; a relationship of trust, loyalty, and commitment with the members of our communities; ethical guidelines and an enriched personal identity. Since the dictionary cooperates, why is our movement ambivalent about identifying itself as a religion?

With good reason we abhor the dogmatism, intolerance, and exclusivity we have at times found in both theistic and secular religions. When we call ourselves a religion, we risk becoming associated with ideological aggression and chauvinism. However, we Secular and Humanistic Jews are just as prone to stubbornness, orthodoxy, and snobbery as any other group of human beings, perhaps more so because we are so desirous of philosophical consistency. This is and will be so, whether we are organized as a loose federation of *kindershulen* (children's schools) or as a religious movement. It is something we must be vigilant in controlling. In the public eye, it will not be our label (as a religion or otherwise) that will separate us from these afflictions; it will be our deeds.

When we call ourselves a religion, we risk being identified with the more common usage of the word as "the service of God or a god." It is difficult enough to promote something new in Judaism. If we call ourselves another branch of the Jewish religion, won't we jeopardize our growth by confusing people? Regardless of what the dictionary says, most people hear "religion" and think of God and worship. They also hear "culture" and think of bagels and lox. Some people hear "rational" and think it implies being unemotional. That does not mean we should avoid calling ourselves cultural Jews or rationalists. The same kind of misunderstanding arises even from the word Jewish because many people do not understand how one can be secular and a Jew or humanistic and a Jew. Avoiding the "R" word will not lessen the confusion. . . .

If we want to be perceived as legitimate providers of Jewish spirituality, ceremonies, and teachings, we need to be seen as a religious movement. It is equally vital that we have this vision and this will for ourselves. Secular Humanistic Judaism is a religion with common practices based on a set of commonly believed principles. These principles are in our head, heart, and gut every day. They are held with ardor, devotion, conscientiousness, and faith. We are dedicated to achieving the ethical goals of a secular religion with beliefs and rituals resting upon naturalism and humanism.[9]

7

Welcoming and Inclusion

Early leaders in Humanistic Judaism were mostly a breakaway generation: while some had been raised in secular Jewish communities, most came from more traditionally religious Judaisms and defined themselves and the movement in clear opposition to Conservative, Reconstructionist, or Reform Judaism (see the introduction). If this meant risking misunderstanding at best and outright hostility from other denominations at worst, that was the inevitable and acceptable cost of establishing a new Secular Judaism.

This is most easily seen in the change from the traditional centering of a god concept to exclusively nontheistic language that centers human beings in liturgy, life cycle, and holiday celebrations. This distinction is the primary rationale for a Humanistic Judaism: creating an inclusive and welcoming community for Jews and families who share its nontheistic values and approach, from its broad self-definition of who is a Jew (see chapter 6) to its unconditional acceptance of interfaith couples and families (see Jerris below). Humanistic Judaism broadly and joyfully welcomes anyone who identifies as a Humanistic Jew or is part of a Humanistic Jewish family, however that family is defined, and includes every member of such families in every aspect of Humanistic Jewish communal life.

In the early decades of the movement, its acceptance of interfaith weddings and families engendered conflict with the Jewish establishment. As one example, for many years, the *Detroit Jewish News* would not publish announcements of either interfaith or Jewish-only weddings officiated by founding movement rabbi Sherwin Wine. Yet for Humanistic Judaism, the principles of affirming the individual choice to marry for love and welcoming all who wanted to be part of Jewish life were more important than social acceptance.

In the three generations since the founding of Humanistic Judaism, more recent leadership has had more success in creating broader Jewish connections. While the Michigan Board of Rabbis attempted to expel Sherwin Wine in the 1960s, in the early 2000s they accepted ordainees of the International Institute for Secular Humanistic Judaism's rabbinic program as full members. The acceptance went both ways: the Autumn 2000/Winter 2001 issue of the movement journal *Humanistic Judaism* was dedicated to "Building Bridges to the Wider Jewish Community." Diversity was now being heralded as a value not just within Humanistic Judaism, but in Humanistic Judaism's relationship to the other Jewish denominations.

Today, Humanistic Jewish rabbis and educators serve as members of local rabbinical boards, interfaith clergy organizations, and local boards of Jewish education in many metropolitan areas, and often on committees of such boards. Similarly, other liberal branches of Judaism have grown to recognize Humanistic Judaism as a valid Jewish alternative. In some measure, other liberal branches of Judaism have caught up with Humanistic Judaism: interfaith families are more welcomed in Reform and Reconstructionist congregations, and increasing numbers of Reform and Reconstructionist rabbis are willing to officiate at their wedding ceremonies.

This chapter focuses on two distinct issues related to welcoming and inclusion. We begin with the challenges presented to Humanistic Judaism as it welcomes pluralism while maintaining its unique identity: the tension between promoting a humanistic universalism that risks swallowing Judaism entirely and maintaining a particularism that risks unacceptable notions of chosenness. The first two essays address these issues. Second, there are the positive values and outcomes inherent in unqualified acceptance of intermarriage and complete inclusion of interfaith and intercultural families, addressed by the third and fourth selections. A diverse Jewish community is a positive good, both within Humanistic Judaism and in the wider Jewish world.

Humanistic Judaism as One Judaism among Many

Jewish unity in diversity recognizes that modern Judaism has many flavors and there is no arguing about taste. Rabbi Sherwin Wine often remarked that being, and living as, a Humanistic Jew requires a life of courage: the courage to stay true to one's beliefs even when these diverge from Jewish norms, the courage to live a Humanistic Jewish life that reflects those beliefs even if it means making unconventional Jewish choices, and the courage to always say what one means and mean what one says in any Jewish language. Diversity can be achieved without compromise when Jews holding multiple Jewish approaches confidently assert the validity of their beliefs and practices while also accepting other Jewish choices as nonthreatening. Jewish pluralism is the positive result of this diversity.

Early articulations of Humanistic Judaism had a tendency to denigrate the religious denominations they were rejecting and by which they had been rejected. By contrast, Rabbi Tamara Kolton's essay, published in the movement journal *Humanistic Judaism* in 2005, represents a next-generation approach to Jewish diversity and the place of Humanistic Judaism in the Jewish landscape.

Kolton (b. 1970) was raised as a Humanistic Jew at the movement's founding congregation, The Birmingham Temple in Farmington Hills, Michigan. In 1992 she joined the first class of rabbinic students at the International Institute for Secular Humanistic Judaism and earned an MA in clinical psychology and a PhD in rabbinic studies as part of her rabbinic program. In 1999 she became the first Humanistic rabbi ordained by the movement. She served for twenty years at The Birmingham Temple as assistant and then full rabbi until 2012, when her personal evolution took her beyond the movement toward what she describes as "the Feminine Divine." Her advocacy of a pluralistic Jewish community in which Humanistic Judaism is accepted as an equally worthy option remains vital to the movement.

Tamara Kolton, "Healing the Jewish People through Pluralism" (2005)

A Judaism that does not recognize all of its members as equal and worthy of spirituality, a Judaism in which there is fighting amongst Jews who judge and devalue each other's Jewish identities, a Judaism that does not evolve over time so that it can remain meaningful and relevant to the lives of the Jews, a Judaism that does not always encourage people to lead lives of goodness, truth, and love, this Judaism, which I believe is the Judaism of today, needs to be healed. . . .

Being a Humanistic Jew is the life of courage. It is a training program in being able to stand against the pressure of the crowd and affirm your own beliefs even if they do not conform to the fashion of the day.

This is a discussion I have with our children all the time, especially during the seventh grade when they are actively visiting each other's temples for their *b'nai mitsva*. You would be amazed and proud to hear how clear our children are about their identities as Humanistic Jews. They are proud of their temple. They feel that their *b'nai mitsva* are meaningful, and they are excited to share the experience with their friends. They have no need to back down and apologize or launch a counterattack against someone else's beliefs. They know that, although we may disagree, we are all equally Jewish. . . .

Each of us is faced with our own challenges. I must be able to say to the Orthodox woman sitting beside me, "Your life choices are no less legitimate or correct than mine," and I must mean it. I cannot ask for a dignity that I am not willing to afford. I must be willing to give you your dignity by understanding that the way you live your life and practice your religion is your best guess at the right path. I will also give it my best guess. We must be willing to see the value in all the movements in Judaism. I may totally disagree with the way other Jews live their lives or understand the nature of the world. We can debate each other and disagree until daylight. That is just fine. We do not need consensus. What we cannot do is delegitimize each other. We are all present in the Jewish experience; no one is more or less legitimate. We are all giving it our best guess. We must be comfortable being a tree with many branches, knowing that we all share the same roots.

The real threat to Judaism is not intermarriage or antisemitism. The real threat to Judaism is the fighting that occurs between Jews. If we cannot be a cohesive people, accepting each other's differences but remaining one people, then we will not survive....

Today there are thirteen million Jews in the world. We are never going to agree. Agreement should not be our goal. Judaism must be a great tent large enough to give shelter to its entire people.[1]

Cosmopolitan and Particular

Since its founding, Humanistic Judaism has occupied two distinct yet overlapping realms: particular and universal. The challenge has been to strike an appropriate balance between the particularism of being Jewish and the universalism of being part of a wider humanity. Humanistic Judaism has resisted demands from partisans of both Judaism and general Humanism to choose one or the other; the movement affirms that one can be Jewish *and* a Humanist.

This integrated duality reflects the notion of Humanistic Jewish identity generally wherein one can be Jewish *and* other ethnic or cultural identities: Italian, Japanese, etc. The different labels inform and amplify each other rather than creating a contradiction. The very name of the movement, Humanistic Judaism, demonstrates that there are two foundational components: philosophical humanism and cultural Judaism. Adherents to Humanistic Judaism are both humanists and Jews.

Rabbi Jeffrey Falick (b. 1962) is rabbi of the Congregation for Humanistic Judaism of Metro Detroit (formerly The Birmingham Temple). Ordained as a Reform rabbi, he worked in various rabbinic roles including as a Hillel director and a Jewish community center educator before joining Humanistic Judaism. He is also a frequent contributor to *Moment*'s "Ask the Rabbis" column, where he represents Humanistic Judaism in his answers.

In this essay, originally delivered as a 2014 Rosh Hashanah sermon, Falick draws an analogy to the Yiddish aphorism about dancing at two weddings to demonstrate the tension inherent in these two sources of a Humanistic Jewish identity.

Jeffrey Falick, "Dancing at Two Weddings" (2014)

There is a Yiddish maxim that says, "You cannot dance at two weddings with one *tuches* [rear end]." Yet for more than fifty years, this is precisely what Humanistic Jews have been attempting to do. . . .

If there is one thing that characterizes our small movement, it is realism. Humanism is a philosophy that insists upon rigorous honesty and a straightforward evaluation of all the facts in evidence.

The accepted wisdom of most conventional Jews is that the only way for Jews to survive and thrive as Jews is to focus inward. Classical Reform Judaism, the one grand attempt to swing the doors of our community completely outward, was a failure. Owing to its theistic frame of reference and its reverence for the past, its pilots steered it back toward particularistic shores.

Humanistic Jews do not have this option. By our very nature we reject the supremacy of accepted wisdom. So we must ask ourselves, would looking inward serve our purposes? Could we do so without betraying our humanism? And to what end? . . .

Consider the popularity in many of our congregations of that great humanistic anthem, John Lennon's "Imagine." Here is a song that expresses a longing for the ultimate unity of humanity. It lauds the disappearance of boundaries; of nations and religions. Like many humanists, I, too, love this song.

Yet for a movement that is committed to saying what we mean and meaning what we say, we should pause for a moment to consider its vision. Is this what we want for the Jewish people? Is it the disappearance of differences? That vision rejects tribalism in favor of a strong universalism. It is not the vision of the Jewish federations, bureaus of Jewish education, or boards of rabbis.

Most of us would say that we want the best of both worlds. We rightly see very little conflict in our day-to-day simultaneous embrace of universalistic humanism and particularistic Judaism. But our children—at least those who take these things seriously—are increasingly attracted to one or the other.

Those seeking Jewish immersion find little of value in our movement. They are far more attracted to Orthodox Judaism, though liberals among them will find a comfortable home with the other movements. Those who identify most strongly with the goals of humanism find little of interest in particularistic Judaism. For them Humanistic Judaism is insufficiently universalist.

Traditional Judaism holds that prophecy is dead. We believe that it never existed. For that reason I won't even attempt to predict what lies ahead for us. Perhaps we will win the day as more and more thinking Jews reject the lessons of their establishment rabbis and flock to our rational shores. Perhaps we will slowly disappear into the larger humanistic world, becoming nothing more than an interesting footnote in the history of humanism.

For now we have no choice but to continue our efforts to defy that Yiddish maxim. We've placed these two weddings as close to each other as possible. We can't dance at both with one tuches, so we'll just have to keep moving our tuches from one to the other, doing the best we can to honor our commitments to both Judaism and humanism.[2]

Celebrating Intermarriage with Dignity

Where the abstract debate of universalism versus particularism hits reality is intermarriage.

A general rejection of interfaith marriages persisted well into the 1980s, even among liberal rabbis. For example, in 1983 the Reform rabbinate issued a statement reaffirming their opposition to rabbinic officiation at "mixed marriages."³ Nevertheless, the opposition of more conventional denominations of Judaism was unsuccessful in preventing intermarriage. Major Jewish demographic studies in 1990, 2001, 2010, and 2020 showed Jewish intermarriage rates among non-Orthodox Jews at or over 50 percent. Intermarriage was becoming both a fact of modern Jewish life and increasingly the norm in liberal Judaisms. Some liberal Jews belonged to synagogues for years only to find that "their rabbi" refused to marry them or their children. Many experienced great relief upon learning that intermarriage is not an obstacle in Humanistic Judaism, only an opportunity to affirm a loving partnership.

Humanistic Judaism unequivocally endorses the premise that marriage for love is good. Same-sex marriages and intermarriages are validated. Intermarriage in particular is an inevitable consequence of Jews living in an open society. Since its founding, Humanistic Judaism has been fully welcoming of interfaith or intercultural couples in every aspect of Jewish life without exceptions. As a moral principle, the movement has argued that if people are in charge of their own lives, this includes the freedom to choose a marriage partner, and Jews who intermarry do not cease being Jewish if they love someone from another heritage. Hence, recognizing and welcoming intermarried couples by officiating at their weddings and celebrating future life-cycle events, such as baby namings, with them has been a fundamental moral imperative for Humanistic Judaism from the outset.

On a practical level, too, welcoming interfaith couples into Humanistic Jewish communities is mutually beneficial, as the couples find a Jewish home and the community grows with them.

Rabbi Miriam Jerris (b. 1949) is rabbi of the Society for Humanistic Judaism. She holds rabbinic ordination from the International Institute for Humanistic Judaism (IISHJ) and graduate degrees in Near Eastern studies and humanistic psychology and a PhD in Judaic studies. Her experience with intermarriage is both professional and personal: her doctoral dissertation was on clergy providing pastoral support to intermarried couples, she has officiated at scores of interfaith weddings, and she is in an interfaith marriage herself.

In this essay, responding to the 2012 IISHJ Colloquium "'Half Jewish?' The Heirs of Intermarriage," Jerris rejects the role of gatekeeper in favor of being a "gate opener," someone who welcomes both the individual interfaith couple and the entire notion of interfaith marriage. Being a gate opener allows former boundaries to be expanded and previous borders to be taken down. All the more, the commitment to providing a welcoming Jewish home for interfaith couples and their children benefits the entire Jewish community.

Miriam Jerris, "Gate Openers: Reaching Out to the Next Generation of Children from Intermarriage" (2017)

"Hello, rabbi?"

"Yes, speaking."

"Hi, my name is Josh Cohen and I'm getting married next October, but my fiancée is not Jewish."

"Mazel tov, Josh. I'm so happy for you."

DEAD SILENCE on the other end of the phone.

"Josh?"

"Yes, rabbi, I'm here."

"Are you okay?"

"Yes, rabbi, I am, but you are the third (fourth, fifth) phone call I've made, and you are the first one to congratulate me."

For more than thirty years, I have been championing the rights of individuals to choose their life partner based on the quality of their relationship. The measure I use when considering whether I will involve myself in a couple's wedding ceremony is the couple's love and their desire to have a Jewish presence at their ceremony, rather than any label that might be ascribed to them as a consequence of birth and ancestry. I honor their right to choose their life partner freely and, as a rabbi, I choose to celebrate with them.

When you ask a young couple in love to decide between Judaism and the person they love most in the world, there is no contest. How could there be? In addition, turning young Jews away because they live in a free and open society and have fallen in love with someone not Jewish is not a way to create a positive connection to Judaism or the Jewish community. Thus, Secular Humanistic rabbis and ceremonialists prefer to hold the gates to the Jewish community open, rather than slam them shut. Our welcoming and acceptance is often significantly appreciated, and has helped assure that countless numbers of Jewish kids feel that they have access to their Jewish identity, regardless of their partners' cultural or religious backgrounds. A lifetime of involvement with a family often flows from our acceptance and willingness to welcome Jews who are intermarrying.

This is why I choose to be a "gate opener," and not a "gatekeeper." A most profound example of this "gate-opening" stance is that the International Institute for Secular Humanistic Judaism is one of three rabbinical programs that expressly opens admissions to Jews married to or in committed relationships with a non-Jewish partner [as of 2017]. This doesn't come without controversy. Many Jewish community leaders have asked me, "What kind of a model are you providing to the Jewish community if you are married to someone who is not a Jew by birth or choice?" My answer: I am modeling that you can retain your Jewish identity and remain a significant part of the Jewish community, marry the person you love, and not expect that they change their identity to fit into your world. I am proud to be part of a movement that supports my message.

Once, at a Michigan Board of Rabbis meeting, one of the younger rabbis said to me, "Miriam, you'll marry anyone won't you?" My response? "My goal is to keep the gates open to all Jews who want access, however limited, to their Jewish identity and community, rather than slam them shut in their face."

We do this, first, by broadening the definition of who is a Jew. Our movement has long subscribed to the International Federation of Secular Humanistic Judaism's 1988 declaration [see chapter 6]: "A Jew is a person of Jewish descent or any person who declares himself or herself to be a Jew and who identifies with the history, ethical values, culture, civilization, community, and fate of the Jewish people."

The intermarriage rate has been nearly 50% for more than three decades, and there are now thousands of children born from these marriages. Secular Humanistic Judaism recognizes the need many of these children feel to explore their Jewish identities. In 2012, the Colloquium of the International Institute for Secular Humanistic Judaism addressed the issue with "'Half Jewish?' The Heirs of Intermarriage." Addressing multiple identities is not a popular approach to the issue of intermarriage in the North American Jewish community today. But Secular Humanistic Judaism has never been as much about popularity as it has been about grappling with the realities of modern Jewish life and meeting the needs of real people. And that means recognizing and addressing the needs of individuals with multiple identities.

At the 2012 Colloquium, Paul Golin, then Assistant Executive Director of the Jewish Outreach Institute ("JOI") and now Executive Director of the Society for Humanistic Judaism, described eloquently what he calls "intermarriage math." If you begin with four Jews and 50% of them intermarry, then two of the four Jews will marry one another, while the other two Jews marry someone from a different background. The two Jews who intermarry will create one household each, while the other two each create their own household. This results in three households, doubling the number of intermarried families compared to in-married households. The upshot? Intermarriage is increasing the Jewish population. Given the birth rate among most Jews, intermarriage may be the best option for increasing the number of Jewish households today. If the Jewish community is open, welcoming, creative, and willing to consider a different kind of Judaism for the future, it can potentially draw a majority of those families into the Jewish community.

And make no mistake: many of these families want a Jewish identity. In a 2011 JOI study of young adults who are the products of intermarriage, more than 70% of the respondents to the survey said that "being Jewish" is "somewhat" or "very" important to them, while 65% of them said that they want to pass on "Jewish ethnic identity to their kids."[4] And I have seen this phenomenon personally: I once facilitated a Shabbat meeting in a college town; four young people arrived. All of them were the products of Jewish/Christian intermarriage, none had a Jewish upbringing, and all were curious about their Jewish identities as young adults.

What we heard in a variety of different ways over the weekend of the 2012 Colloquium was that the greater threat to the Jewish people is not intermarriage, but the superficiality of Judaism today. The Jewish communal challenge is not to stop intermarriage—it is to create Jewish options that will engage and excite Jewish youth and young adults enough to learn more about Jewish history and Judaism, and then have meaningful, relevant Jewish experiences.[5]

Diversity as a Positive Value

In biological evolution, diversity within a species is a survival asset, enabling flexibility to respond to new environments, challenges, and possibilities. In social evolution, diversity also represents a strength, not a fault line.

The Jewish people has always been diverse and is growing more so with ongoing intermarriage, conversion, and acceptance. While some fear the changes that result from this increasing diversity, Humanistic Judaism welcomes a multiplicity of family configurations and identities, believing that standing up for all Jews when others may turn them away is the moral thing to do.

The Society for Humanistic Judaism (SHJ), founded in 1969 as the congregational and community-organizing arm for Humanistic Judaism in North America, is composed of both members of affiliated communities and congregations and individuals at large. In addition to publishing philosophical and celebrational resources and the movement's quarterly magazine, *Humanistic Judaism*, SHJ provides community development support and issues statements on ethical, religious, and general matters on behalf of its members. This statement from 2021 affirms the movement's stance on acceptance and inclusion based on its Humanistic Jewish philosophy.

Society for Humanistic Judaism, "Radical Inclusion" (2021)

Intermarriage between someone who is not Jewish and someone who's Jewish is good, period. Humanistic Judaism is the only Jewish denomination that can say so with no strings attached.

We celebrate love. All love. Our rabbis and celebrants do not have restrictions on the type of people for whom we will officiate at Humanistic Jewish lifecycle events.

We believe in full LGBTQ equality.

We believe that diversity is a positive value and a strength, whether racial, gender, financial, or neurodiversity.

Our inclusivity does not emerge from a need to make accommodation to demographic trends; it stems from our strongly-held convictions about full equality and the dignity of all people....

By determining what is right for us today, we are not breaking with Judaism but rather continuing the ongoing tradition that's existed within Judaism for thousands of years, of grappling with what came before and modifying it to meet current interests and needs.

Judaism is always what the Jews make of it. By recognizing that Judaism has been a culture all along—by, for, and about people—we no longer need to claim a divine imprimatur to act on what we know is right. To some that might seem a radical inclusion. We just call it Humanistic Judaism.[6]

8

Israel/Zionism and Diaspora

The relationship between American Jews and the State of Israel has faced complications and contradictions, some of which especially impact Humanistic Jews. Before World War II, factions within secularist Jewish socialism and Reform Judaism (not to mention Orthodox Judaism) expressed substantial resistance to Zionism. Jewish socialists felt Zionism was parochial as they pursued internationalism, while some Reform Jews identified primarily as political citizens of the Jewish religion but not Jewish nationality. After Israel's establishment in 1948, broad American Jewish support for Israel was not accompanied by mass *aliyah* (move to Israel), since by then Jews generally felt at home in the United States, rather than in exile or diaspora from a homeland in Israel. While tremendous pride and excitement were evident at the founding of the State of Israel and its victory in the 1967 Six-Day War, relations since have become strained, largely due to Israel's occupation of the West Bank and Gaza, especially after the first *intifada* in 1987 and ongoing conflicts with Palestinians in the subsequent decades.

Humanistic Judaism's philosophical commitment to universal human rights often clashed with commitments based on ethnic solidarity to Israel's prosperity and security. Israeli and American Jewry's increasingly divergent perspectives on politics, religion-state separation, and Jewish pluralism further heightened tensions, as did Israel's continued rejection of non-Orthodox Judaism, patrilineal Jews, and shared public spaces like the Western Wall by the Ministry of Religious Affairs and right-wing coalition governments.

In the twenty-first century, when 90 percent of world Jewry lives more or less evenly divided between Israel and the United States, attempts to bridge the gap between American and Israeli Jews, from Birthright Israel to increased efforts to connect Israeli Americans with the organized American Jewish community, have had mixed success. The 2020 Pew survey of Jewish Americans showed American Jews' levels of attachment to Israel vary by a two-to-one margin between those who define themselves either as Jews by religion or as Jews of no religion. Indeed, "six-in-ten Jews with no particular denominational affiliation (59%) say they are either 'not too' or 'not at all' emotionally attached to Israel."[1]

Despite these challenges, Humanistic Jews in America have much in common with secular Israelis and have generally maintained a positive connection with the state and its Jewish culture.[2] Many early Zionists and founders of Israel were secular and acted from the same nontheistic convictions and values then as Humanistic Jews do now. The creativity of kibbutz Judaism in reenvisioning life-cycle events and holidays with secular Jewish framing and content parallels similar creativity within Humanistic Judaism. An attachment to Jewish peoplehood and a global Jewish family necessarily must include the vibrant and diverse expressions of Judaism in Israel. Contemporary Israeli Jewish culture, from food to music to poetry to Hebrew as a living language, can be an important part of the Jewish culture that forms the basis of Humanistic Jewish identity (see part 3). Can one embrace this secular Israeli Jewish history and culture despite significant political disagreements? Israel is one more example of the Humanistic Jewish balancing act between universal human commitments and identification with a particular people in a particular ancestral homeland.

This chapter explores how Humanistic Judaism grapples with the challenges of diaspora, Zionism, and Israel. The first selection describes the movement's ongoing positive commitment to a global Jewish identity—with or without a deep connection with Israel—as the key not only to diaspora Jewish survival, but to its thriving. The second comes from a longtime Israeli supporter of Humanistic Judaism whose progressive Zionism articulates both the critiques and positive affirmations of Humanistic Jewish identification with Israel. The third describes the challenges and possibilities of talking about Israel given the spectrum of opinions within a Humanistic Jewish congregation.

A World People

How do Humanistic Jews in North America define their relationship to where they live? "Exile" (in Hebrew, *galut*) does not reflect the rootedness they generally feel as acculturated citizens of democratic societies. "Diaspora" implies dispersion from a homeland or "old country," but for them, precisely which ancestral homeland is most significant varies depending on the individual Jew: Eastern and Central Europe, Aleppo (Syria), even New York City (among other locales) are all viable candidates to a Jewish individual's "family homeland" in addition to—or even instead of—Israel.[3]

The question then becomes whether a cultural Jewish identity *without* a shared center can last and be transmitted outside of Israel. A self-sufficient global Jewish identity requires the confidence to assert that the Diaspora is not inferior to Israel because the former has its own powerful and exciting story to tell.

Some of the early Israeli participants in the International Federation of Secular Humanistic Jews (established in 1986; see chapter 6) agreed with Humanistic Judaism's beliefs and practices but continued to express skepticism about furthering secular Jewish identity without linguistic and cultural context—something they believed was only possible in Israel or, in earlier generations, within Yiddish- or Ladino-speaking communities. In this essay, delivered at a 1992 IFSHJ conference in Jerusalem, Rabbi Sherwin Wine (see chapter 1) articulates both the challenges faced by non-Israeli Humanistic Judaism and its potential to draw on both the global nature of the Jewish experience and the lessons in humanism taught by that experience.

Sherwin Wine, "Being a Secular Humanistic Jew in the Diaspora" (1993)

The word *diaspora* has a problem built into it. It implies that the Jewish people is a people whose extension flows out from the land of Israel, and in many respects historically that was true. But the reality of Jewish history in the twentieth century was not the way it is with most diasporas. Normally the homeland creates the diaspora. In this case the Diaspora created the homeland....

I start out with a very important premise: that we are a world people. If we don't start out with that premise, then the communities in the Diaspora have a very inferior reality, and if we accept that self-image, we cannot grow, we cannot be what we want to be....

The Jewish people started out as a nation in our own land, a territorial nation. And even when we were dispersed, we still viewed ourselves as one nation, though in reality we had become several. The Jews of Eastern Europe were not Polish or Russian; they belonged to the Ashkenazic Jewish nation. It had a language all its own called Yiddish. It was dispersed over a discrete territory. There were certain towns and villages and shtetls that were completely Yiddish-speaking. That language and culture, which developed in Eastern Europe, is very different from the culture that developed in Spain, from the culture that developed in the Jewish Arabic world, from the culture that developed in the Jewish Persian world. Each was built around a Jewish language....

So, although in our consciousness we were one nation, in our experience there was diversity. And then came the French Revolution.... All of a sudden Jews had to confront a new situation. Somebody said to them, we welcome you into a secular state. Secularism altered the character of the Jewish people.... Religion and culture became private matters. There are certain things that you as a citizen of the state must conform to, but your roots, your culture, and your religion are private matters....

One of the realities of life in the Diaspora is that Jewish identity is not always the primary concern of Jews. They are involved in the political, social, and economic life of their countries. In our country, in the United States of America, most people are in a sense the children of the Enlightenment. The Enlightenment gave us reason, it gave us secularism, it gave us a loss of interest in the supernatural... and it gave us individualism. In fact, individualism, which is so pervasive in North American life, constitutes to a large degree one of the problems we have to deal with. The other is an intermarriage rate of more than 40 percent. That means that in two generations, people who identify with Judaism—and there is a fairly high rate of retention among intermarried couples—will not have the same kinds of ethnic memories (borscht and blintzes) that many of us grew up with. We're already encountering that problem. So we're struggling with effective ways to express our Jewish identity. Let me mention a couple of ways in which people do it.

First, people display an increasing identification with the culture of the State of Israel. That is a perfectly appropriate thing to do; the problem is that it is a vicarious experience.... Part of the problem with Zionism for the Diaspora is that Zionism does not really allow for the Diaspora. The great wish of those who are committed to the Zionist movement is that ultimately all Jews who live in the Diaspora will come to the land of Israel. That relationship, therefore, creates a certain inequality. Nevertheless, one of the ways to express a secular Jewish identity—and it is very appropriate—is to increase identification with the culture of the State of Israel.

A second way is what I call "residual ritual." You do *Hanukka*, you do *Purim*, you do *Pesakh*, you may do *Rosh Hashana*, *Yom Kippur*. You do a series of holidays, and people feel very Jewish around the holidays, but the holidays aren't attached to anything. They hang in limbo. And after a while, there are so many holidays coming from elsewhere in the environment that they simply fade into other holidays....

I believe that the only way we can create any kind of intense commitment or intense feeling about being Jewish in the Diaspora is for people to feel they are part of an exciting world people. In fact, the reason Jews are interesting is that we are a world people. We are an interesting world people with an interesting history, and if you are going to be a Secular Humanistic Jew, you need to master the alternative history. You have to master the history of the Jewish people and of the Jewish experience from a secular humanistic point of view. Then you can tack holidays onto that if you want to....

In order for Jewish identity to last, people have to feel that being Jewish is significant, and the only way they can feel that being Jewish is significant is if they feel that being part of the Jewish people is significant. And the only way they can feel that being part of the Jewish people is significant is to feel identified with Jewish history and informed of that history....

If we told the alternative story of the Jewish experience, if we created it so it doesn't appear only in scholarly journals, somebody who was a teacher in a school in the Diaspora or even in Israel could pick it up, and there would be the story told from the other point of view. Our story would say that being a world people is significant. If Judaism is identified only with the State of Israel and its concerns and culture, then there is no reason to make a distinction between Judaism and Israelism. Judaism means that the people of the State of Israel who are Jews wish to identify with the civilization that embraces this world people....

Our problem is our self-hate. We can't write about our history because the things we did for the past two thousand years are things we are embarrassed about. What we can write about are people milking cows on *kibbutzim* (collective farms). Just show a Jew handling soil, and all of a sudden he is real, he's useful. All the Jews I know, the psychiatrists, the accountants, everybody, they are not real. They're not part of Jewish history. If we wrote that alternative history, we wouldn't be trapped by the literature of the past. As secular Jews in the Diaspora, we live (as Mordecai Kaplan said) in two civilizations. We have the American civilization and we have the Jewish civilization. My heroes consist of two sets of people. The only way we will ever give Jews in the Diaspora a sense of strong Jewish identity is if they become masters of Jewish history; but if they become masters of the old history, they will either reject it or they will not want to be secular Jews. So we have to write a new history, and all the heroes of that history are my heroes. Those heroes include Baruch Spinoza, Albert Einstein, Theodor Herzl, and David Ben-Gurion. They include the vast spectrum of people, modern, medieval, or ancient, that are part of this tradition.

Finally, we need to make a connection between humanism and Judaism. There is a universal humanism, and I subscribe to its wisdom, but my humanism is reinforced by my identification with the Jewish experience. The meaning of Jewish history is not that we are in the hands of a loving and just Providence. The meaning of Jewish history is humanism. The meaning of Jewish history, certainly during the past two thousand years, is that we live in a world in which nobody out there gives a damn whether we live or die. The meaning of it is that we have to rely on ourselves. For me, Jewish ethics does not come from somebody coming down on a mountain. I don't care how many thunderbolts he has—that's not authority. Ultimately the authority for ethics lies in the Jewish experience. For me, it is inconceivable that we should oppress other peoples given the history of our people, given all that we have suffered and endured.

So, we have to find a way of connecting to Jewish history that's very intense. We have to be the masters of a second Jewish history, and then we can attach whatever cultural items we want to that. Then we can live in a world that is multilingual and multinational as a world Jewish people. Unless we can achieve that, we in the Diaspora will not survive; if we do, then we will.[4]

A Jewish and Democratic State

Can Israel truly be both democratic and a Jewish state? For Humanistic Jews, having to choose one or the other would be like choosing between their universal humanist values and their particular cultural Jewish identity—a binary choice they refuse. Over a century ago, secular Jewish socialists like the Bund argued that "bourgeois nationalism" like Zionism will inevitably fail as a democracy and "like every nationalism, it could lead to chauvinism."[5] While tension remains high between "democratic" and "Jewish" in contemporary Israel, it is also true that many other self-declared democracies privilege particular ethnic or religious majorities, allow and encourage diaspora repatriation, or have political parties representing various ethnic communities. Israel also hosts a robust free-speech tradition of its citizenry criticizing the state on political, moral, and religious grounds across the political spectrum.

Shulamit Aloni (1928–2014) was an Israeli activist for human and women's rights and a politician who consistently advocated for the democracy side of the Jewish/democratic balance. Having fought in Israel's War of Independence, she was first elected to the Knesset in 1965 representing a precursor of the Labor Party and then on her own as the founder of the Movement for Civil Rights and Peace (Ratz) in 1973. She and her party argued for the separation of religion and state and for civil rights, especially women's rights, throughout her thirty-one years in office. Recognizing her early advocacy for dialogue with Palestinians, a foundation in her name grants an annual award to cultural creators (in both Hebrew and Arabic) whose work promotes human rights.

Aloni became actively involved in Humanistic Judaism in the early 1980s as the North American movement made positive connections in Israel. This essay, adapted from her presentation at the 1999 Colloquium of the International Institute for Secular Humanistic Judaism, demonstrates both the promises and the perils of Zionism and modern Israel for Humanistic Jews by highlighting successes and failures of secular Jewish Israelis.

Shulamit Aloni, "One Hundred Years of Zionism, Fifty Years of Statehood" (2000)

> The Zionist ideal, of which the founding fathers dreamed and for which they fought, was the creation of a democratic state, liberal

and open to the world. A state in which universal humanism and moral values—which Jews throughout the world identify as Jewish values and Jewish ethics—would be respected. The idea was to cease being a reclusive, frightened, and persecuted community, constantly building safeguards for itself and concerned only for itself and its continued existence in a hostile world, and to become a nation among the nations of the world. A nation that develops its own culture, identity, and resources in its own land. A nation that conscientiously cares for the rights of all its citizens. A healthy nation, free of the paranoia engendered by persecution.

These ideals are embodied in the Declaration of Independence, in which Israel is identified as a sovereign state, Jewish and democratic. The Declaration promises citizenship to every Jew who comes here to settle and grants complete social and political equality to all citizens, making "no distinction between creed, race, or sex" and "guaranteeing freedom of religion and conscience, of language, education, and culture."

The basic guidelines of the first elected government elaborated on these rights. In order to avoid any misconception about the secular character of the state, the guidelines promise that the "State will supply the religious needs of all its inhabitants, but will, itself, refrain from all matters of religion." Aside from establishing the Sabbath and other Jewish holidays as days of rest, no ritual of any kind is imposed; nor are any hints made of religious coercion. Nor is a Jewish citizen granted any advantage over a non-Jewish citizen....

The reality is that the State of Israel did not create a constitution to protect its principles. Nor did it undergo, upon its founding, the transition from a coalition of parties to a constitutional democracy. We do not have a human rights charter; the supposedly progressive law known as "Basic Law: Human Dignity and Liberty" does not include a clause on equality. This clause was removed from the draft legislation in response to demands by the religious and nationalist parties.

Thus it has happened that discrimination based on ethnic origin, nationality, race, religion, and gender exists. Discrimination is anchored in laws, still valid, left over from Ottoman and British rule, as well as in original Israeli jurisdiction and in administrative decisions and acts.

From birth to death, Israelis are subject to segregation in all aspects of personal status, marriage, and divorce. The citizens are divided into twelve religious, ethnic groups (what was once the Ottoman "Millet"). All members of each ethnic group are subject to its own conservative and coercive clerical authority, which draws both its power and its funds from the state, but whose codes and decisions originate in religious rulings. These systems border on racism and have gained force in recent years with the growing nationalism of the far right, religious-messianic nationalism, and ultra-Orthodox groups, including the noisy, messianic Habad movement. . . .

We are the only country in the free world that requires of people (mainly new immigrants from the former Soviet Union) that they undergo conversion—a purely religious ritual—in order to obtain citizenship. Registration is conducted on the basis of religious identity. Husbands and wives, parents and children, are separated in accordance with what the rabbis and government clerks define as their religious affiliation. In other words, it is *they* who decide whether or not these people are "pure" Jews according to *halakha* (Jewish religious law); and this is openly indicated on the official identity card.

The State of Israel has become two entities, one Jewish, the other democratic. This split has resulted in many conflicts over the years. The liberal Israeli population, which believes in the democratic vision, is trapped in the hands of fundamentalist nationalism. There are those who claim that *Jewish* means religion, tradition, *halakha*—in short, religious ethnocentrism rather than a sovereign state for all its inhabitants.

My own post-Zionism requires that we return to the collective credo for which we fought—the credo in whose name we brought in immigrants from all corners of the world and called upon the world's nations to stand by our side.

We are strong enough to understand the limitations of power and make peace with our neighbors. We have caused them much injustice—some unconsciously, some consciously, and some which has been their own fault. We shall never know true peace until we rid ourselves of paranoia and begin to understand the needs of our counterparts as human beings and as a national entity. . . .

We must become what we wanted to be, and what we are capable of being. We have to shake off the fears, the ethnic-racist seclusion, and the glut of religious functionaries and return to the values of the prophets: to peace, equality, justice and judgment, science and research, knowledge and wisdom. We must be rational; we must understand the limitations of power and release ourselves from territorial, nationalistic, and religious greed. Only under the umbrella of a tolerant democracy that promises equality to all people and recognizes social and religious pluralism can everyone in Israel live according to his or her own beliefs.

Together we shall be able to realize the Zionist dream: that the Jewish people can maintain a normal sovereign state, like each and every other nation in its own land, developing its own culture and language, taking care of its citizens, and living in peace and cooperation with its neighbors and the rest of the world. Thus we can also become a source of attraction, a bridge and a connection to all the various Jewish communities in the Diaspora. They, too, want to see in Israel a modern and advanced democracy, one that maintains traditional Jewish values with pride and assures the rights of all its citizens, without discriminating against minorities.

As someone who has followed the state from the time before it was founded, as one who fought in the War of Independence and served as a minister in the Rabin and Peres governments, and as a former member of the Ministerial Committee for Defense, I say that now, after two thousand years, the fate of Israel is entirely in our own hands.⁶

Israel/Palestine: Seeing Both Sides

While Humanistic Judaism differs from other Jewish denominations in its understanding of Torah, chosenness, and God, it is similar to other liberal Judaisms when it comes to Israel. Some are centrist and left-wing Zionists, others are non- and even anti-Zionists, and still others are conflicted or indifferent.

Generally speaking, through the 1990s and 2000s the movement supported a two-state solution for Israel/Palestine. For example, the 2014 statement "SHJ Stands with Israel" concludes:

> The SHJ encourages all involved parties to seek a solution that will bring peace with justice to the entire region. A negotiated solution that assures a secure State of Israel and a demilitarized sovereign Palestinian state must be secured. We encourage the United States and the countries of the world to take a vigorous stand in bringing ... involved parties to the negotiating table. Only then will the region find a lasting peace.⁷

As of this writing, however, that possibility seems increasingly remote.

Humanistic Jews may view the government of Israel as acting antithetically to their democratic values even as the people of Israel may be their friends, family, and colleagues. In other words, the very issue of Israel is a thorny one, and anything approaching consensus is unlikely. Sometimes, respectful dialogue on controversial issues is itself an achievement.

Rabbi Tzemah Yoreh (b. 1978) was raised in a religious Zionist family before secularizing as an adult. He earned his first PhD in biblical criticism at the Hebrew University of Jerusalem and a second PhD in ancient wisdom literature from the University of Toronto. Ordained in 2015 in Jerusalem by Tmura-IISHJ, the Israeli partner of the International Institute for Secular Humanistic Judaism, he is now rabbi of The City Congregation of New York and author of several books of biblical criticism, poetry, and humanist liturgy. In this essay, based on his 2019 presentation to the Society for Humanistic Judaism's fiftieth anniversary conference, Yoreh explores how to hold constructive conversations about Israel in Humanistic congregations.

Tzemah Yoreh, "Constructive Conversations about Israel" (2019)

Since I love Israel and I love the Bible (even if I regard it as "only" a piece of literature), two of the pieces are already in place, and it is not such a leap for me to see the right-wing, even the extreme right-wing, perspective. It does help that I attended a religious seminary in Israel for two years and my roomies were from the territories. When you've read about Jerusalem, about Hebron, about Bethel in the Bible, and then you see these places and live in them, the Bible becomes real for you. Though much of the Bible is elaboration and extrapolation, and some of it is fabricated, there is still much that is not, and then these same biblical places are right across the street, literally.

When you walk upon Emek Refaim, you ask yourself, was it here that David fought the Philistines (though the biblical account of King David is almost exclusively literary extrapolation)? When you walk on Derekh Hebron, you ask, was this the ancient path taken by so many of our ancestors? Did Abraham walk among these mountains and promise to sacrifice his son? (To be fair there is no evidence whatsoever that Abraham or any of the patriarchs actually existed, and they are most likely literary fabrications, but Hebron definitely does [exist].) I cannot describe the connectedness you feel, the validation of your heritage, and it is so much greater when you believe wholeheartedly in a personal God who granted this land to your ancestors. Now people are trying to make you give it up, trying to make you move away from Hebron, trying to bulldoze your house in Ofrah, because some upstart Palestinians know how to effectively manipulate world sympathies for victims. You cry out, haven't we been victims our whole existence? Didn't my grandparents survive Auschwitz, my great-grandparents survive the pogroms of Russia, my ancestors survive untold expulsions? Let me have my little scrap of land! Arabs have so many countries of their own; can't Egypt or Jordan, or Syria, or Iraq take them?

Now this narrative may seem to be unfair to you, but that doesn't take away from its potency and from the fact that so many people believe in it. And whether you like it or not, this narrative has validity if you are a liberal, since every group has the right to self-definition.

SPEAKING ABOUT ISRAEL IN CONGREGATIONS

Accepting and tolerating the views of others is the key to productive conversations about Israel, but how is this achieved? Speaking about Israel in congregational settings in North America is just getting more difficult in this day and age. Unquestioning support for Israel is no longer a given. Times are changing. . . . Feelings regarding Israel run high, and for many congregations Israel is a toxic issue. Yet people feel passionately about Israel and want to help. What can be done? . . .

[A key principle is recognizing that] the Palestinians [are] human beings who should be treated with dignity. . . . This I believe should be the common ground that should be sought in any congregational discussion about Israel or about allocation of charitable funds. The inhabitants twixt the Jordan and the Sea are all human beings and should be treated with dignity and respect, whether they be Arab or Jewish. . . .

Today, security—the ultimate precondition for everything—prevails. Neither Jews nor Palestinians are threatened by en masse eviction; the economies are thriving; a new Palestinian city, Rawabi, is being built north of Ramallah; Jewish communities are growing; checkpoints are being removed; and tourists of all nationalities are again visiting Bethlehem and Shiloh. While the status quo is not anyone's ideal, it is immeasurably better than any other feasible alternative. And there is room for improvement. Checkpoints are a necessity only if terror exists; otherwise, there should be full freedom of movement. And the fact that the great-grandchildren of the original Palestinian refugees still live in squalid camps after sixty-four years is a disgrace that should be corrected by improving their living conditions....

As a high school student, I was deeply affected by the settler narrative, since it was the only narrative I ever heard and I became fairly right-wing. That changed after one semester at university, where I was suddenly exposed to so many other choices. The only way to get other people to consider an opinion that is not their own is to force them to become acquainted with this counter opinion. Just like an academic paper where you are forced to bring the other side of the story and examine the pros and cons....

Thus if a genuine conversation about Israel is to take place [there] must [be] a framework wherein each person reads or interacts with perspectives that are not their own. The way I suggest it be done is through exchange of reading material or other media. Each side (and there can be more than two) should recommend materials the others should read, listen [to], or see. Then the others have to commit to engaging with these materials. A critical step in this endeavor is to have people present the side of the argument that they disagree with. This way they have to engage critically with the narratives and arguments of the other. When you engage critically with the other's narratives, it forces you to take the other seriously, to stop disparaging them, to stop blindly hating them.[8]

PART 3

Culture

Introduction

When a 2020 Pew survey of American Jews asked if being Jewish was mainly about ancestry, religion, or culture, 22 percent responded with only "culture," while another 33 percent included "culture" with one or more of the other options.[1]

If a majority of American Jews define their Judaism as at least partly based on Jewish culture and one-fifth do so exclusively, then understanding how Jewish culture defines, supports, and expresses modern Jewish identity is essential to understanding American Judaism. It is even more essential to understanding Humanistic Judaism, a movement that both views religion as only a part of Jewish culture, not something separate or superior, and expressly roots its Jewish identity in Jewish culture rather than in theology, revelation, and commandment.

Judaism rooted in Jewish culture both reflects actual contemporary Jewish practice and enables contemporary creativity and a broader approach to what is considered Jewish practice. Extending considerably beyond the traditional canons of Bible, Talmud, halakhah (Jewish law), and Jewish philosophy, culture is defined as "Jewish" even if it doesn't conform to Jewish religious law or belief. For cultural Jews, food can be as Jewish as fasting on Yom Kippur, and what qualifies as "Jewish food" varies widely across geography, outside cultural influences, and personal choice; both a nonkosher Jewish deli and a kosher Chinese restaurant express Jewish culture in their own ways. American movies, Israeli music, Yemenite clothing, Yiddish literature, etc.—whether particular works express religious beliefs is less salient than the fact that they enrich our understanding of the Jewish experience. Novels, short stories, and poetry expressing love, lust, and atheism by Jewish characters or in Jewish settings can be Jewish literature. Holidays adapted to new languages, cultural expressions, and family identities are still religious inheritance when treated as malleable culture; for example, a seder plate for intercultural families might feature wasabi for *maror* (bitter herbs) and, for vegetarians, a roasted beet rather than a lamb shank. Some might even choose to consume cheeseburgers on matzah during Passover week. The Humanistic Jewish cultural "canon" is thus more expansive than fixed religious texts such as the Bible and Talmud. Although paradoxical, given the conventional meaning of "canon" as a fixed body of culture, the Humanistic Jewish "canon" is open-ended, with new material in various media constantly being added.

Literary theory describes a dynamic called intertextuality in which later texts draw on motifs, characters, symbols, and stories of earlier texts in the same tradition to provide added meaning and cultural resonance that affect the reading of both. Like John Milton's *Paradise Lost*, which works only if the reader is familiar with Genesis in a Christian understanding, so does the Jewish past inform much of the Jewish cultural present. Jews retell biblical stories in new creative narratives and utilize ancient symbols like the tallit and the Star of David to create new ones, such as the Israeli flag. The 2009 film *A Serious Man* parallels the biblical book of Job, and George Segal's 1978 sculpture *Abraham and Isaac: In Memory of May 4, 1970, Kent State* depicts the biblical *Akedah* (the Binding of Isaac) in Genesis 22 in modern terms. Allusions to the traditional narrative activate Jewish cultural connections and thereby recast the tradition in more identifiable and meaningful ways.

Of course, many Jews who are not part of Humanistic Judaism create and consume such Jewish culture today. Other liberal Jewish congregations, Jewish community centers, and public Jewish cultural events like movie festivals and book fairs offer Jewish culture programming. What makes Humanistic Judaism distinct is its centering of Jewish culture in its identity and communal life. High Holiday services include both adapted traditional liturgy and modern Jewish poetry and Broadway music (most by Jewish composers). A book club may be just as important as a Shabbat service. Learning to cook new Jewish foods or sing contemporary Jewish music is practicing Humanistic Judaism as much as studying Torah or reciting Hebrew.

With its understanding of Jewish identity as an extended family (see chapter 6), Humanistic Judaism feels comfortable drawing from all Jewish cultures, not only its particular Jewish subcultural background (which has been predominantly Ashkenazic/European so far). Global Jewish culture includes the experiences and customs of Ashkenazic, Sephardic, and *Mizrahi* (Jews from the Orient) Jews, in addition to other diaspora communities as well as contemporary Israel. Jewish culture also includes diverse Jewish foods like *moufletot* (pancake eaten after Passover by North African Jews), *orejas di Haman* ("Haman's ears," fried strips of dough coated with powdered sugar from Italy eaten during Purim), and *cassola* (sweet cheese pancakes from Spain for Hanukkah).

Just as Humanistic Jewish identity is more open to the outside world (also see part 2), the limits of what is included as Jewish culture are likewise permeable. The debates on such questions—"Is it anything created by Jews, or must it relate in some way to Jewish identity?"; "Must it be accepted by Jewish communities as Jewish, and if so, who in the community decides?"—are themselves Jewish conversations.

Sometimes culture created by the outside world today can become Jewish through its use in Jewish life, just as the Roman feast became the Passover seder centuries ago. For example, Yeshiva University's a cappella men's singing group the Maccabeats' adaptation of "Dynamite" by Taio Cruz into a Hanukkah song called "Candlelight" has been viewed on YouTube over seventeen million times since 2011; this has led to many other Jewish a cappella singing groups periodically going viral on social media by adapting contemporary pop song lyrics to feature Jewish content.[2] Many weddings between two Jewish partners now include a mutual exchange of vows/promises and rings for both partners as in Christian weddings, a change from the Jewish tradition of no spoken vows and a ring given only from the groom to the bride, who did not speak.

This section first demonstrates how "cultural Judaism" (chapter 9) functions as a basis of Jewish identity for secular and Humanistic Jews and then describes the parameters of "a cultural Jewish canon" (chapter 10), with both general explorations of literature, music, and art and specific examples of contemporary Jewish literary culture. Recommendations of non-textual Jewish movies, music, art, and food that Humanistic Jews have found meaningful appear in the "Go Forth and Learn" section concluding this volume.

One final thought: Because Humanistic Jewish services include both adapted traditional liturgy and contemporary Jewish cultural creations in music, poetry, and art, and because the line between religion and culture fades when religion is understood as part of culture, Jewish culture itself can become a source of inspiration for "religious" experiences. Part 4 will explore this in greater detail.

9

Cultural Judaism

As discussed, Humanistic Judaism was founded on both humanism and Judaism (see chapter 6). This chapter expands on the second foundational component—namely cultural Judaism.

Unlike secular Jews without a clear ideology, who tend to define themselves in negative, subtractive terms vis-à-vis the traditions they do not observe—"I don't keep kosher," "I don't go to synagogue," "I don't fast on Yom Kippur," and so on—Humanistic Judaism provides a positive ideological basis for unconventional Jewish choices. Humanistic Jews stress that Jewish culture can be a strong Jewish foundation for a positive secularized Judaism, just as positive humanism (see Epstein, chapter 3) and positive self-definition (see Wine, chapter 3) allow for a stronger Jewish identity than negative non-beliefs ("I don't believe in a personal, interventionist God," "I don't believe Israel is the divinely 'promised land,'" etc.). Importantly, the choice to create a Jewish experience on one's own terms amounts to a Jewish tradition in and of itself. In fact, one could say the shift to Jewish culture reflects an additive process of creativity, discernment, and critical thinking. Choosing to read a poem by Israeli poet Yehuda Amichai or an original meditation in a Humanistic Jewish service or ceremony is as valid as a traditional Jew's choice to use centuries-old liturgy. Moreover, for Humanistic Jews, the choice need not be one or the other; they are free to also choose from the tradition when it provides relevant, meaningful texts.

In addition to the values of positive expression and choice, cultural Judaism reflects Humanistic Jewish values of diversity and inclusion.

Jewish culture is considered, very broadly, as works by Jews that relate in some way to the Jewish experience, independent of religious sensibilities. Here, Humanistic Judaism strives for the converse of the traditional Jewish approach, in which contrary voices like the second-century-CE rabbi Elisha ben Abuya (who was often referred to as *acher*, "the other," rather than by name in the Babylonian Talmud, because he questioned whether God was just) and Baruch Spinoza (who was excommunicated in 1656 for challenging rabbinic authority, divine revelation, and a transcendent god) are spurned. Humanistic Judaism aims for an expansive and radical inclusion of Jews *and* Jewish culture. Acknowledging that the first generation of Humanistic Jewish leadership was largely white, male, and Ashkenazic, defining Humanistic Jewish expression as Jewish culture now means including Jews of all ethnicities, genders, and locales. New and meaningful Jewish culture in the twenty-first century is being created by Jews of color, LGBTQ+ Jews, Jewish women, and Jews from all genres of Judaism's cultural heritage.

Cultural Judaism is seen, too, in a diversity of media. It is not limited to the written word, though that of course is of continuing importance. It includes music in many Jewish languages, graphic art in various forms, drama on stage and screen, movement and dance, and other modalities. These varying expressions address the diversity of individual Humanistic Jews: how they think, learn, articulate, and express their Judaism. A kinesthetic learner exploring Jewish dance may find just as much meaning as a verbal learner studying Jewish text or a musical learner playing Ladino songs. Cultural Judaism thus demonstrates yet another Humanistic Jewish value: meeting the needs of individual Jews to express their Judaism—and themselves—in the creative and personal ways that speak most to them.

Thus it is that a Jewish cultural canon provides alternatives to the traditional religious canon; from the perspective of cultural Judaism, all of Jewish religion is already included in Jewish culture, while not everything that is accepted as Jewish culture is religious. Secularized Jews rarely, if ever, study Talmud and Rabbinic law, yet they do read novels and watch videos about the Jewish experience that may include religious Jewish subjects and characters, consume art and music with Jewish subjects, prepare and eat foods connected to Jewish cultural expression, and more. Jewish Scripture still has much to offer when put into a secular context (e.g., Bible as literature). The extensive content of a cultural Jewish identity connects Humanistic Jews to their heritage across historical time and geographical space. The diversity of global Jewish cultures and the creativity of Jewish art, language, food, music, and more enrich Humanistic Jewish identity, education, and celebration.

Each of the four readings that follow explores how the cultural Judaism of Humanistic Jews is a vital and vibrant part of Jewish tradition and a tradition that belongs to these Jewish writers as much as to any other Jews. Humanistic Jews (and other secular Jews) are rightful and legitimate, even if skeptical or critical, heirs to the tradition. Representative of this approach, Amos Oz rejects the idea that Jewish culture beyond the synagogue represents an "empty cart" devoid of seriousness or meaning; he focuses on positive expressions of cultural Judaism that enrich Jewish identity. Yehuda Bauer illustrates how cultural Judaism encompasses religion and so much more, while also asserting that "religion" is insufficient to encompass all of Jewish life. In "Recovering Our Stories," Daniel Friedman underscores the importance of biblical stories as a medium for conveying important lessons and that, as stories, they need not be taken at face value. Instead, claiming ancient texts as "our stories" rightfully places Humanistic Jews among those who gain much from them as cultural foundations. Finally, Sivan Malkin Maas argues the ironic truth that Humanistic Jews are doing what Jews conventionally have always done: reinterpreting and reimagining the texts and institutions from the Jewish past to make them relevant for modernity.

A Jewish Cultural Inheritance

The distinction between a Judaism solely rooted in and defined by religious tradition and a secular Jewish culture that breaks those boundaries has been derisively described as the difference between a "full cart" and an "empty cart." Israeli author Amos Oz (see chapter 4) recounts a meeting between secular Israeli founding father David Ben-Gurion

(1886–1973) and Orthodox rabbi Avraham Yeshayahu Kerlitz (1878–1953) in which the latter extolled the superior canon of halakhah as a "full cart" of laws and traditions that should supersede the "empty cart" of secular Jews, and Ben-Gurion did not defend secularism. Oz objected to both Kerlitz's characterization and Ben-Gurion's silence, writing, "The Jewish culture that evolved outside the synagogue over the past few centuries is no empty cart. [Israeli cultural icons such as] Bialik and Agnon . . . Rachel the Poetess . . . and Yehuda Amichai [among others] all tow carts of Jewish heritage no less full than those of the great religious adjudicators."[1] Kerlitz is simply wrong; the secular cart is not and never was empty.

Oz was an articulate proponent of a vibrant and creative secular Judaism in active dialogue with its Jewish inheritance. In this 1983 essay describing Judaism as a living civilization comprising much more than religion, he places secular Jews as legitimate heirs to Jewish civilization. As heirs rather than curators, secular Jews have many options when considering whether to accept the tradition, and if so, how much of it to accept.

Amos Oz, "A Full Cart or an Empty One? Thoughts on Jewish Culture" (1983)

> Judaism is a civilization, and one of the few civilizations that have left their mark on all of mankind. Religion is a central element in the Jewish civilization, perhaps even its origin, but that civilization cannot be presented as nothing more than religion. From the religious source of that civilization grew spiritual manifestations that enhanced the religious experience, changed it, and even reacted against it: language, customs, life styles, characteristic sensitivities (or, perhaps it should be said, sensitivities that used to be characteristic), and literature and art and ideas and opinions. All of this is Judaism. The rebellion and apostasy in our history and in recent generations—they are Judaism, too. A broad and abundant inheritance. And I see myself as one of the legitimate heirs:

not as a stepson, or a disloyal and defiant son, or a bastard, but as a lawful heir. . . .

For it follows that I am free to decide what I will choose from this great inheritance, to decide what I will place in my living room and what I will relegate to the attic. Certainly our children have the right to move the floor plan around and furnish their lives as they see fit. . . .

A museum curator relates ritualistically to his ancestral heritage: on tiptoe, in awe, he arranges and rearranges the artifacts, polishes the glass cases, cautiously interprets the significance of the items in the collection, guides the astonished visitors, convinces the public, and seeks, in due time, to pass on the keys of the museum to his sons after him. The museum curator will proclaim, Holy Holy Holy. And he will proclaim, I am too humble to determine what is important here. It is my lot only to see that the light of the inheritance shall shine in as many eyes as possible, and that nothing is damaged or lost. . . . But I believe there can be no vital existence for a museum civilization. Eventually it is bound to shrivel and to cut off its creative energies: at first it permits innovation only on the foundations of the old, then freedom is restricted to the freedom to interpret, after that it becomes permissible only to interpret the meaning of the interpretations, until finally all that is left is to polish the artifacts in their cases.

A living civilization is a drama of struggle between interpretations, outside influences, and emphases, an unrelenting struggle over what is wheat and what is the chaff, rebellion for the sake of innovation, dismantling for the purpose of reassembling differently, and even putting things in storage to clear the stage for experiment and for new creativity. And it is permissible to seek inspiration from, and be fertilized by, other civilizations as well. This implies a realization that struggle and pluralism are not just an eclipse or a temporary aberration but, rather, the natural climate for a living culture. And the heretic and the prober are, sometimes, the harbingers of the creator and the innovator.[2]

What Counts as Judaism?

Yehuda Bauer (b. 1926) has been a leading voice in the Secular Humanistic Jewish movement since the 1980s. Born in Prague, he emigrated with his family to British Mandatory Palestine in 1939 and obtained his PhD at Hebrew University in 1960. An expert in Holocaust studies, he is professor emeritus of history and Holocaust studies at the Avraham Harman Institute of Contemporary Jewry at the Hebrew University of Jerusalem and academic advisor to Israel's Holocaust memorial museum Yad Vashem.

In this excerpt from Bauer's introduction to *Judaism in a Secular Age* (1995), an anthology of leading thinkers of secular and Humanistic Judaism from the late nineteenth century through the then present, Bauer succinctly points out that religion (particularly in its Western cultural understanding, focused on theological beliefs, Scripture, liturgy, and ritual practices) is insufficient to encompass all of the cultural expressions of the Jewish people over the centuries. All the more so, without Jewish culture in its many varieties as part of the equation, a purely religious Judaism would be incomplete.

Yehuda Bauer, "Judaism Is..." (1995)

> Bible is Judaism, Talmud is Judaism, everyday life is Judaism, Jewish history is Judaism, Jewish poetry is Judaism, Jewish customs are Judaism, Jewish food is Judaism, Jewish jokes are Judaism; just as religion is Judaism. But you cannot argue that Judaism equals the religious beliefs of Jews; first, because these beliefs were and are different, even mutually contradictory; and second, because religion was and is just one aspect of Jewish existence; today, for many Jews, it is not even that. Judaism, then, is everything that the Jewish people in their very long history have produced. Judaism is Jewish civilization, Judaism is Jewish culture.[3]

Biblical Narratives as Cultural Myths

Humanistic Jews understand the TANAKH (Hebrew Bible) as having been written by people. Therefore, they feel no need to cast biblical texts aside or reject them in toto simply because the texts reflect theistic beliefs. Rather, because ethical pronouncements that claim to have been decreed by a god were nevertheless written by people in response to the human condition, these texts can still have meaning for secular people today. Similarly, biblical narratives do not need to be edited to reflect Humanistic values that are not there. Instead, stories are seen as stories; characters, including the biblical god, are literary characters. Sometimes, and to some readers, the stories have modern resonance; at other times they may not. One of the freedoms of Humanistic Judaism is choosing what is relevant and meaningful from Jewish inheritance rather than feeling compelled to justify and defend everything in the traditional canon.

But before one can even do that, one must acquire the cultural literacy needed to make those decisions.

Rabbi Daniel Friedman (see chapter 4) served as a congregational Humanistic rabbi for over thirty years. In this essay from a volume of the movement journal *Humanistic Judaism* focused on Humanistic observances of Shavuot as "discovering our literature," he emphasizes the importance of recovering and retelling "our stories" in such a way that young Humanistic Jews gain both cultural literacy and meaning from them. Before one may choose from one's literary heritage, one must first know what it is and claim it as one's own.

Daniel Friedman, "Recovering Our Stories" (1995)

Father Andrew Greeley offers an intriguing answer to the question: How can an intelligent, well-educated person believe in religion? What is there about Catholicism in particular that explains its enormous appeal, even to men and women who think the Pope is out of touch and the bishops and priests are fools? His answer: "Catholics like their heritage because it has great stories."[4]

Judaism has wonderful stories, too, but Jews—especially Humanistic Jews—are losing touch with them. . . . Our Humanistic Jewish children may have a better grasp of the nature of Jewish identity than we did when we were their age, but they are likely to know little or nothing about Korah's rebellion or Absalom's death. In our eagerness to communicate the essential features of a *humanistic* Judaism, we may be too quick to ignore or reject that which is of value in the legacy of theistic Judaism: its rich treasury of legends and myths. In avoiding Bible stories or minimizing their significance, we may be depriving our children of a precious heritage of images and metaphors that could be as meaningful to them as to theistic Jews—perhaps more so.

We, after all, are free to consider biblical personalities without preconceptions about their virtues or faults. As with characters in Shakespeare, we may study biblical personalities as prototypes, heroic or flawed—as admirable or pitiful or despicable examples of human possibilities. We may see in them what our experiences have enabled us to see. Or, we may see in them what our experiences have not enabled us to see for ourselves. These stories offer for us—and for our children—a rich metaphorical vocabulary that makes possible what rational philosophic discourse cannot: the dramatic display of human emotions, values, and dilemmas in time-honored scenarios featuring compelling characters.

If we are to use biblical stories humanistically, we must, of course, deal with the Bible's central character, Yahveh [Hebrew name for God in the TANAKH]. This is not difficult. Yahveh is, and may be presented to children as, a fictional character whom they easily can understand and enjoy, just as they can understand and enjoy stories about giants, witches, and fairies. The very fact that Yahveh is not real makes him all the more interesting. Among the questions children can consider in discussing a Bible story are: What do you most like or dislike about Yahveh in the story? What human characteristics does he exhibit? Jealousy? Anger? Love? Power? Who is more admirable: Abraham or Yahveh? Moses or Yahveh?

The great Bible stories provide opportunities to see universal human experiences vividly portrayed: Job's anguish over undeserved misery, Esau's hatred of his brother, Joseph's urge toward revenge and his joy when he reconciled with his brothers. Guilt, sorrow, rage, frustration, fulfillment, redemption—the full range of feelings is presented in timeless tales that may be used humanistically to inspire and instruct.

And to remember: Long after the reading or discussion, the images remain. The biblical characters become part of one's cultural background. The metaphors resonate throughout one's lifetime.

Father Greeley suggests that stories are the way humans explain reality to themselves. Among the most profound stories ever told are those in the Hebrew Bible. We need to recover and retell them or we shall lose them.[5]

Jewish Choice as Jewish Tradition

Should we understand cultural Judaism—which extends Judaism beyond religion and views religious texts as cultural creations of the Jewish people—as an entirely new approach to Judaism or as a variation on a historic theme ever present in Jewish history: the need for both continuity and change?

Humanistic Judaism cannot center the entire Jewish religious tradition, because that includes an active personal God, worship, and miraculous intervention. At the same time, this tradition cannot be entirely disregarded, because it includes ethics, wisdom, and cultural heritage. The positive Humanistic approach has been to underscore the religious elements consistent with its own core tenets and to reimagine some that are not. Doing so puts Humanistic Judaism squarely in the ongoing tradition and convention of Jews of every generation to reinterpret their cultural inheritance in order to make choices for the present and future.

Sivan Malkin Maas (b. 1958) was the first Secular Humanistic Israeli rabbi ordained by the International Institute for Secular Humanistic Judaism (IISHJ) in 2003. Rabbi Maas serves as the dean of Tmura-IISHJ in Jerusalem; president of Secular Judaism, a coalition of Secular Humanistic projects and organizations in Israel; and director of the Secular Library, publishing works on Judaism as culture. While serving as the Jewish Agency emissary to the Jewish Federation of Metropolitan Detroit in the early 1990s, she encountered Humanistic Judaism founder Sherwin Wine (see chapter 1) and his congregation and realized that Humanistic Judaism was a close cousin to the cultural Judaism of self-aware secular Israeli Jews. In her presentation at IISHJ's Colloquium 2009, "Challenging Convention: Secular and Humanist and Jew," Maas argued that Cultural Judaism is part of the tradition and convention of other Judaisms. Cultural Judaism chooses and makes relevant those parts of Jewish inheritance that resonate with a cultural approach to Jewish identity. As she notes, the core of lived Jewish life is the real tradition; values are expressed in the choices one makes about what to celebrate from it.

Sivan Malkin Maas, "Cultural Zionism: Reclaiming Convention" (2009)

I am here to reclaim convention. It might not be conventional to try and reclaim convention, but that is what I am trying to do. I do not want to be presumptuous, to say that is what all of us are trying to do, but that is what Cultural Judaism is all about. We declare that we are mainstream. We are not just another stream of Judaism; you need a pool or you need a body of water from which the stream emerges. What is it? If all the others are streams of Judaism, then maybe Cultural Judaism is what encompasses all the various ways of being Jewish. Each person decides what is valid for him- or herself, but the ability to encompass all into a culture is the view of Cultural Judaism. Therefore, that is the convention. The convention is that we are all part of a culture....

Tzvi Herman Shapira, a math professor active in Hovevei Zion,[6] wrote in 1882, "What we want to build is a *beit midrash*," a term usually used for the rabbinic yeshiva; from Shapira's *beit midrash*, the Torah of wisdom and morals would be preached to the entire Israeli nation; and also a *beit mikdash*, a new temple. Ahad Ha-Am, who believed in the Jewish state as a Jewish spiritual center, claimed at the Eleventh Zionist Congress that twenty-five hundred years ago the Jewish national temple of God on the hill of Moriah was destroyed. And now we come charged with belief and hope to build a new national temple, the *heikhal*, the great hall of wisdom and science on Mount Zion—a University of Zion, the third Temple. Judah Leib Magnes, president of the Hebrew University and a Reform rabbi, described it as a *mikdash*, a temple, free of religion!

There are those who believe that God wrote the Torah. There are those who believe it was written by people. There are Jewish people who believe in God and there are Jewish people who believe in man-made values. Some may even be the same people. Each and every one of us is a believer.... We believe in justice, so we create a judicial system and hope it works, but sometimes it does not. The value of something goes up when there are more people who believe in it—a law of intellectual supply and demand. Past generations bequeath their values and their heritage to us. It is up to us, as Sherwin Wine used to say, to tell the story and to interpret their values and our inheritance in the light of our beliefs.

Jewish culture is an array of options, a pluralistic entity from which we choose our expression. Today we talk about the vision, the blessing, and the curse of normality. I talked about the striving for a normal Jew, as well as the realization of the dream using the terminology of a Third Temple. And what is the name of the Parliament of Israel? "Knesset" sounds fine, but that is not the full name. It is really called *Mishkan ha-Knesset*. *Mishkan* [tabernacle] was the first temple where God supposedly *shakhan*, lived and existed among the Jewish people. Is that not presumptuous, for a few Israeli parliamentarians to name the place where they work "the *mishkan*"? But it's not—that's what Zionism does. It reclaims the norm; it declares, "*This* is the norm, therefore I can decide what it means to me."...

Do we have *k'dushah*, "holiness," in our ceremonies in Israel? ... *K'dushah* originally means "holiness," "sacredness," and "sanctity." These words do not describe the contemporary meaning in Hebrew. Judaism is alive and so is Hebrew, ever changing and developing. When a lover devotes time to his beloved, he chooses a special moment from all others just for her. This is called in Hebrew *l'hakdish*, "to choose," "to give," as well as "to exalt." It is to sanctify, from the term *k'ddishah*. When an author dedicates a book, he chooses a person from all other people in the world. He elevates him to the special occasion; that, too, is called *l'hakdish*, from the word *k'dushah*. When a bride and groom *mikadshim*, marry each other, they too choose especially one person from all other people in the world to share their future and to be their partner for life. They are *mikudashim*—they have singled each other out to be united and sanctified. In the story of Creation when time was defined into days and clustered into a week, just one day from all others was sanctified *kidesh*. All the other names of the days of the week remained nameless in Hebrew, not like in English where you have the day of the sun and the day of the moon—in Hebrew you just count them. *Rishon*, *sheni*, first, second, third, and then you hit Shabbat. But the last day of the week, the seventh one, received *k'dushah*. It was hallowed; it comes from a concept of *l'hakdish z'man*, "to dedicate and sanctify time." May we be free to choose to dedicate our time, to adorn it with *k'dushah*, to celebrate our heritage. These words in Hebrew are so much a part of this heritage that we cannot think of . . . doing anything without that heritage. . . .

Consider the story of the expulsion from Egypt, a biblical story we share around the table during Pesach. If we tell the story using the traditional Haggadah, it's not the same story. The story in the Bible, like every other body of literature, has heroes. We know who the heroes are. There's God and Moses, Aaron, Miriam, the people, etc. When we open the Haggadah and we look at the heroes, oops, it's a different story. There is no Moses and Aaron. Who wrote that story in the Haggadah? Rabbis. Why did they write that? Because these were their values; they believed in a story they needed to tell.

Therefore we *are* traditional rabbis because we are doing the same thing. We are telling the story according to our set of beliefs—in other words, we are traditional rabbis. That's part of convention. That is why I see myself as part of the Jewish cultural convention of what a rabbi should really do....

Our core is our tradition; our values are how we choose from it.[7]

10

A Cultural Jewish Canon

Judaism can often be understood as a religion of memory; we retell our stories regardless of their historicity, and we add our own stories to the collective library. And by telling these stories about ourselves, our identity becomes rooted in a narrated cultural past even more than in our actual history.[1]

Judaism's encounter with modernity changed both what Jews chose to remember and how those memories would be expressed through new forms of culture, from literature to theater and movies and beyond. With increased secularization, the importance of the Jewish author rose as the relevance of the rabbi diminished. The intellectual space formerly occupied by religious texts increasingly filled with secular literature. Likewise, the Yiddish theater was described as the "secular synagogue."[2]

By the early twentieth century, Jewish literature had come to represent the Jewish experience, not only for newly expressed secular Jewish identities, but also for inspiration and the armature on which to build Jewish memory, ceremony, and ritual. Passages from the Hebrew Bible and rabbinic literature were reframed and understood differently through allusions in contemporary secular Jewish literature, with the new text often taking precedence. The Jewish canon was no longer limited to religious sources either; rather, it was growing ever wider by building on and going beyond them. The Yiddish stories about Tevye the milkman by Sholem Aleichem (1859–1916), first published in 1894, questioned divine justice in the spirit of Job. In 1989, nearly a century later, *Mr. Mani* by Israeli author A. B. Yehoshua (1936–2022) presented the *Akedah* (the Binding of Isaac) as the central traumatic narrative in modern Israel, where fathers were still willing to sacrifice their children all too easily.

Seeing the Hebrew Bible as the beginning of Jewish literature rather than the foundation of Jewish religion enables Humanistic Jews to access that text with more ease and integrity, without cognitive dissonance. For them, both ancient and modern Jewish literature express Jewish culture—informing and educating while reflecting and entertaining.

This chapter spotlights the cultural Jewish canon across many media. Essays by Julian Levinson, Jodi Kornfeld, and Jonathan Friedmann show how important definitions are to fully appreciating Jewish literature, Jewish art, and Jewish music. Merely putting the word "Jewish" before any medium cannot convey the breadth and scope of Jewish cultural output; to understand what makes it Jewish requires explanation and nuance.

However, definitions only go so far; examples are needed to demonstrate how Jewish culture can both express and reinforce Jewish identity. Literary excerpts by Nathan Englander, Etgar Keret, and Nicole Krauss speak to the secular Jewish experience, including the tensions that can arise between secular and traditional Jews.

To go beyond the printed word, readers are encouraged to turn to "Go Forth and Learn" at the end of this volume for recommended music, art, and films that resonate with cultural Judaism.

Defining Jewish Literature

Jewish writers reflect Jewish experiences in many literary genres, yet defining the library of "Jewish literature" today is challenging. Nineteenth- and early twentieth-century Yiddish literature highlighted stories of the average East European Jewish "everyman" with humor and pathos. The rebirth of Hebrew literature during the Haskalah (Enlightenment) gave way to Zionist and then Israeli literature, much of it reflecting the secular Israeli experience. In North America, Jewish fiction, memoir, poetry, and essays grappled with the diasporic experience of immigration and life in new lands. Less well-known modern Jewish literature in Ladino and other Jewish languages reflected these Jews' diasporic experiences and identities. Rabbinic literature before the twentieth century was written and almost exclusively read by men; this new literature was written by both men (e.g., Sholem Aleichem) and women (e.g., Anna Margolin, 1887–1952; Kadya Molodowsky, 1894–1975) and has been read by both, even if the women writing in Yiddish are less known. The same philosophical issues Humanistic Jews wrestle with, including finding meaning in the Holocaust, assessing the importance of modern Israel, navigating the challenges and promises of integration, and defining one's Jewishness, all appear in this new Jewish library.

As Jews integrated with their surrounding cultures, a new challenge arose: defining the boundaries (if any) of Jewish literature. What about works written for general audiences in non-Jewish languages such as French, Spanish, or German? Are the novels and short stories of Franz Kafka (1883–1924) Jewish literature because of the author's biography and identity, German literature because of their original language of publication, Czech literature because Kafka lived and wrote in Prague, or all of these? What factors ought to define "Jewish literature"? Is its content or its author determinative? Must it include clear references to Jewish tradition, or can it be freestanding as reflective of its own time? Is a secular narrative devoid of religious allusion disqualified? Or, indeed, is all this a part of Jewish culture?

In this contribution to a 2009 volume of essays on secular Jewishness, Julian Levinson (b. 1969) demonstrates the complexities of these literary definitions. An associate professor of English and Judaic studies at the University of Michigan who has also taught North American Jewish culture and literature in the International Institute for Secular Humanistic Judaism rabbinic program, Levinson describes his work as the study of how Jewish culture has transformed as a result of its intense, sustained, partly harmonious, partly acrimonious dialogue with American culture.

Levinson's attempt to define boundaries for Jewish literature beyond Scripture, liturgy, and religious law could also apply to Jewish music, Jewish movies, and Jewish art. If Humanistic Judaism self-defines as a cultural Jewish identity, then the boundaries of that culture are vital to clarify.

Julian Levinson, "People of the (Secular) Book: Literary Anthologies and the Making of Jewish Identity in Postwar America" (2009)

If secular Jewish culture exists, then it would seem to possess identifiable content. It should be possible, that is, to find practices, ideas, or texts that might be defined at once as Jewish and nonreligious. This is obvious, perhaps, and yet little agreement exists on how to define the content of secular Jewish culture. One possibility, suggested over the years by various scholars and intellectuals, has been through literature—not in the sense of rabbinic commentary, ethical literature (e.g., *musar*), or any other genre sanctioned by religious tradition—but rather in the sense of Jewish *belles lettres*. If the religious Jew reads the rabbinic *Pirke Avot* [Ethics of the Fathers] on Shabbat afternoon, the argument goes, his or her secular counterpart would spend the same time with a novel by Saul Bellow.

Jewish literature conceived along these lines is notoriously difficult to define, but it is generally understood to include novels, stories, plays, or poems by Jews on Jewish themes or possessing an identifiable relation to ideas, images, or values associated with Judaism. Unlike religious texts, however, these texts do not derive sanction for their views or values from divine revelation or any communally sanctioned tradition of commentary. They are considered to be solely products of human creativity, expressing the subjective opinions, outlook, or "vision" of the author. According to this definition, a novel by an American Jew about a man struggling to understand his place in the modern world (such as Bellow's *Herzog*) might well qualify as secular Jewish culture. Part of the appeal of this notion of secular Jewish literature, we might add, is that it preserves the traditional image of Jews as the "people of the book," while broadening the definition of "the book."

No sooner are such propositions put forth, however, than a host of definitional problems appear. What qualities must a work include before it is accepted as "Jewish"? Must it be written by a Jew? Must it be explicitly about Jews? How might one demonstrate that a work derives from a specifically Jewish sensibility rather than some other source? ... Moreover, to get to the heart of our concerns here, even if a given work seems close enough to Jewish life to qualify as *Jewish* literature, how can we confidently place it under the *secular* rubric? Allen Ginsberg's autobiographical poem about his mother, "Kaddish," includes transliterated passages from the Aramaic prayer. But its primary theme is his mother's descent into schizophrenia and his personal development as a poet. Henry Roth's *Call It Sleep* features a protagonist obsessed with the Book of Isaiah, and yet the text continually reminds the reader that he is but a young, vulnerable boy. The novel's style and overall aims share much more with the High Modernism of James Joyce than any Jewish source. E.L. Doctorow's *The Book of Daniel* also pivots around allusions to biblical prophets, even though Doctorow's main point is to retell the story of the Rosenbergs' trial and execution. None of these works would generally be classified among Judaism's religious texts. If they contain some religious sentiments or yearnings, these are more properly associated with "religiosity" (vague feelings connected with the supernatural) than with Judaism proper. Thus their Judaic motifs seem only to function metaphorically: the Kaddish becomes a type of lament, and the figure of the prophet stands for the defiant critic of the status quo.

And yet this seems too easy. A religious allusion does not get automatically separated from the traditions of Judaism simply because of the ostensibly (secular) purpose of the work. After all, the meaning of any metaphor derives from its original context, which remains present even in the new context as a tacit frame of reference.... And, finally, were one to argue that, allusions and motifs notwithstanding, a form like the novel is somehow inherently secular, one would have to contend with the fact that for every theory of the novel as a secular or at least agnostic form... countless readers have found religious teachings encoded within novels (consider, for example Gershom Scholem's argument that Kafka's *The Trial* allegorically recapitulates key insights of the Kabbalah). Thus one would be hard pressed to determine the status of a given work as secular or religious solely on the basis of its internal, formal characteristics.

A further complication is introduced when we consider the institutional contexts in which works are presented. Countless examples abound of texts being brought into liturgical or other sacral contexts even though their religious content is debatable. A classic case is the Song of Songs, which is considered appropriate for the biblical canon only when its erotic motif is read allegorically to recount the love affair between Israel and God. Similarly, poems or other kinds of writing that might be read as secular in one context can be introduced into religious services, where they are suddenly read with an eye toward their religious significance....

On the other hand, texts generally used in religious contexts may be brought into secular contexts, where once again they take on different meanings. Perhaps the most unambiguously religious Jewish text is the Pentateuch, traditionally ascribed to Moses' authorship under God's direction. Indeed, to bolster its status as divine scripture, the Talmud provides lengthy explanations of the ontological division separating words of Torah from mere poetry. And yet, beginning as early as Longinus's first century treatise *On the Sublime*, we observe an approach to the Bible "as literature," namely a body of writing studied primarily for its stylistic devices and patterns of imagery....

Why, we might ask, does imaginative literature figure so centrally in this model of Jewishness as "ethnicity" or "culture"? What do stories and poems offer that other kinds of Jewish texts do not? The answer may lie in the association of literature with individual subjectivity. If the central metaphors for Jewishness are the debate, the struggle, and the bridge, and if the authority of the normative religious tradition has been unseated, the only remaining mediating force becomes human consciousness, which itself becomes the final arbiter of meaning. . . . Finally, it appears that a Jewish identity supported by literature may not be necessarily secular, but neither can it ever be truly religious, since its proposals will be inevitably mutable.[3]

In the Image of Jews

Despite some readings of the Second Commandment prohibiting graven or drawn images, figurative art by and for Jews has existed from the biblical era to modern times. Jewish religion and culture rejected idolatry, but not all imagery was understood as idolatry. From Hebrew statues created before Judean monotheism to later ritual objects, synagogue decorations, text illustrations, and modern sculpture, Jews have always been both the proverbial "people of the book" and the "people of images."

This real history of Jewish artistic creativity despite religious and ideological restrictions supports Humanistic Judaism's ongoing creativity in Jewish ritual, practice, and expression. The artistic "heresies" of medieval illuminated *Haggadot*, which included human images, both expand our understanding of historical Jewish practices and justify contemporary changes to texts. Humanistic Jews also draw on the wide range of past and present Jewish artistic expressions to add beauty, insight, and meaning to life.

Rabbi Jodi Kornfeld (b. 1956) was raised in Conservative Judaism but found Humanistic Judaism more resonant for raising her own family. Ordained by the International Institute for Secular Humanistic Judaism in 2009 and holding a MSJS and a DSJS from Spertus College, she is rabbi of Beth Chaverim Humanistic Jewish Community in Deerfield, Illinois, which she founded, and has been a Jewish educator for more than twenty-five years. In this selection, adapted from her doctoral work on Jewish art, Kornfeld explores both the boundaries and the wide range of Jewish artistic work through the centuries, spotlighting how this cultural creativity can provide a nonreligious avenue for Jewish connection and expression.

Jodi Kornfeld, "Of Course There's Jewish Art!" (2022)

Since ancient times through the present, art records, reflects and restates the actual and imagined reality of its cultures. From a Jewish perspective, art often added the component of providing cohesion and coalescence to the experience of being the minority wherever Jews lived, living both within a Jewish environment and as a minority variously tolerated, persecuted, segregated or assimilated. Jews have a rich cultural heritage within Jewish communities, and also as part of the wider culture. The cultural output that can be considered "art" has provided cohesion in that it transcends geographical boundaries and historical delineations, serving to unify otherwise disparate Jewish experiences. When applied to Jewish art, coalescence represents the integration of outside methods, techniques and iconography to become a genuine part of the Jewish corpus. It allows for an expansive view of the Jewish experience, over time and geographical space, by which elements of the dominant culture in which Jews have existed become Judaicized for various reasons and purposes. Whatever its iteration, Jewish art has a long and rich history unfettered by the Second Commandment because when properly read, the prohibition against graven images found there applies only to idolatry of those images, not the production of them.

Apart from its various purposes such as polemical, educative or simply decorative, when one speaks of art, it encompasses a variety of media. It is distinguished from the written word found in traditional texts, literature and poetry. Art can appear architecturally as part of buildings, or on buildings as murals. It can be two-dimensional such as paintings or mosaics; or it can be three-dimensional, such as a statue or a relief on an object; or as a ritual object itself.

The intersection between art and its sub-category of Jewish art is reflected in the words of sculptor Jacques Lipchitz (1891–1973) who said: "Jewish art? Art is Jewish if a Jew creates it."[4] Marc Chagall (1887–1985) explained, "If a painter is Jewish and paints life, how can he help having Jewish elements in his work? But if he is a good painter, there will be more than that. The Jewish element will be there, but his art will tend to be universal."⁵ Jews have been influenced by their surrounding cultures throughout history even when they acted in contradistinction to those cultures to maintain a separate identity. Since Jewish culture is made up of the entire output of Jews throughout history, it is evident that every form of material art is a part of it.

Jewish art, like Judaism itself, is given wide definitional latitude because the precise definition may be difficult to state with certainty. It is important to think of Jewish art in the broadest possible terms, and not take a myopic view of only the inside of museums. Jewish art can be political such as Zionist propaganda posters of pre-state Israel showing the so-called muscular Jew armed with a spade and/or a rifle; it can be additions to the walls and floors of synagogues and other buildings such as the ancient wall paintings of the third century CE Dura-Europos synagogue and the floor mosaics of fifth century CE Sepphoris synagogue, or Chagall's stained glass windows at Hadassah Hospital in Jerusalem; or it can be embellishments to ritual objects such as a Torah cover or a *ketubah*.

To fall within the purview of "Jewish art," regardless of media, echoing Lipchitz, the art needs to be created by those identifiable as Jewish regardless of the artist's religiosity or the subject matter portrayed. Both Jewish and secular themes shown by Jewish artists are part of Jewish culture. To that end, an Impressionist work depicting a peasant girl by Camille Pissarro (1830–1903), who was born Jewish, identified as an atheist and did not practice Judaism, would be part of the genre of Jewish art whereas a work by Rembrandt (1606–1669), who was not Jewish but painted portraits of Jews, would not. Included would be the pre-modern realism work of Moritz Oppenheim (1800–1882), a religious Jew who sought to depict and thereby preserve Jewish life in mid-nineteenth century Germany as an example in which both the artist and the subject matter are identifiably Jewish. In contrast to Oppenheim but nonetheless part of the category of Jewish art is the Abstract Expressionism of Mark Rothko (1903–1970), the sculpture and assemblages of Louise Nevelson (1899–1988), and the cubism of Amadeo Modigliani (1884–1920), all of which often lack a readily discernible Jewish subject matter but were created by Jews. There are works that fall in-between but can be defensibly part of Jewish art. Specifically, the illuminated manuscripts of the medieval period found in *Haggadot* and *siddurim* either created by Jews or commissioned by them and created by non-Jews would be considered "Jewish art" based on the Jewish context of personal, familial and ritual use of these manuscripts.

The notion of Jewish artists creating artworks that are both particularistic and universalistic, namely on Jewish and other subjects, is a "modern" phenomenon. This mirrors the experience of Jews as they moved from the particularistic to the universalistic in other realms of Jewish life. The images Jewish artists created included both Jewish and non-Jewish subjects as their world and worldview expanded. The explosion of Jewish artists can be traced to many of the developments stemming from the Enlightenment, from Jewish emancipation, and from the French and Industrial Revolutions. New ideas took hold as the philosophies and theologies of prior times were questioned and supplanted. Old social barriers keeping Jews out of certain professions such as art guilds fell. Jews, like other artists, were able to benefit from the technological advances of the times. For example, paint became inexpensive and portable with the invention of the metal tube, and as a result, Impressionism became possible. Artists, Jewish and not, could move outdoors to their subjects, rather than try to recreate them indoors.

As Jews became assimilated into the society at large on other levels, their entry into visual arts followed. This is not to say that Jewish art with Jewish subjects was no longer created in the modern era. The pop art sculpture of George Segal (1924–2000) has distinctly Jewish themes, including for example a kosher butcher shop, and a modern interpretation of the *Akedah* showing it as Abraham dressed in jeans, about to sacrifice his son dressed in running shorts, in his "Abraham and Isaac: In Memory of May 4, 1970 Kent State." Marc Chagall sought to memorialize his childhood in Vitebsk with identifiably Jewish scenes and interpretations of uniquely Jewish expressions. For example, his "Self-Portrait with Seven Fingers" is a visual depiction of the Yiddish expression that to do something well is to do it with seven fingers.

Jewish art in all of its forms and varieties, in all of the eras of Jewish history, comprises an important part of Jewish culture. The artistic expression of Jewish artists reflects their experiences, their own time, and the interaction with the wider cultures in which Jews lived. It can no longer be viewed as a question, "is there such a thing as Jewish art?", but instead as a resounding affirmation of the ongoing Jewish experience.[6]

Humanistic Judaism beyond Words

Music is an integral component of the Jewish experience. The chants and melodies of traditional Jewish liturgy can be beautiful and haunting even if the listener has no understanding of the Hebrew words being sung. Jewish songs have also been used outside of synagogue settings to establish sociopolitical ties and communal bonds; for example, the Jewish socialist Bund anthem *Di Shvue* written in 1902 by S. Ansky (1863–1920), the well-known modern folk song *Hava Nagila* written in 1918 by Abraham Zvi Idelsohn (1882–1938), and the Israeli national anthem *Hatikvah* written in 1877 by Naftali Imber (1856–1909) have served various Jewish populations well.

For Humanistic Jewish celebrations, the aim is to choose songs that are both philosophically consistent in any language and meet more subjective criteria such as inspiration, connection, and beauty. Music enhances the individual and communal Jewish experience all the more when lyrics and beliefs are in harmony.

Cantor Jonathan L. Friedmann (b. 1980) is the author or editor of thirty books on music, Jewish history, and the Hebrew Bible. Friedmann serves as community leader of Adat Chaverim—Congregation for Humanistic Judaism, Los Angeles and was academic dean of the Master of Jewish Studies Program and Rabbinical School at the transdenominational Academy for Jewish Religion–California. He is also president of the Western States Jewish History Association, director of the Jewish Museum of the American West, editor of *Western States Jewish History*, and co-host of the podcast/YouTube interview show *Amusing Jews*, celebrating Jewish contributors and contributions to American popular culture. This essay, original to this volume, explains the importance and influence of Jewish music on Humanistic Jewish identity and congregational life.

Jonathan L. Friedmann, "Music by, for, as Humanistic Jews" (2023)

"Music is the universal language of [hu]mankind."[7] This oft-repeated phrase, coined by Henry Wadsworth Longfellow, is usually misinterpreted to mean that music—in contrast to the more than seven thousand languages spoken today—is intuitively understood the same way across cultures. Any cursory knowledge of world music, or even music subcultures in one's own city, dispels this romantic notion. Instead, like language, music exists in many family groups and dialects. The fact that some of the best-known "happy songs" in the Ashkenazic corpus use minor scales—*Heiveinu Shalom Aleichem, Siman Tov u'Mazal Tov,* "Chanukah, O Chanukah/*Khanike Oy Khanike*," etc.—tells us that minor is not always sad and that tempo can be more important than tonality in conveying musical moods. Looking beyond the European context, the Arabic *maqam kurd*, a melodic mode closely resembling the minor, is used to convey romance, gentleness, and freedom—responses lost on listeners outside of that culture. This is one of the reasons why ethnomusicologists speak of "musics" in the plural, steering us away from false, monolithic, de-regionalized assumptions about music(s) and its meanings.

Longfellow did not intend his phrase to be taken the way it typically is. It appears in an essay, "Ancient Spanish Ballads," exploring shared *functions* of music across populations. Specifically, Longfellow describes work songs belonging to mule drivers, grape harvesters, fishermen, ploughers, gondoliers, and goatherds. Although sonically distinct, the ubiquity of work songs in different settings suggests a human universal. The same is true for other general (and sometimes overlapping) song types: healing, dance, love, war, ritual, didactic, infant-directed, mourning, celebration, and so on. Songs can also contain a host of associational components and attachments: nostalgia, inspiration, solidarity, identity marking, emotional cues, personal and collective memories, connections to something greater (real or imagined), and more.

Since the mid-twentieth century, Jewish music scholars have followed this functional approach, looking not at what is unique about the music of the Jews—a dizzyingly complex assortment of sounds borrowed from, adapted to, and in conversation with sounds of surrounding peoples—but rather how Jews *use* music for Jewish purposes, however broadly defined. At the First International Congress of Jewish Music in 1957, musicologist Curt Sachs reportedly gave this utilitarian approach a slogan, calling Jewish music "that music which is made by Jews, for Jews, as Jews." While this improved on earlier sentimental scholarship, which posited but never proved a melodic ethos underlying all Jewish musical expressions, Sachs's ostensibly inclusive definition fell short in several ways. Not only have non-Jews contributed works on Jewish themes, but listeners of Jewish music need not be Jews themselves, and what qualifies as making music "as Jews" is ambiguous. A further complication arises when we interrogate bigger questions of what constitutes a "Jew" or "doing Jewish": the answers tend to reveal more about personal biases than anything else. There are, in fact, multiple Judaisms and multiple Jewish musics.

This brings us to Humanist Jewish music—or that music which is made (or used) by, for, as Humanistic Jews, especially for Shabbat and holiday celebrations, life-cycle events, and other communal gatherings. Humanistic Jews seek to express themselves Jewishly, adhering to the ritual calendar, but without reference or appeal to the supernatural. This requires alternatives to the conventional liturgy, as well as music to accompany those alternatives. Although there is no rigid framework for accomplishing this task, Humanistic Jewish communities deliberately curate and sometimes invent musical selections that serve their emotional and ideological aims.

There are seven main sources of music for Humanistic Jewish gatherings. First are familiar texts and melodies that happen to be humanistic despite being from theocentric sources, such as *Mah Tovu* (Num. 24:5), *Hinneh Mah Tov* (Ps. 133:1), and *Lo Yissa Goy* (Isa. 2:4; Mic. 4:3). Second are prayer-songs with modified lyrics, such as rewording *Oseh Shalom* as *Na'aseh Shalom* ("We will make peace") and *Shema* as *Shema Yisrael, echad aminu, adam echad* ("Hear, O Israel: our people is one, humanity is one"). Third are select Jewish folk songs and old favorites, sometimes reinterpreted with more overtly humanistic meanings, like *Tumbalalaika* and *Am Yisrael Chai*. Fourth are popular Israeli songs with thoughtful, uplifting, and/or nostalgic appeal, such as *Zum Gali Gali* and *Hava Nagila*. Fifth are relevant songs from American musicals and popular music, like "Somewhere over the Rainbow" (Harold Arlen and Yip Harburg) and "I Won't Back Down" (Tom Petty). Sixth are *nigunim*, or wordless songs, including some that preserve familiar liturgical melodies but replace texts with various syllables, like "la la la" or "ai dai dai." Seventh are songs original to Humanistic Judaism, such as the movement's anthem, *Ayfo Oree* ("Where Is My Light?"), with lyrics by Rabbi Sherwin Wine.

What unites these sources, and connects them to the wider human experience, is that they use specific musical and textual vocabularies to achieve culturally particularistic yet universal musical functions—namely, group demarcation, self-assertion, communal cohesion, emotional uplift, inspiration, and aspiration. Following pioneer Jewish musicologist Abraham Z. Idelsohn, who wrote that "Jewish music is the song of Judaism through the lips of the Jew,"[8] Humanistic Jewish music is the song of Humanistic Judaism through the lips of Humanistic Jews.

Jewish Literature as Mirror

The modern Jewish experience is neither monolithic nor static. The lines between Orthodox and secular, Israel and Diaspora, religious and cultural blur within families, between friends, even within an individual's life journey.

For Humanistic Jews, Jewish literature can provide a mirror in which to see one's own experiences. Contemporary Jewish literature often challenges traditional notions and tropes thought to be essential to Judaism and Jewish identity and also reflects the experiences of secular Jews navigating their place in the long history of the Jews.

Nathan Englander (b. 1970) is an American Jewish writer who grew up in an Orthodox household. A Distinguished Writer in Residence at New York University, he writes about the complicated relationships between Jewishness, humanity, and the individual. In the title story from his 2012 collection, excerpted here, Englander describes the reuniting of two couples, one of whom has become even more Orthodox, while the other has become even more secular. In reflecting on the couples' disagreements over what it means to be Jewish, Humanistic Jewish readers may hear their own life stories, challenges other Jews offer, and questions they just might ask themselves.

Nathan Englander, "What We Talk About When We Talk About Anne Frank" (2012)

> Facebook and Skype brought Deb and Lauren back together.... They stayed best friends forever until I married Deb and turned her secular, and soon after that Lauren met Mark and they went off to the Holy Land and went from Orthodox to *ultra-Orthodox*, which to me sounds like a repackaged detergent—ORTHODOX

ULTRA®, now with more deep-healing power. Because of that, we're supposed to call them Shoshana and Yerucham. Deb's been doing that. I'm just not saying their names....

"Your son, he seems like a nice boy."

"Do not talk about their son," Shoshana says.

"Do not talk about our son," Deb says. This time I reach across and lay a hand on her elbow.

"Talk," I say.

"He does not," Mark says, "seem Jewish to me."

"How can you say that?" Deb says. "What is wrong with you?" But Deb's upset draws less attention than my response. I am laughing so hard that everyone turns toward me.

"What?" Mark says.

"Jewish to you?" I say. "The hat, the beard, the blocky shoes. A lot of pressure, I'd venture, to look Jewish to you. Like, say, maybe, Ozzy Osbourne, or the guys from Kiss, like them telling Paul Simon, saying, 'You do not look like a musician to me.'"

"It is not about the outfit," Mark says. "It's about building life in a vacuum. Do you know what I saw on the drive over here? Supermarket, supermarket, adult bookstore, supermarket, supermarket, firing range."

"Floridians do like their guns and porn," I say. "And their supermarkets."...

"What I'm trying to say, whether you want to take it seriously or not, is that you can't build Judaism only on the foundation of one terrible crime. It is about this obsession with the Holocaust as a necessary sign of identity. As your only educational tool. Because for the children, there is no connection otherwise. Nothing Jewish that binds."

"Wow, that's offensive," Deb says. "And close-minded. There is such a thing as Jewish culture. One can live a culturally rich life."

"Not if it's supposed to be a Jewish life. Judaism is a religion. And with religion comes ritual. Culture is nothing. Culture is some construction of the modern world. And because of that, it is not fixed; it is ever-changing, and a weak way to bind generations. It's like taking two pieces of metal, and instead of making a nice weld, you hold them together with glue."⁹

Secular and Orthodox in One Family

Generally speaking, the trajectory in Jewish identity over the last 150 years has been from more traditionally religious to more secular. Yet, in some families, the journey is reversed. Those who remain secular Jews grapple with how to relate to relatives who have chosen to become more traditional, more ritually bound, and more pious. Who judges whom and which side is more secure in their Jewishness and personal beliefs can change from moment to moment.

Etgar Keret (b. 1967) is an Israeli author who has written short stories, graphic novels, and screenplays. His parents were Polish Holocaust survivors who emigrated to Israel after World War II. His work is often surreal, reflecting the absurdities of life.

Keret's memoir, *The Seven Good Years*, reflects both personal experience and his literary creativity, since memoir as a literary genre resides between fiction and essay. In the passage excerpted here, Keret inverts the practice of some Orthodox Jews who treat those who have become secular as dead, even to the point of sitting shivah (seven days of mourning) for them, by describing his sister, who went from secular to Orthodox, and their relationship since. What accommodations will secular and Orthodox Jewish relatives make for each other, and what is a bridge too far?

Etgar Keret, "My Lamented Sister" (2016)

Nineteen years ago, in a small wedding hall in Bnei Brak, my older sister died, and she now lives in the most Orthodox neighborhood in Jerusalem. I recently spent a weekend at her house. It was my first Shabbat there. I often go to visit her in the middle of the week, but that month, with all the work I had and my trips abroad, it was either Saturday or nothing. "Take care of yourself," my wife said as I was leaving. "You're not in such great shape now, you know. Make sure they don't talk you into turning religious or something." I told her she had nothing to worry about. Me, when it comes to religion, I have no God. When I'm cool, I don't need anyone, and when I'm feeling shitty and this big empty hole opens up inside me, I just know there's never been a god that could fill it and there never will be. So even if a hundred rabbis pray for my lost soul, it won't do them any good. I have no God, but my sister does, and I love her, so I try to show him some respect. . . .

Whenever we met, I'd study her closely, trying to figure out how she'd changed. Had they replaced the look in her eyes, her smile? We'd talk the way we always did. . . . But my cousin Gili, who belonged to the youth section of the Movement Against Religious Coercion and knew a lot about rabbis and stuff, told me it was just a matter of time. . . . Once she was married, she might continue breathing, but from our point of view, it would be just as if she'd died. . . .

Gili also promised me at the time, about twenty years ago, that my sister would have hordes of children and that every time I'd hear them speaking Yiddish like they were living in some god-forsaken shtetl in eastern Europe, I'd feel like crying. On that subject, too, he was only half right, because she really does have lots of children, one cuter than another, but when they speak Yiddish it just makes me smile. . . .

The fact that my sister will never read a single story of mine upsets me, I admit, but the fact that I don't observe the Sabbath or keep kosher upsets her even more. . . .

Nineteen years ago, in a small wedding hall in Bnei Brak, my older sister died, and she now lives in the most Orthodox neighborhood in Jerusalem. . . . "I'll pray for you to meet someone you'll be happy with instead," she said, and gave me a smile that tried to be comforting. "I'll pray for you every day. I promise." I could see she wanted to give me a hug and was sorry she wasn't allowed to, or maybe I was just imagining it. Ten years later I met my wife, and being with her really did make me happy. Who said that prayers aren't answered?[10]

Jewish Writer as Interpreter

Modern Jewish writers grappling with their literary inheritance live in two realities: factual history and literary imagination. As for the latter, it can be said that words create whenever an author decrees—in the words of Genesis 1, "Let there be...."

If contemporary Jewish readers welcome Jewish literature as an opportunity to reflect on and express their identity, what purpose do these works serve for the contemporary Jewish writer? It may be similar to the choices Humanistic Jews make from their heritage: opportunities for self-definition.

Nicole Krauss (b. 1974) is an American Jewish author of short stories and novels. In 2020 she was the first writer-in-residence at the Zuckerman Mind Brain Behavior Institute at Columbia University, and in 2021 she was awarded the Sami Rohr Inspiration Award for career achievement. These excerpts from her novel *Forest Dark* relate the fictional author's reasons for her writing, her place in the Jewish canon, and the very notion of Jewish literature after accepting that even the first stories in the Torah were created by human hands and minds.

Nicole Krauss, "Adding to the Jewish Story" (2017)

"I've read your novels. We all have," he said, gesturing toward the other tables in the restaurant. "You're adding to the Jewish story. For this, we're very proud of you."...

I wanted to write what I wanted to write, however much it offended, bored, challenged, or disappointed people, and disliked the part of myself that wished to please. I'd tried to rid myself of it, and on a certain level had succeeded: my previous novel had bored, challenged, and disappointed an impressive number of readers. But because the book, like the ones before it, was still undeniably Jewish, filled with Jewish characters and the echoes of two thousand years of Jewish history, I'd avoided sloughing off the pride of my landsmen. If anything, I'd managed to increase it, as part of me must have secretly hoped to do....

But if David's palace was the dream of the writer of Samuel, just as the brilliant insight into political power was his, what did it matter in the grand scheme of things? David, who might have been only the tribal leader of a hill clan, had brought his people to a high culture that has since given shape to nearly three thousand years of history. Before him, Hebrew literature didn't exist. But because of David, two hundred years after his death, Friedman said, the writers of Genesis and Samuel established the sublime limits of literature almost at its beginning. It's there in the story they wrote about him: a man who begins as a shepherd, becomes a warrior and a ruthless warlord, and dies a poet....

"What goals do you mean, exactly? To cast Jewish experience in a certain light? To put a spin on it in order to influence how we're seen? Sounds to me more like PR than literature."

"You're looking at it too narrowly. What we're talking about is much larger than perception. It's the idea of self-invention. Event, time, experience: these are the things that happen to us. One can look at the history of mankind as a progression from extreme passivity—daily life as an immediate response to drought, cold, hunger, physical urges, without a sense of past or future—to a greater and greater exercise of will and control over our lives and our destiny. In that paradigm, the development of writing represented a huge leap. When the Jews began to compose the central texts on which their identity would be founded, they were enacting that will, consciously defining themselves—*inventing* themselves—as no one had before."

"Sure, put like that, it seems extremely radical. But you could also just say that the earliest Jewish writers were at the frontier of that natural evolution. Humanity had begun to think and write on a more elevated plane, giving people greater sophistication and subtlety in how they defined themselves. To suggest a level of self-awareness that would allow for self-invention, as you say, is assuming a lot about the intentions of the earliest writers."[11]

PART 4

Jewish Life

Introduction

Humanistic Judaism's approaches to ethics, identity, and culture (described in parts 1–3 of this volume) articulate the movement's core beliefs and define the individual Humanistic Jew. Yet it is within our next and final subject—part 4, the actualization of the abstract through services, life-cycle celebrations, education, and lived community—that Humanistic Judaism is fully realized.

Living Humanistic Judaism, the subject of chapter 11, means grounding one's Jewish identity in Jewish culture. It calls for drawing on the wider Jewish cultural canon to create rituals, texts, and practices that reflect Humanistic Jewish values and beliefs, and not just remove or reframe traditional teachings. It encourages Humanistic Jews to become well-educated about their Jewish inheritance in order to make informed decisions that enrich their individual and collective Jewish practice.

One of the clearest differences between Humanistic Judaism and other streams of Judaism is its clear, consistent, and positive focus on the human experience in the natural world. Living as a Humanistic Jew involves celebrating life-cycle events in human-centered ways. Services, ceremonies, and blessings center on human beings generally and on the individual people involved in a particular event specifically. All celebrations are nontheistic, meaning a personal god is not addressed.

Chapter 12 expressly addresses liturgy for services and holidays. Humanistic Judaism's willingness to change traditional Jewish liturgy and practice to reflect its values parallels similar secularizing creativity in the kibbutz movement, the adaptation of God language in Jewish feminism, and to some extent the ideologically motivated liturgical changes early in the Reform and Reconstructing Judaism movements. Humanistic Jewish services do include several elements found in other denominations, such as blessings over candles, wine, and bread at a Shabbat service; blowing a shofar (ram's horn) and singing *Kol Nidrei* (the traditional song for the Yom Kippur Eve service) at High Holiday observances; and reciting names to mark yahrzeits (death anniversaries) in community. However, the language of these and other blessings and observances is changed to not address, praise, or thank a personal god. For example, *Yizkor*, "He [God] will remember," becomes *Nizkor*, "we will remember"—a declaration that the obligation to remember rests on each of us as human beings rather than on the Divine. Hebrew and other Jewish languages like Yiddish and Ladino may occasionally appear in services and ceremonies, but less frequently than in other denominations, in the attempt to balance Jewish roots and the personal inspiration that comes from clear comprehension. When Jewish languages are used, the same standard of philosophical integrity applies: saying what one believes, and believing what one says. Liturgy, whether original or derived from traditional religious texts, reflects creativity rather than uniformity and includes a mix of poetry, prose, and music from both the Jewish and the universal repertoire. There is no one movement siddur (prayer book) or Haggadah. Holiday celebrations emphasize Humanistic themes inherent within them—self-liberation (and helping to free others) for Passover, self-judgment for Yom Kippur, the very human need for rest in the ever busyness of modern life for Shabbat—and as a result holiday liturgy integrates these messages throughout a service.

Humanistic Jews' liturgical texts and rituals serve many purposes: to connect them with their heritage, to give purpose to their lives, to express values and beliefs, and to provide pathways to mark growth and the passage of time. Traditional Jewish texts and rituals may be welcomed if these are understood to be philosophically consistent with nontheistic language and personal dignity. If, by contrast, a Jewish ritual does not provide meaning or comfort, or if it is performed only because traditionally "we've always done it this way," or if its performance might be more alienating than inspiring, then Humanistic Jews may opt out of that ritual as they choose how to celebrate their own Jewish lives. Conformity and continuity are not inherent values in themselves; only if they serve to further meaning, inspiration, or comfort are they positive.

So it is that the variety of ritual practices one experiences at services and celebrations operate on multiple levels. Any original purpose behind them may have little to do with its rationale for later generations, while emotional attachment, behavioral habit, social convention, personal meaning, and rational evaluation all exert their own influences (see "Humanistic Judaism Facebook Discussion on Ritual Practice," chapter 5).

Similarly, Humanistic Jewish life-cycle events, the subject of chapter 13, focus in human-centered ways on individuals and families through the stages of their lives. Praise of God is replaced with the elation of welcoming a baby, the importance of a teenager coming of age, the joyful narrative of a loving partnership, the lasting meaning of a life well lived. A coming-of-age ceremony (conventionally bar or bat mitzvah) may include a Torah reading or a research project and presentation chosen as meaningful to the young adult; a wedding ceremony may include a Humanistic version of the *Sheva Brachot* (Seven Blessings) or original blessings composed by family or friends; and a funeral may include one of several Humanistic versions of the *Kaddish* prayer or a modern Hebrew or English poem about loving memory instead. Each life-cycle event is enhanced in meaning by the shift in focus from a personal god to the particular person or people for whom it is celebrated. This shift, in turn, enriches the significance of Humanistic Jewish life-cycle events as a whole.

Humanistic Judaism is not only aimed at present practices and ceremonies; it also looks to the future. A Humanistic Jewish education, the subject of chapter 14, passes on its values to and develops Jewish cultural literacy in Humanistic Jewish children. It reflects the language used in the movement's liturgy, the meanings and celebratory practices of its holiday observances, and the movement's positive focus on human action in Jewish history and the world. Successive generations of Humanistic Jews have been educated to be fully participating Jews who, in turn, live their lives and raise their own children with Humanistic Jewish values. The stories from the Jewish library that Humanistic Jews tell can reinforce their beliefs in the human experience and the natural world, as well as connect the listeners and readers to Jews past, present, and future.

11

Living Humanistic Judaism

If Judaism is a human creation rather than a supernatural gift, why bother continuing it into the future? "Continuity" is not a self-evident good in a world where new technologies, family structures, and values demand new creative possibilities. A Judaism worth preserving and passing on to future generations must have as much meaning and relevance today as it did in antiquity. It must stand for positive shared values and adapt to changing times and demographics. It must not merely—and nostalgically—perpetuate old norms, definitions, and practices.

In reality it must continue the change, reflecting the resiliency of the Jewish people, that has always been a part of Judaism. There have always been multiple Judaisms. The Judaism of biblical Israel is different from the Judaism of the Rabbinic era, and that Judaism is different from the many varieties of Judaism in the modern era. Each successive generation raises its own questions and answers them in ways that suit its present needs.

In advancing change to meet people where they are, Humanistic Judaism contains a paradox: it emphasizes the right and responsibility of individuals to make up their own minds and direct their own lives, and it celebrates shared values and collective action to improve the world, consequently requiring agreement among those individuals. A movement of freethinking Humanistic Jews is thus continuously navigating delicate balances between the particular and the universal, the individual and the collective, and internal reflections and external activism.

This chapter sets forth two readings that reflect these themes, describing the essential needs, approaches, and values of a Humanistic Judaism worth celebrating and carrying forward.

Why Preserve Judaism?

Rabbi Eva Goldfinger asks a basic question for twenty-first-century liberal Judaism: is Judaism worth preserving? Her answer is that it is. However, the Judaism to be preserved is not static or stale or exclusively the Judaism of the religious; rather it is vibrant, meaningful, and responsive to the Jews who compose the majority of the non-Orthodox Jewish community. Such a Judaism will improve the life of the individual, the Jewish community, and the broader world.

Raised in an Orthodox family, Goldfinger (b. 1950) graduated from a Bais Yaakov High School, received a master's degree in Jewish studies, and was subsequently ordained by the International Institute for Secular Humanistic Judaism in 2005. Today she is both a practicing psychotherapist and counselor and the life cycle director and adult educator at Oraynu Congregation for Humanistic Judaism in Toronto. She is one of many Jews who have left more traditional Jewish upbringings to discover a form of Judaism personally meaningful to them. Her 1995 textbook *Basic Ideas of Secular Humanistic Judaism*, from which this essay is excerpted, remains a key resource for movement adult learning and professional leadership training.

Eva Goldfinger, "Is Judaism Worth Preserving?" (1995)

> Jewish continuity is the buzzword in all our communities today. There is suddenly a crisis of faith among the leadership of the Jewish community about the viability of Jewish continuity in our open society. Many are encouraging a return to "traditional" religious Jewish values and practices, to stem the tide of assimilation.
>
> We believe that many Jews are choosing to assimilate or to ignore their Jewishness precisely because traditional Judaism has no relevance for the majority of Jews in contemporary society.

We need to create a contemporary Judaism that suits the needs of modern liberal Jews. We believe that Secular Humanistic Judaism may in fact fill the Jewish void for a large percentage of disenchanted Jews.

Continuity is defined as "persistence without essential change." Jewish civilization has in fact persisted for thousands of years, but it evolved and continues to change. What in one era was normative became outlawed in another. What was considered heretical in one generation became accepted and desired in the next.

We have always been a nation of heretics and dissenters from establishment dogma, beginning with the story of Eve and Adam's rebellion against God's authority. This rebellious streak asserts itself repeatedly throughout Jewish history in our Israelite kings, prophets, priests and of course the rabbis, who replaced the priestly sacrificial cult with Rabbinic Judaism, a profoundly different cult. This astounding change was accomplished by Talmudic interpretation and reinterpretation—a quiet revolution of the pen, rather than the sword!

All the progressive Jewish movements have continued this process of reinterpretation to make Judaism compatible with contemporary ideas and an urban life outside the Land of Israel. As Secular Humanistic Jews we concern ourselves not with continuity or persistence without essential change, but rather the perpetuation of the Jewish people. *We want to continue the age-old process of heresy or interpretation of the civilization of the Jewish people so that in each generation it will continue to have meaning and relevance.*[1]

As long as we continue to tell our story, to celebrate the rhythms of life as Jews in a meaningful and relevant way either in our homes or in warm accepting communities, to provide profound humanistic insights and guidelines for creating personal happiness, and to work for the common good, Judaism will continue to have a positive impact on ourselves and on our world and will continue to be worth preserving.[2]

Positive Values without Dogma

Proverbially, two Jews hold three opinions. Can one organization of Humanistic Jews encapsulate the beliefs and values of independent-minded individualists and communities in one statement of values?

Even as Humanistic Jews are encouraged to make up their own minds about ritual practice, personal beliefs, and ethical choices, they do find common ground and values from that diversity. These shared values define the purpose of their community and provide boundaries for community practice, even as individuals remain free to live their own Jewish and ethical lives. They also inform social and political action in the public square.

The Society for Humanistic Judaism (see chapter 7), the national organization for Humanistic Jewish congregations and communities in North America, regularly issues statements addressing current events, ethical concerns, and the needs of its members. Its 2021 "Statement of Values," excerpted here, sets forth the key commitments of Humanistic Judaism in both celebrating Jewish life and applying shared values to personal actions. These values balance particular Jewish identity with universal human lessons regarding personal dignity, the collective human quest for knowledge, and the importance of social justice for all people. The statement's focus on human rights, anti-racism, and the separation of religion and government reflects consensus issues across the political and economic diversity of individual secular Humanistic Jews.

Society for Humanistic Judaism,
"Statement of Values" (2021)

> Jewish Cultural Identity: Judaism is [comprised of] the evolving, concurrent cultures of the Jewish people, with religion being just one facet. We draw strength from aspects of our history, rituals, achievements, literature, music, arts, food, humor, and wisdom tradition, and we view the Jewish story as testament to the continuing struggle for human dignity.
>
> Community: Coming together in times of celebration and loss improves lives by offering belonging, support, and meaning. We

center nontheistic expressions of Judaism that elsewhere may be marginalized, providing uniquely secular and humanistic celebrations of Jewish holidays and lifecycle events reflecting our ethical core. . . .

Critical Thinking: We rely on science, evidence, reason, experimentation, empathy, creativity, and artistic expression to address Jewish and universal human questions and to help improve the world and ourselves. We are committed to passing these values on to present and future generations through education and by our example.

Social Justice: We seek a future where the dignity and freedom of every human being is upheld. We must repair the world through community service and by advancing human rights, anti-racism, and the separation of church and state.[3]

12

Liturgy

As social creatures, Jews of many kinds feel the universal human need to come together communally in joy as well as sorrow. When Humanistic Jews gather for holidays and life-cycle events, however, the liturgy, ritual actions, and meaning of these celebrations often differ. Just as Reform, Reconstructing, and feminist Judaisms explicitly changed traditional blessings and prayers to reflect their ideologies, Humanistic Judaism creates its own liturgy that reflects its core values. For Humanistic Jews, a fundamental value is liturgical integrity: people-centered beliefs are best expressed through people-centered liturgy. Because the traditional liturgy was written to meet pre-modern theological and psychological needs, that liturgy can and should be reframed, revised, and recreated as people's needs change.

Instead of petition, praise, or gratitude to a god, Humanistic Jewish liturgy celebrates the natural world and the power of people to do good. A creative amalgamation of the movement's blessings, songs and meditations as well as the entire Jewish (and human) cultural canon of poetry, music, and prose can provide meaning and inspiration for celebrations.

Humanistic Jewish communities produce their own liturgies (such as Shabbat service booklets) rather than look to their own central bodies (Society for Humanistic Judaism or the Association of Humanistic Rabbis) to create "top-down" prayer books. Some communities follow a traditional service structure, including Humanistic versions of traditional passages like the *Shema*, while others diverge significantly from that model in both structure and content. Most congregational services include some standard elements, such as the *Hinneh Mah Tov* ("Behold how good") song derived from Psalm 133:1 and sung in many Jewish denominations ("Behold how good and pleasant it is / for siblings to dwell together"). Another common inclusion specific to Humanistic Jewish celebrations is Rabbi Sherwin Wine's 1976 song *Ayfo Oree*, "Where Is My Light," which expresses the movement's philosophy of individual self-actualization and mutual responsibility:

> *Ayfo Oree? Oree Bee.*
> *Ayfo Tikvatee? Tikvatee Bee.*
> *Ayfo Kochee? Kochee Bee. V'gam Bakh.*
> Where is my light? My light is in me.
> Where is my hope? My hope is in me.
> Where is my strength? My strength is in me. And in you.[1]

So it is that a core philosophical principle of Humanistic Judaism—insight, inspiration, and the power to act in the world are within each person and in community—is expressed in word and song, formalized as liturgy, and reinforced by its regular use at Shabbat and holiday services.

Humanistic Jewish holiday observances also reflect the movement's human-centered approach to cultural Jewish identity. Many (though not all) Jewish holidays are celebrated in Humanistic Jewish communities through this lens. Shabbat supports individual choices for rest, reflection, and rejuvenation rather than recalling the day God rested from Creation. The High Holidays of Rosh Hashanah and Yom Kippur are opportunities to repair human relationships through asking for and giving forgiveness, as well as a time for introspection and self-forgiveness. Sukkot is a reminder of the beauty and benefaction of nature and encourages gratitude to those who preserve the earth and help produce its bounty. Simchat Torah celebrates Jewish learning in all forms and from all eras, from Torah to today. Hanukkah emphasizes the religious freedom to believe as one chooses, while recognizing the inconvenient historical truth that the Hellenistic Jews of that era were precursors to today's secular and Humanistic Jews and their Maccabean opponents were militant Jewish religious fundamentalists. Passover inspires empathy with those who suffer and motivates action to promote freedom while recalling the Passover narrative and centuries of Jewish historical experience. Shavuot can be understood as celebrating literature and learning broadly considered, beginning but not ending with the Torah. And so on through other events in the Jewish calendar (such as Yom ha-Shoah/Holocaust Remembrance Day), life-cycle celebrations, and times of personal reflection. The framing of Humanistic Jewish holidays and the liturgy used to observe them embody the movement's synthesis of Jewish culture with human knowledge, power, and responsibility.

Humanistic Jewish liturgy additionally demonstrates the positive value of consistency between belief and action, ritual and integrity, words and meaning. The first selection in this chapter, by Marcia Falk, explains the contemporary phenomenon of creating liturgy from both feminist and humanistic motivation. The second essay, by Adam Chalom, articulates why the liberal religious Jewish approach of creative translation without changing traditional Hebrew does not work for Humanistic Judaism, and thus why Humanistic Judaism needed to establish its own creative Humanistic liturgy that diverges from traditional blessing and prayer formulae. This leads directly to the third selection: passages by several Humanistic rabbis that demonstrate what such innovative liturgy looks like. The fourth selection exemplifies the kind of poetry used in Humanistic Jewish celebrations as secular liturgy. The last passage, from a Humanistic Haggadah, demonstrates the reframing of holiday symbols through inventive lenses.

Creative Contemporary Liturgy
Modern prayer-book editing began in the nineteenth century by deleting texts deemed obsolete, repetitive, or ideologically problematic. For example, the Reform movement was inspired by its commitment to national citizenship, its rejection of miraculous messianic deliverance, and its distaste for "primitive" ritual practice to eliminate prayers calling for the Jewish people's return to Israel and the restoration of animal

sacrifices (at the future rebuilt Jerusalem Temple). So, too, twentieth-century Reconstructionist Judaism removed prayers and blessings referring to the idea of chosenness (such as the Shabbat *Kiddush* text "'Indeed, Thou has chosen us and hallowed us above all nations' [which Reconstructionist movement founder and liturgist Mordecai] Kaplan replaced . . . with 'for Thou has brought us nigh to Thy service'"),[2] because these texts did not reflect the movement's beliefs that a Reconstructionist God would not choose one particular people for reward, punishment, and exclusive revelation.

By the twenty-first century, liberal Jewish denominations moved beyond cutting or adding to the liturgy to actually changing the texts themselves, sometimes radically. In particular, Jewish feminism has motivated liturgical innovation in many liberal Jewish denominations, from including the Matriarchs in the *Amidah* prayer ("Blessed are you, THE ANCIENT ONE, our God, God of our ancestors, / God of Abraham / God of Sarah / God of Isaac / God of Rebecca / God of Jacob / God of Rachel and God of Leah" in Reconstructionist practice)[3] to revamping God language to refer either to a feminine divinity or sometimes to none at all.

The poet, liturgist, and Judaic scholar Marica Falk (b. 1946) brings a feminist perspective to all of her work. As a featured speaker at "Beyond Tradition: The Struggle for a New Jewish Identity," the International Institute for Secular Humanistic Judaism's Colloquium 1999, she described her work as a bridge between secular and religious frameworks: she reimagines liturgy in novel ways and also provides access to traditional text enhanced by new insights into their meanings. Her ceremonial poetry for Shabbat, the High Holidays, and Passover reenvisions liturgy to make it gender *and* theologically neutral, blessing "the source of life" rather than a personal god of any gender. In her collections *The Book of Blessings: New Jewish Prayers for Daily Life, the Sabbath, and the New Moon Festival* and *The Days Between: Blessings, Poems, and Directions of the Heart for the Jewish High Holiday Season*, Falk invites readers to use the liturgy she has written, and many Humanistic Jewish communities and congregations do just that. Because its writing is both informational and inspirational, this passage from *The Book of Blessings* has been used liturgically in Humanistic Jewish congregations to introduce Torah readings or simply to encourage reflection.

Marcia Falk, "Honoring Torah" (1996)

In a tradition that views Torah as sacred and values the study of Torah beyond all else, we consider with utmost care what is Torah and what it means to honor it. . . .

We must keep asking: Whose text is it? For whom does it speak, whom does it represent? Whose story does it tell, and whose does it erase? Whose values does it convey, whose power preserve? How do we feel—indeed what shall we do—about the patriarchal portrayals of divinity that are so pervasive in the Bible? About the ethnocentricity so profoundly embedded there? About the sweeping erasures of women as full human agents from our history? Can *this* be *our* Torah?

We are told that this Torah is ours, our people's. But to which of our people has it been taught? Which of our people teach it? How much of it did our mothers and grandmothers—and the mothers before them—learn? How much did these women participate in handing it on, contributing their own insights to the tradition? Did any of them gain entrance to the community we call *rabbeynu*, our most esteemed teachers of Torah?

Still, can we entirely abandon what has become emblematic of our people's identity, even of our people's survival? If it is not all we wish it were, it remains what history has bequeathed us; it is, for the most part, what we have. Where, then, is its proper place today?

The rabbis said, "Turn it, turn it, for all is contained in it." We turn, and we turn—but *not* all is in it. We find we have more to add. We cannot read all our truths into a place where they have never been. So we invent and inscribe, and we ask: Can new texts, too, become sacred? Can our own voices become Torah?

And throughout the process, we ask what it means to us to keep on wrestling with tradition—with what is difficult and causes us pain. How do we know when we have wrestled enough? How do we know when it is time to let go, time to free ourselves for something new?

We ask these questions here today, in the context of our service, because questioning—in pursuit of our deepest truths—is itself a form of Torah. We ask our questions, fully realizing that well-meaning people among us may differ—perhaps vehemently—in their answers. It is not our purpose to be divisive. But we are already of many minds. Silencing the concerns will not diminish them; it will not make them go away.

Dare we ask these questions? Dare we not ask them? If not now, when?[4]

Consistency between Belief and Liturgy

Revamping liturgy by prioritizing philosophical consistency over cultural continuity or emotional nostalgia has been a hallmark of Humanistic Judaism from its early days. As both a congregational rabbi and as dean for North America of the International Institute for Secular Humanistic Judaism, Adam Chalom (see chapter 4) has addressed Humanistic Judaism's approach to liturgy both through teaching future Humanistic rabbis and creating *Shabbat* and holiday services for his congregation. This essay, from an issue of the movement's journal *Humanistic Judaism* titled "Beyond God, Beyond No God," summarizes the distinction between Humanistic Jewish liturgy, with its substantial changes to blessings, songs, and concepts to more clearly reflect its beliefs, and the common practice in liberal religious Judaism of maintaining traditional Hebrew texts while using creative translation or interpretation to reflect less traditional theology.

As we have seen (chapter 2), Humanistic Judaism rejects multiple God concepts: a conventional biblical or Rabbinic concept of a commanding *melekh* (king) as well as the Gods of twenty-first-century liberal Jewish theology, including process theology, divine-human partnership, the imminent God of divine sparks, and the transcendent yet impersonal God of spiritual forces. Humanistic Judaism's emphasis on philosophical consistency between stated beliefs and Hebrew liturgy provides the satisfaction of clear integrity, though admittedly at some cost to ritual continuity. Nonetheless, a clearer approach to expressing what one actually believes, in any language, is more meaningful for Humanistic Jews.

Adam Chalom, "Our Quarterback, Our King: Two Problems with Liberal Theology" (2007)

THE QUARTERBACK

"Do not forget YHWH your God . . . lest when you have eaten and are full, and have built goodly houses . . . You may say in your heart, 'My power and the might of my hand has gotten me this wealth.' And you shall remember YHWH your God; for he is who gives you power to get wealth. . . ." (Deut. 8:11–18)

In the Bible and traditional Jewish liturgy, YHWH, the God of the Hebrews who evolved into the one God of Biblical monotheism, runs the show like a quarterback who calls his own plays. While some fans of the Indianapolis Colts might have said that Peyton Manning was like God, in traditional Judaism, God is like Peyton Manning.

Even though promoted to God of the entire universe, YHWH clearly takes sides and has a "chosen team." He calls all of the plays, and like a quarterback he makes them happen himself "with a mighty hand, and with an outstretched arm."[5] If you do what he tells you and you perform well, he will help the "chosen team" win again and again.[6] If you fall short of his ideals, or worse yet disobey his instructions, he will punish you by sending you to the bench and withdrawing his protection[7] or even by kicking you off his team.[8] And if the entire team fails to listen to him, he may throw the ball to the other team and help them win just to punish you.[9] We even know from which side he throws: "Your right hand, YHWH, is glorious in power; your right hand, YHWH, has dashed the enemy in pieces. And in the greatness of your excellence you have overthrown those that rose up against."[10]

One problem with modern liberal theology is that their God works more like a coach or a cheerleader—he may have planned how things should run, but he has no direct impact on how they turn out. The "God" imagined behind "intelligent design" works at most on the molecular level, hardly parting the Red Sea or writing a Torah. More important, such a god cannot impact what actually happens on the field. Once the actual game (i.e. real life) starts, he can encourage you along by cheering you up and by being with you, but that's about it. No miracles, no mighty hand and outstretched arm, no direct intervention that could be proven or disproven. This may work to make a plausible modern theology, but not if you keep talking to the cheerleader as if he is the quarterback.

Here is one summary of some theological options within Reform Judaism:

> Some may be fortified by accepting all things as God's will, fulfilling a purpose that may take time to fathom, if we can ever fathom it.... Some may be fortified by a belief that God is limited in power, so that illness and death and loss do not come from God nor can God prevent them. Some may be fortified by a faith that God cares about them and suffers with them even when God, like a parent, cannot always make things better.[11]

And here is a selection from a Reform *Birkat ha-Mazon* (grace after meal):

> Sovereign God of the universe, we praise You: Your goodness sustains the world. You are the God of grace, love, and compassion, the Source of bread for all who live; for Your love is everlasting. In Your great goodness we need never lack for food; You provide food enough for all. We praise You, O God, Source of food for all who live.[12]

Is this the same God? In prose he is a limited God, a coach at the most and a cheerleader at the least. But in liturgy he is the quarterback, doing everything and lacking nothing, never failing. Will people believe the prose, or will they believe what they're told at summer camp to say after every meal? For those who believe in the importance of clear thinking, the risk is too great to leave the liturgy alone.

THE KING

Sometimes theology echoes politics; just as we create our gods in our image, we imagine a god's authority as we see power exercised among us.

At one time, it made sense to imagine a god as a King—after all, every land one could see had a king. On the rare occasion that queens ruled independently, their authority was no less absolute. The exception might have been Athenian democracy, which had a city council made up of rich elites, but that system paralleled the Pantheon of the Greek gods. In Babylonia, Egypt, and Israel, kings ruled directly and completely. And just as an emperor, or ruler of many lands, could be described as a "king of many kings," God was easily understandable as "king of kings, and lord of lords."[13]

This imagery is basic to traditional Jewish liturgy, from *avinu malkeinu* (Our Father, Our King) to the basic blessing phrase *melekh ha-olam* (king of the universe). And it is totally foreign to the Jewish experience today, whether in Western Europe, Israel or the Americas. Why does the Reform *Birkat Hamazon* cited above translate "king" as "sovereign"? It avoids both gender identification and political alienation.

Consider one way of looking at the world from the Jewish Renewal movement: "Reality is merged; all is one. This is the world of essence, where we recognize ourselves as being a spark of God's fire. It is not we who pray; rather, God prays in us. With God's own eye we see ourselves."[14] Now hear it put into political terms: we are one nation, *e pluribus unum* [from many, one]. We are citizens, each an essential element of political authority. The authority does not rule us; rather, it rules through us. It is a government of the people, by the people.[15] By saying each person is a piece of God, God is now compatible with a democracy where each person has a vote and a voice. No one ever voted for or had a real say with God the King.

Of course, just like the quarterback, king imagery is rarely removed from the liturgy, and thus creeps back into theology. If there is one lesson that Humanistic Judaism can learn from these examples, it is this: words have meaning, and if you don't say what you believe and believe what you say, the lack of integrity between the two creates problems and conflicts. If your highest ideals are neither a supernatural quarterback nor a cosmic king, but rather human effort and human achievement, then it is both right and wise to say so.[16]

Nontheistic Jewish Liturgy

If the Talmudic maxim *she-lo y'daber echad ba-peh v'echad ba-lev*, "one should not say one thing in the mouth and another in the heart,"[17] applies to Humanistic Jewish celebrations, then blessings and liturgical texts require new wording in Hebrew as well as English. Accepting Jewish identity as cultural inheritance rather than divine decree empowers contemporary creativity for Jewish celebration.

Here Is Our Light: Humanistic Jewish Holiday and Life-Cycle Liturgy for Inspiration and Reflection, published in 2019 for the fiftieth anniversary of the Society for Humanistic Judaism (see chapter 7), draws from fifty years of original Humanistic Jewish liturgy. As was the case with the 1988 *Celebration: A Ceremonial and Philosophic Guide for Humanists and Humanistic Jews* by Humanistic Judaism founding thinker Rabbi Sherwin Wine, *Here Is Our Light* is not treated like a siddur (prayer book), with texts recited verbatim and in fixed order by Humanistic Jewish communities. Instead, the volume serves as a resource for communities and individuals to choose from for their own celebrations.

At times Humanistic blessings can be sung with a similar cadence to traditional versions, so that even if some continuity with traditional texts is lost by changing words, some is maintained through melodies. Preserving some traditional phrasing helps maintain continuity where possible, with revisions as needed for philosophical consistency. For example, the opening of the traditional blessing *Baruch atah Adonai, Eloheinu melekh ha-olam* ("Blessed are You, YHVH our God, King of the world") is always replaced by a Humanistic alternative such as *Baruch ha-or ba-olam, baruch ha-or ba-adam* ("Blessed is the light of the world, blessed is the light in humanity"). Conventional text for what is being blessed, such as *boray p'ri ha-gafen* ("that brings forth the fruit of the vine"), often follows.

While such blessings are generally uncredited in Humanistic Jewish liturgy, the later prose and poetry selections reproduced here were authored by Humanistic rabbis Adam Chalom (see chapter 4), Jodi Kornfeld (see chapter 10), Jeremy Kridel (rabbi of Machar: The Secular Humanistic Jewish Congregation of Greater Washington DC), Peter Schweitzer (see chapter 3), and Frank Tamburello (rabbi of the Westchester, New York, Congregation for Humanistic Judaism).

Adam Chalom, Jodi Kornfeld, Jeremy Kridel, Peter Schweitzer, and Frank Tamburello, "Liturgical Readings" (2019)

SHABBAT

Blessing over wine:
B'ruchim boray p'ri hagafen.
Blessed are those who bring forth the fruit of the vine.

Blessing over candles:
Barukh haor baolam.
Barukh haor baadam.
Barukh haor baShabbat.
Radiant is the light of the world.
Radiant is the light within each person.
Radiant is the light of Shabbat.

Blessing over bread:
B'ruchim ha motziim lechem min haaretz.
Blessed are those who bring forth bread from the earth.[18]

ROSH HASHANAH MORNING READING

Last night, a new year was born.

Like a child, a new year already has within it the seeds of the year it may become. Just as our DNA is not our fate, the past does not absolutely determine the future. As we nurture this New Year to maturity, we may yet learn from our mistakes, make wiser choices, do good and then do better.

We are the sum of our yesterdays, but we are also the potential of our tomorrows.[19]

A TASHLIKH MEDITATION [A Rosh Hashanah ritual of casting bread onto open water to symbolically release past failures and correct bad tendencies]

Community:
We arrive bearing the last year's load of leaven.
Triumphs and failures,
Missed chances,
Joys and sorrows.

Reader:
At tashlikh, we cast away the staler bits;
Throw aside our regrets,
Like so many breadcrumbs
Carried off in water.

Community:
If we cast away our ills, what do we lose?
Can we learn from mistakes?
Might good turn bad?
Might bad be made good?

This tashlikh let's not cast ourselves away.
We'll keep the crumbs of our pasts,
Hold tight these few morsels—
The bread of our lives.[20]

A HUMANIST AL CHET [for the sins] [based on a traditional Yom Kippur confession of sins]

Reader: By giving in to anger, we have cheated ourselves of peace, joy, and satisfaction with life.

Community: By giving in to envy, we have cheated ourselves of commitment and gratitude.

Reader: By giving in to jealousy, we have cheated ourselves of self-worth.

Community: By giving in to hate, we cheat ourselves of love, health, and strength of spirit.

Reader: By giving in to fear, we cheat ourselves of adventure and joyful achievement.

Community: By giving in to impatience, we cheat ourselves of the enjoyment of the fruits of our labors.

Reader: By giving in to laziness, we do not make full use of the powers we have.

Community: By giving in to worry, we cheat ourselves of serenity, confidence, and power.

Reader: By giving in to mistrust, we cheat ourselves of the security that friendships give us.

Community: By giving in to greed, we fail to appreciate our gifts and blessings.

Together: *How wonderful it is to realize that the strength, the goodness, the joy, the serenity, and the power over our own lives that we seek is already within us!*[21]

B MITZVAH: READING BEFORE THE TORAH

Hand made
Man made;

Teller of stories
Maker of myths.

Unroll it.
Unbind it.
Approach it.
Unwind it.

Symbol of wisdom,
Source of tradition.
Look deep within it.
Find your own truth.[22]

FUNERAL: MODERN KADDISH

May the glory of life be extolled. L'chaim. [To life.]

May the world be blessed with peace, all life hallowed by love and respect. L'chaim.

Let life be blessed, and glorified, exalted and honored. L'chaim.

Though beyond praises, songs, and adorations we may utter, let life be celebrated. L'chaim.

For us, for all Israel, for all people, may the promise and the gift of life come true. L'chaim.

May peace embrace all of us, all Israel, and all the world. L'chaim.

May peace be granted us, we who mourn, and be a comfort to all who are bereaved, and let us say, L'chaim.[23]

Poetry as Secular Liturgy

Jewish liturgical poetry is a well-rooted Jewish tradition, both inside and beyond the conventional siddur. For many decades, both Reform and Reconstructing Judaism have included contemporary poetry in their prayer books as alternative readings. Where Humanistic Judaism differs is in its use of secular poetry (by both Jewish and non-Jewish authors) as primary rather than supplementary inspirational readings for holiday and life-cycle events. A meaningful poem may replace—and not just supplement—the *Kaddish* memorial prayer in a memorial service.

The poetry of Yehuda Amichai (1924–2000) makes frequent appearances in this role. Raised Orthodox, Amichai immigrated with his family to Mandate Palestine as a child and served in World War II as well as Israel's wars in 1947–49, 1956, and 1973. Nominated several times for the Nobel Prize in Literature, he received the 1982 Israel Prize and many other accolades over his long career. The inaugural Colloquium of the International Institute for Secular Humanistic Judaism in Farmington Hills, Michigan, recognized him for artistic achievement in 1995.

Amichai's accessible yet multilayered conversational Hebrew language includes allusions to biblical and rabbinic intertexts; personal experience with war, love, and death; the complexities of life in Israel and particularly Jerusalem; and the emotional attachments to family and tradition that continue far beyond secularization and theological doubts.

The following two selections, "A Man Doesn't Have Time" and "The Waters Cannot Return in Repentance," exemplify the kinds of poems Humanistic Jews use for secular inspiration in their ceremonies. "A Man Doesn't Have Time" enhances a Rosh Hashanah observance, an appropriate setting for a poem on the turning of the seasons and the beginning of a new year in the autumn. "The Waters Cannot Return in Repentance," when read on Yom Kippur, expresses the limits of repentance and thus the need for self-forgiveness.

Yehuda Amichai, "A Man Doesn't Have Time" (1986)

A man doesn't have time
to have time for everything.
He doesn't have seasons enough to have
a season for every purpose. Ecclesiastes
was wrong about that.

A man needs to love and to hate at the same moment,
to laugh and cry with the same eyes,
with the same hands to cast away stones and to gather them,
to make love in war and war in love.

And to hate and forgive and remember and forget,
to set in order and confuse, to eat and to digest
what history
takes years and years to do.

A man doesn't have time.
When he loses he seeks, when he finds
he forgets, when he forgets he loves, when he loves
he begins to forget.

And his soul is experienced, his soul
is very professional.
Only his body remains forever
an amateur. It tries and it misses,
gets muddled, doesn't learn a thing,
drunk and blind in its pleasures
and in its pains.

He will die as figs die in autumn,
shriveled and full of himself and sweet,
the leaves growing dry on the ground,
the bare branches pointing to the place
where there's time for everything.

Yehuda Amichai, "The Waters Cannot
Return in Repentance" (1986)

The waters cannot return in repentance
To where would they return?
To the faucet, the sources, the ground, the roots,
the cloud, the sea, into my mouth?
The waters cannot return in repentance,
every place is their seas / days of old, their waters of old,
every place a beginning and end, and a beginning.

Reinterpreting Jewish Symbols

There are more versions of the Passover Haggadah than any other Jewish text.[24] From the medieval era forward, there have been illustrated *Haggadot* such as *The Birds' Head Haggadah* (fourteenth century), the *Golden Haggadah* (c. 1320–30), and in modern times, the *Szyk Haggadah* (1940) and Marcia Falk's *Night of Beginnings: A Passover Haggadah* (2022). Contemporary *Haggadot* reflect Jewish feminism, Israeli kibbutzim, various Jewish religious denominations, LGBTQ+ Jews, and children. The themes of self-liberation and freeing others are universal, and virtually any Jew of any persuasion can find a Haggadah that speaks to and for them.

Many Humanistic Jews choose to use *The Liberated Haggadah: A Passover Celebration for Cultural, Secular and Humanistic Jews* (2003) by Rabbi Peter Schweitzer (see chapter 3) for their home seders, as well as at some congregational seders. The excerpt below speaks to the balance Humanistic Jews seek in holiday commemorations: to tell their truth by engaging creatively with tradition. To this point, Schweitzer offers multiple meanings for the same Passover symbols.[25]

Peter Schweitzer, "The Passover Symbols" (2003)

> What do all these symbols mean? There are many answers. Some are preserved as part of our tradition and are explained by the legend we have told. Others are provided by biblical scholars who remind us of the origins of the Spring festival that are the root of this celebration. And finally, there are the modern interpretations that we write ourselves. These give voice to our own imagination and creativity in keeping with the idea that the haggadah is forever new. [Leader points to each in turn]
>
> PESACH
>
> *Pesach*—Why did our ancestors eat the Passover lamb?
>   To remind ourselves that we were passed over (*pasach*) and saved when the Egyptians were plagued and ruined.

And to teach us that the lamb, newly born in the spring, is a reminder that at this season we celebrate the joy of birth, new life, and continued sustenance.

And to remind us, too, that we have not always been passed over, but too often have met with the same fate of slaughter as the innocent lamb.

MATZOH (UNLEAVENED BREAD)

Matzoh—Why do we eat matzoh tonight?

To remind us that when our ancestors fled Egypt they had no time to bake their bread. They could not wait for the yeast to rise.

And to remind us that matzoh is the bread of new life. In ancient Israel, flat bread was baked from the unfermented grain of the new spring harvest to celebrate the newness of the reborn earth. We reject the cold slavery of winter and affirm the warm vitality of spring.

And to teach us, too, that we will gladly give up the comforts of Egypt, with its pretense of luxury, for the simplicity of liberty and the bread of freedom....

MAROR (BITTER HERB)

Maror—Why do we eat maror tonight?

To remind us of the bitterness of our slavery and the gift of our freedom that we too often take for granted.

And to remind us that our ancestors ate bitter herbs at the time of the spring festival. The sharpness of the taste awakened their senses and made them feel as one with the revival of nature.

And to teach us, too, that not all know the taste of freedom. Let us also remember the embittered lives of all those in the world who remain in bondage, physically and mentally, and continue to suffer without relief.

HAROSET (FRUIT/NUT MIXTURE)

Haroset—Why do we eat haroset tonight?

To remind us of our bondage in Egypt when we mixed clay to make mortar and bricks for Pharaoh.

And to remind us that just as the parsley is dipped in salt water to sharpen its flavor, so do we dip the unleavened bread and bitter herb into the haroset to sweeten our taste. In this season of life, we remember the goodness of life.

And to teach us, too, that our foremothers took risks for freedom and acted courageously when they gave birth to the next generation under the shade of the Egyptian apple trees. . . .

BAYTSA (EGG)

Baytsa—Why do we eat baytsa tonight?

To remind us of the special Festival Offering by which the priests, in Temple days, expressed their gratitude for the well-being of the people.

And to remind us that eggs are the symbol of life, of birth and rebirth. As all around us nature dances with new life, so may this season stir within us new strength, new hope, and new joy.

And to teach us, too, that the egg, which becomes harder and tougher when heat is applied, symbolizes the toughness of the Jewish people to endure and persevere despite our suffering.

ORANGE

Orange—Why is there an orange on the Seder Plate?

To remind us that the Seder is always growing and that new symbols can be included in our celebration with evolving messages of their own.

And to remind us that all people have a legitimate place in Jewish life, no less than an orange on the seder plate, regardless of gender or sexual identity.

And to teach us, too, how absurd it is to exclude anyone who wants to sit at our table, partake of our meal, and celebrate with us the gift of life and the gift of freedom.[26]

13

Life Cycle

Humanistic Judaism honors the agency individual Jews have to live their own Jewish lives with philosophical integrity. Each will choose or develop rituals designed to meet one's emotional, social, and spiritual needs throughout a lifetime. Each will decide whether to continue, reject, or adapt traditional Jewish customs—essentially, to find a personal balance between Humanistic beliefs and values and continuity with traditional Jewish practice. Every life-cycle celebration centers on the individual, couple, or family rather than God and affirms these three central tenets: individual agency, living Humanistic Jewish values, and meeting human needs. For example, families with diverse religious and ethnic heritage will typically involve all their relatives in a celebration as active participants, often by drawing from those cultures and traditions.

Rituals surrounding the birth of children celebrate the arrival of new lives into families, the Jewish people, and humanity. Baby-welcoming ceremonies often include wine sharing, poetry, messages from parents (and sometimes grandparents) to the children, and the conferral and explanation of a Hebrew (or Yiddish, Ladino, etc.) name. These ceremonies are offered equally to all genders, independent of parental decisions regarding infant male circumcision. Families who choose to have their sons circumcised do so in a hospital or with a *mohel/mohelet* (one who performs ritual circumcisions), either separately or in conjunction with a Humanistic naming ceremony designed to affirm the newborn's Jewish identity in the joyful presence of family and friends.

A b mitzvah (preferred gender-neutral term for bar/bat/b'nai mitzvah) is a Jewish coming-of-age ceremony. While many cultures celebrate this transition from childhood to emerging adulthood, a Humanistic Jewish b mitzvah demonstrates the young person's connection to Jewish heritage and growing maturity and responsibility. After a process of studying Jewish history and culture (which varies depending on the Humanistic Jewish community), often paired with the study of Hebrew, the student chooses a focus for a b mitzvah presentation. Options include reading from the Torah (which may or may not be from the traditional Torah portion of the week) and delivering an original commentary; reading and commenting on another piece of Hebrew literature, from the Bible through modern poetry; or selecting an issue, person, or topic from the broad sweep of Jewish experience. In the last case, Hebrew readings are often included as supportive texts. Because the b mitzvah ceremony celebrates both Jewish identity and growing responsibility, community service work (sometimes related to the b mitzvah focus) is generally required. Humanistic Jewish b mitzvah students experience a personalized connection to their Jewish identity as they grow more confident in their knowledge and ability to participate in Jewish life.

A Humanistic Jewish wedding celebrates love and commitment regardless of the religions or genders of the loving partners. Together with the couple, Humanistic Jewish officiants create personalized ceremonies that incorporate the Jewish wedding traditions the partners find meaningful, along with texts and symbols from the wider world of human culture that celebrate love. Jewish wedding rituals may be revised or reinterpreted, from mutual circling under the *huppah* (wedding canopy) to reimagined, creative texts for *ketubot* (marriage contracts) and the Seven Blessings to the partners each breaking a glass. For intermarriages (see chapter 7), this openness extends to including non-Jewish elements in the ceremony (such as the African American tradition of jumping the broom) and to co-officiating balanced ceremonies with other clergy. Humanistic Jewish weddings empower loving partners to celebrate their shared lives through Jewish culture and personal freedom.

Humanistic Jewish funerals celebrate the deceased by telling the story of their lives and its lasting legacy for their loved ones and community. Through poetry and prose, personal stories and music, family sharing and moments of silent reflection, those present are encouraged to remember the deceased as this individual lived. Some Humanistic Jews choose a conventional memorial service and interment, while others elect cremation, green funerals, donation for medical study, or other nontraditional options accompanied by a Humanistic memorial service. Humanistic Jewish funerals may take place shortly after the death, or the family may choose to hold a memorial service at a later date. Shivah is observed flexibly (see below), as are future memorial moments such as yahrzeit (death anniversary). As with all Humanistic Jewish life-cycle ceremonies, Humanistic Jewish memorials respect the needs, beliefs, and values of the individuals and families involved.

In the twenty-first century, Jewish life includes many more opportunities for life-cycle moments, from celebrating independence to becoming an empty nester to adult b mitzvahs. Humanistic Jewish officiants offer creative ceremonies in collaboration with individuals or communities to mark life-cycle moments such as these in meaningful ways.

When it comes to including Jewish rituals in life-cycle events, Humanistic Jews make their own decisions in accordance with their own beliefs. If, say, a b mitzvah chooses to wear a tallit, it is not to humble oneself before God (a traditional symbolic understanding not in keeping with Humanistic Jewish beliefs), but instead to connect to one's family history/ancestry, with the fringes symbolically tying the generations together. Some mourners may choose to practice *keriah* (ritual tearing of clothing) as an external expression of internal sadness and will choose for themselves how long to wear the torn ribbon or cloth, while others do not find this ritual meaningful. If a compelling new Humanistic meaning cannot be ascribed, the ritual object is not used.

This chapter presents Humanistic Jewish perspectives on the rituals that frame major life-cycle events. A discussion regarding circumcision demonstrates the movement's commitment to gender equality and parental choice in the context of welcoming newborns to their Jewish and human families. An example of a b mitzvah presentation highlights its personal relevance and meaning to the b mitzvah student. Humanistic *ketubah* texts, similar to texts by Reform and Reconstructing Judaism, update the traditional rabbinic marriage contract to speak of love and commitment without references to property or divine creation of the world. Some shivah mourning rituals can provide emotional comfort and community to Humanistic Jews after loss, though practices bereaved families generally consider unhelpful (e.g., covering mirrors, sitting on low stools) are omitted. All of these Jewish experiences meet human needs in creative and personally meaningful ways.

Circumcision

Some Humanistic Jewish families choose to have their sons circumcised (in the hospital or at a formal ceremony), while others do not. The reasons for circumcision vary from family tradition to Jewish cultural identification to health, but do not include the traditional commandment of circumcision as a sign of a covenant with God. Whichever decision parents make, the wider Humanistic Jewish community is supportive, because circumcision is not considered a prerequisite for Jewish identity (see chapter 6). Both infant girls and boys are welcomed with egalitarian baby-naming ceremonies.

The Leadership Conference of Secular and Humanistic Jews (LCSHJ)[1] established ethical standards and professional guidelines for current and future leaders, provided continuing education for lay leaders, and certified new lay ceremonial leaders trained by the International Institute for Secular Humanistic Judaism's (IISHJ) *Madrikh/Vegvayzer*/Leader Program until LCSHJ ceased operations in 2012 and was absorbed into the IISHJ. One of LCSHJ's most important public statements, reprinted here, affirmed freedom of choice for the intimate decision of circumcision. The Association of Humanistic Rabbis (see chapter 6) later endorsed this statement.

Leadership Conference of Secular and Humanistic Jews, "Circumcision and Jewish Identity" (2002)

PREAMBLE

The ceremony of welcoming a child to the world and to the Jewish people can be one of the most meaningful and exciting experiences. It is a tradition of the Jewish people to celebrate the arrival of sons with *Brit Milah* (ritual circumcision or *"Bris"*), yet our commitment to the equality of men and women inspires us to create new welcoming ceremonies. Secular and Humanistic Jews do not see *Milah* (circumcision) as a sign of a *Brit* (covenant), but circumcision may retain cultural or personal significance for some.

STATEMENT

We, the Leadership Conference of Secular and Humanistic Jews, mindful of both our commitments to Jewish identity and to gender equality, affirm that:

We welcome into the Jewish community all who identify with the history, culture and fate of the Jewish people. Circumcision is not required for Jewish identity.

We support parents making informed decisions whether or not to circumcise their sons. We affirm their right to choose, and we accept and respect their choice.

Naming and welcoming ceremonies should be egalitarian. We recommend separating circumcision from welcoming ceremonies.[2]

B Mitzvah

Many cultures have coming-of-age ceremonies. In Judaism, the legal concept of coming of age was understood as becoming bar mitzvah (son of commandment) at age thirteen or bat mitzvah (daughter of commandment) at age twelve. Formal ceremonies to mark this transition for boys began to develop in the Middle Ages, and parallel ceremonies for girls appeared in non-Orthodox Judaisms in the twentieth century.

Humanistic Jewish communities celebrate this milestone in various ways. Some have a group ceremony; others hold individual ceremonies for each b mitzvah. Some students present a Torah reading in Hebrew and in English with original commentary; they may choose the traditional Torah portion or select one they find personally meaningful. Because Humanistic Jewish congregations do not regularly read the conventional weekly Torah portion, b mitzvah students who choose a Torah reading have more freedom. Some communities use a Torah scroll for this ceremony, others a bound volume. Still other communities offer the option of a research project and presentation on a self-selected hero or issue connected to broader Jewish experience, with or without a Hebrew reading from the Torah or other Jewish literature. B mitzvah students preparing to use Hebrew in their celebrations learn reading skills and basic Hebrew language as part of their Jewish education (see chapter 14). The goals of the ceremony are personal relevance, Jewish connection, and youth empowerment. Leading ceremonial gatherings devoted to their self-selected and researched topics helps b mitzvah students experience ownership over their own Judaism, a key principle of Humanistic Judaism.

When Camila Grunberg (b. 2003) celebrated her bat mitzvah in 2016 at The City Congregation for Humanistic Judaism in New York City, she delivered the following talk, "The Meaning of Life," her chosen topic for what she would later describe as "the start of a journey that will continue forever. Although now I am officially a Bat Mitzvah, I will continue to consider my family history and values in my daily life. Not only will I consider them but I will also create my family's history and my own personal values as I continue to grow older. Most importantly, I will make sure to continue to be insightful and thoughtful while completing any work, both academic and non-academic."[3]

Camila Grunberg, "The Meaning of Life" (2016)

The meaning of life, where do I begin? As I picked this topic [for my bat mitzvah], I decided to start my research by asking my family and friends what their opinions were. But first, I asked Siri, "What is the meaning of life?" Her response was, "I don't know.

But I think there is an app for that." This was the moment when I realized that finding the meaning of life was not going to be easy. . . .

Judaism focuses on this world and this life, and not some future world or world to come. Traditional Jewish philosophy emphasizes a commitment to making the world a better place, not to affect God, but to benefit the individual and society. Judaism includes among its fundamental values the pursuit of justice, compassion, peace, kindness, hard work, prosperity, humility and education.

Humanistic Judaism offers a nontheistic alternative in contemporary Jewish life. On The City Congregation website there is a statement that reads:

Humanistic Judaism is a secular Jewish denomination that celebrates the centrality of human judgment and human power from a uniquely Jewish perspective. As humanists we believe that reason, rather than faith, is the source of truth, and that human intelligence and experience are capable of guiding our lives.

Humanistic Judaism focuses on the cultural and historical experience of the Jewish people. It provides a structure for humanistic and secular Jews to celebrate their Jewish identity by participating in Jewish holidays and lifecycle events (such as weddings and bar and bat mitzvahs) with inspirational ceremonies that draw upon but go beyond traditional literature.

The following is a quote about the purpose of life according to Humanistic Judaism, from a Shabbat service that our congregation has used: "We believe that the purpose of life is bringing justice and human dignity. We believe that the purpose of life is in enabling people to live in freedom with autonomy and choice. We believe that the purpose of life is making the most of the lives we have each and every day."

Judaism has often been described as a religion of deed, not creed. This observation applies to Humanistic and traditional Jews alike. Observing religious practices and doing acts of social justice are much more important than embracing specific beliefs.

The meaning of life and the purpose of life are achieved not by what we say or confess, but by how we act and how we behave.

I believe that the meaning of life is not a static concept; it varies from one person to another, throughout a person's life, at different times of history and across geographies. It is defined by internal factors, such as personality and how we process life experiences, as well as by external factors, such as the time and place where we live. Nevertheless, there are universal principles that have withstood the test of time, from the ancient civilizations through today, such as kindness, generosity, respect, fairness, awareness, tolerance, and compassion.

Every person has the opportunity to find meaning in each moment, and to do the best we can to build a positive life with what we are given. In our everyday lives we can pay attention to each experience and try to make the best choices, maybe keeping those universal principles in mind.[4]

Marriage Promises

How can one define a loving partnership in words? This is the challenge of the Humanistic Jewish *ketubah* (marriage contract; pl. *ketubot*). The traditional *ketubah* text involves assets and property, provides a safety net to a divorcée or widow, and does not even include the word "love." In the twenty-first century, for many Jews a *ketubah* is as much a personal aesthetic and emotional expression as it is a reflection of tradition. Between creative designs and revised modern texts that diverge radically from the Aramaic original, today's *ketubot* reflect contemporary values of love, equality, mutual support, and respect for diversity beyond and within the new family home.

The Association of Humanistic Rabbis (see chapter 6) adopted the following texts (originally created by the now-defunct Leadership Conference of Secular and Humanistic Jews; see above) for *ketubot*. Use of these texts is not mandatory—a Humanistic rabbi may sign other *ketubot*—and these versions may be found on *ketubah* websites independent of Humanistic rabbinic officiation. The texts are available in both Hebrew and English, though some couples choose only English or English and another language meaningful to them, based on their cultural heritage.

Why two versions? One speaks to interfaith or intercultural couples, and the other focuses specifically on Jewish culture and heritage in the new marital partnership. The continuity of the tradition of signing a *ketubah* is balanced by these creative responses to new realities.

Association of Humanistic Rabbis, "Wedding *Ketubah* Texts" (1999)

INTRODUCTORY TEXT FOR BOTH VERSIONS 1 AND 2

On the _____ day of the month of _____, in the year _____ of the Jewish calendar, corresponding to the _____ day of the month of _____, in the year _____ of the secular calendar as recorded in _____, _____ and _____ entered into this covenant of marriage.

VERSION 1

We pledge to nurture, trust, and respect each other throughout our married life together. We shall be open and honest, understanding and accepting, loving and forgiving, and loyal to one another.

We promise to work together to build a harmonious relationship of equality. We shall respect each other's uniqueness and help one another to grow to our fullest potential. We will comfort and support each other through life's sorrows and joys.

Together, we shall create a home filled with learning, laughter and compassion, a home wherein we will honor each other's cherished family traditions and values. Let us join hands to help build a world filled with peace and love.

VERSION 2

We pledge to each other our mutual trust and respect. We will offer support and encouragement for personal growth and the fulfillment of our shared dreams.

We will be open, honest, loyal and devoted to one another. We promise to be faithful friends, companions and life partners and to comfort one another through life's sorrows and joys.

We shall honor each other's individual needs, and shall cherish and love one another throughout our married life together.

Let us weave our commitment to the Jewish people and culture into the fabric of our lives. Together, let us build a Jewish home filled with loving affection, laughter, wisdom and a dedication to peace and harmony for all humanity.[5]

Shivah

In times of sorrow, Humanistic Jews also need to balance continuing Jewish tradition and upholding personal and communal integrity. This can be challenging through moments of grief, particularly with non-Humanistic family members and social pressure to follow traditional practices. Still, for Humanistic Jews, performing Jewish life-cycle rituals involving death only because they have "always" been done is not sufficient reason to continue them. Mourners must assess each ritual element's potential to create personal and communal meaning in line with their own Humanistic values.

As a result, some Jewish memorial texts—such as the Twenty-Third Psalm or the traditional Mourner's *Kaddish*—are problematic because of their extensive praise of God and lack of focus on the mourners. Some Humanistic Jewish families may choose to recite the traditional Mourner's *Kaddish* for the sake of family harmony or because it evokes memories of the comfort provided to previous generations of Jews who believed its words. Others may choose a Humanistic adaptation of the *Kaddish*,[6] while still others choose Hebrew or English poetry that speaks of love and loss.

Other practices—such as shivah observance—can hold meaning

and provide comfort to Humanistic Jews once shivah is boldly reinterpreted, reinvented, and reconfigured (an ongoing process for other liberal Jewish denominations as well).

In a 1992 edition of the movement's journal *Humanistic Judaism* titled "The Return to Tradition," Rabbi Sherwin Wine, the principal founding thinker of Humanistic Judaism (see chapter 1), explores how Humanistic Jewish mourners might sit shivah (traditionally defined as seven days of mourning) in meaningful ways for them. Accompanying customs of tearing their clothing, covering mirrors, or sitting uncomfortably close to the ground may not be relevant or useful. What remains beyond ritual, and what Humanistic Judaism emphasizes, is the psychological comfort provided by the positive aspects of the shivah experience: community, family time, even silence with the caring presence of friends as one adjusts to the loss of a loved one. In these ways, the Jewish tradition of shivah meets abiding human needs.

Sherwin Wine, "Sitting Shiva" (1992)

Question: Should Humanistic Jewish mourners sit shiva?

Responsum:[7] The mourning practices of rabbinic Judaism were built around a belief system that no longer generally prevails in the Jewish community. This system began with an all-powerful judgmental God who was the master of life and death. Death was ambiguous. It might be a sign of divine anger and divine punishment. God's displeasure was not trivial. It needed to be countered. The deity needed to be appeased. And the spirit world of the dead, including evil and malevolent spirits, needed to be avoided and even driven away.

This ideology explains the traditional practice. Only the appearance of abject suffering and misery could persuade both God and the spirit world not to strike again. The mourners—the sons, daughters, fathers, mothers, brothers, and sisters of the deceased—must be as pitiable as possible. They must tear their garments. They must sit on the ground or on harsh surfaces. They must not wash or dress in fine clothing. They must abstain from good food. They must not laugh or joke or participate in happy events. They must be confined to their homes during the first seven days (*shiva*) of mourning. If comforters arrive, they must sit in silence until the mourners initiate conversation.

Of course, the ideological basis of traditional mourning practices is unacceptable to us as Humanistic Jews. So is the notion of enforced suffering to ensure protection. Unwashed, uncomfortable, and underfed mourners are inconsistent with our view of dignified grief.

But the traditional mourning procedure had an unintended consequence. The practice of staying home after the burial of loved ones to receive family and friends turned out to be therapeutic for mourners. In liberal circles, where most of the hardship routines were removed, being surrounded by caring friends became a wonderful source of human support.

Humanistic Judaism is very comfortable with a humanistic "shiva." It does not have to last for seven days. It should last as long as the mourners want it. For some, one day may be enough; for others, eight days. Most Humanistic mourners choose three. A small minority find no need for any "shiva."

Humanistic "shiva" is built around the notion that life and death are natural phenomena, with no intrusion by gods or spirits. It is based on the conviction that vulnerable mourners need as much human support as they can find. Mourners should be comfortable. Conversation should be free.

Many Humanistic Jews hold a brief commemorative celebration of the life of the deceased every evening, or one of the evenings, of the "shiva." Family and friends sit in a circle and share stories about the life of the person who died. Prose readings and poetry selections about a humanistic response to death may be read. Inspirational songs may be sung....

History is filled with ironies. What started out to serve one purpose later serves another.

"Shiva" has been transformed and is now ours.[8]

14

Education

How does one create future generations of Humanistic Jews? How does one deepen the knowledge of Humanistic Jewish adults through Jewish learning? Cultural Jewish education is essential.

Outwardly, the youth and adult educational programs of Humanistic Jewish communities resemble those of other denominations, with supplemental schools meeting on Sunday mornings weekly, biweekly, or monthly and regular adult learning programs during Sunday school or weekdays, daytime or evening. Most Sunday schools teach a full curriculum through the year, while adult learning can be either episodic or a sustained course through multiple sessions. Post-mitzvah students can return as classroom aides for younger grades, and some communities offer confirmation classes and ceremonies for older students. There are no Humanistic Jewish day schools, because Humanistic Jews value participation in broader educational settings and communities.

Also like other liberal denominations, Humanistic Judaism strives to educate Jews in a broad range of Jewish practices and beliefs as well as the movement's own approach. What distinguishes a Humanistic Jewish school is the curricular emphasis on evolving cultural Judaism, on Hebrew taught as language rather than as prayer recitation, and Humanistic Jewish philosophy. Learning for both children and adults is highly experiential. Beyond Jewish text study (through literary and historical lenses), Humanistic Jews delve into Jewish culture through art, film, literature, music, television, and museum exhibitions of world Jewry.

At its essence, Humanistic Jewish education aims to foster general Jewish and Humanistic Jewish cultural and philosophical literacy, positive Jewish experiences that imbue emotional attachment to Jewish life, and robust connections between Jews' beliefs and personal background and their lifestyle and Jewish expressions. The emphasis is as much on students "doing Jewish" (spinning dreidels, hearing the shofar/ram's horn, smelling and tasting Jewish cooking, lighting Shabbat candles) as "being Jewish" (i.e., Jewish identification); each approach reinforces the other. Similar to other liberal Jews, Humanistic Jews encourage their students to live out their values by engaging in *tikkun olam*, acts to repair the world, often by working to ameliorate human suffering and improving the human condition here and now. In this endeavor Humanistic Jews may also emphasize human rights and the separation of religion and government more than other liberal Jews (see chapter 11).

The five selections in this chapter delve into the elements of a Humanistic Jewish education and the underlying philosophy of a Humanistic Jewish curriculum. The first essay explores the core issue of transmitting a cultural Jewish identity. The second grapples with one specific challenge of Humanistic Jewish literacy: creating familiarity with traditional Judaism for nontraditional Jews. The third describes a Humanistic Jewish approach to the Torah, with clear implications for its place in Humanistic Jewish learning for children and adults. The fourth, an example of a Humanistic Jewish Torah commentary, demonstrates how Humanistic perspectives applied to Torah study produce novel understandings. Lastly, a statement of educational philosophy for the movement summarizes the key objectives and content to educate a Humanistic Jew of any age.

Transmitting Cultural Jewish Identity

Secular Jewish education did not begin with Humanistic Judaism. Starting in 1910 and reaching their heyday in the 1930s, secular Yiddish schools and camps were an integral part of American Jewish communist, socialist, and Labor Zionist communities and national organizations (see introduction). Many early members and community leaders in Humanistic Judaism were educated in this environment. These institutions faced many of the same challenges then as Humanistic Jewish educational programs do now: how to balance secularism with Jewish cultural literacy, and how to balance universal values with particular Jewish identity.

Mitchell Silver (b. 1950), professor emeritus of philosophy at the University of Massachusetts, Boston, was the educational director of the I. L. Peretz Sunday School of the Boston Workers Circle from 1992 to 2009, as well as cultural director of the children's summer camp, Camp Kinderland, from 1989 to 2006. Silver has also served as faculty for the International Institute for Secular Humanistic Judaism.

His *Respecting the Wicked Child: A Philosophy of Secular Jewish Identity and Education* sets forth the basis for a positive secular Jewish education. In his reframing, the so-called wicked child of the Passover seder who asks, "What has all this to do with me?" is now a secularized Jewish adult who wants to know how to instill positive Jewish identity with secular integrity. The following selections from his work dramatize why preserving and passing on cultural Judaism is essential for Humanistic Jewish education.

Mitchell Silver, "Treasures of the Legacy" (1998)

> Beyond the blood of the martyrs, there are the treasures of the legacy. Few Wicked Children are aware of the depth and breadth of Jewish civilization. It contains traditions rich in music, poetry, folktales, philosophy, theology, mysticism, liturgies, sacred objects, ornaments, rituals, homilies, myths, legends, and law. For drama and variety Jewish history is not easily matched. Earlier I made the general point that particular cultures have aesthetic and moral value and therefore merit preservation. Now I make the specific claim that Jewish culture is of great value and merits preservation. But it will not be preserved by the Chinese or Hopi or Quebecois. It will be preserved by Jews or not at all. So Jews are under some obligation to do some preserving....

This is a duty that should prove far more enriching than arduous. The most straightforward reason to be a Jew is also one of the strongest; *es iz gut tsu zayn a Yid*, "it is good to be a Jew." ...

Why maintain and attempt to pass on a Jewish identity? Because human cultures are valuable; because Jewish culture is valuable; because only Jews will maintain Jewish culture; because people have suffered to maintain Jewish culture; because Jew-haters want to see the death of Jewish culture; because you cannot help living in some culture, and a Jewish American one will feel most natural (unless American consumerism does, but that will leave you isolated and alienated); because Jewish culture can provide you with a place in a community and history, and it can give substance to many of your ingrained attitudes and habits; because Jewish culture can ground your progressive politics and moral commitments; because it gives you something that you like to give to your children, making them less likely to seek what you do not like; because it does not prevent you from appropriating anything that is of value or appealing to you from all of human culture (indeed, the secular Jewish culture described in this book positively encourages, nay enjoins you, to appreciate the riches and integrity of other cultures); finally, because it in no way prevents you from being a tolerant, rational, good citizen of the world who treats all humans as equals and with respect. ...

Jewish history is the Torah of Secular Jewish education; it is not the sole object of study, but it is the backbone of the curriculum. To Jewish history we attach all the flesh that makes up the body of Secular Jewish culture. None of the contents of Secular Judaism fails to find a place in the historical curriculum. As we teach the story of the Jews, we can explain Jewish customs, Jewish languages, Jewish literature, Jewish morals, and the varied fates of Jews.[1]

Jewish Literacy

There is an inherent tension between teaching Humanistic Jewish children the values, beliefs, and practices of Humanistic Judaism and teaching them about religious Judaism more generally when many traditional practices and texts do not reflect Humanistic Jewish beliefs. A Humanistic Jewish curriculum naturally emphasizes, in positive terms, what Humanistic Jews believe and how and why they believe and celebrate as they do. Meanwhile, given limited time and resources, Humanistic Jewish education does touch on traditional prayers and rituals to familiarize Humanistic Jews with practices they are likely to encounter in other Jewish settings. Given a choice between repeatedly reciting the traditional *Amidah* prayer, which is not used in Humanistic Jewish services, and experiencing Sephardic Jewish food, a Humanistic Jewish educational program will mention the former and dive into the latter. As a result, when Humanistic Jews later find themselves in the wider Jewish community at a life-cycle event or holiday celebration, they are likely to recognize elements of the traditional service and liturgy such as the Mourner's *Kaddish* but not know it well enough to recite it at full speed.

Additionally, Humanistic Judaism does not teach traditional subjects through traditional lenses. Humanistic Jews view religious texts and rituals as cultural creations, to be taught along with many other subjects for cultural Jewish literacy, and stress choice and creativity. For example, students may create their own "Ten Commandments" based on their personal values after studying—and discussing whether or not they agree with—the original commandments. They may make their own mezuzah, learning first about the traditional object and its required text (that appears inside) and then choosing or creating their own texts to insert. They may not become as familiar with the traditional text as students taught about *mezuzot* in other Jewish denominations; instead, Humanistic Judaism emphasizes personally meaningful experience.

The challenge of achieving broad Jewish cultural literacy beyond Humanistic Jewish practice has been an ongoing debate in Humanistic Jewish education. At times, those focused on Humanistic philosophy have de-emphasized learning about traditional Judaism, even as those pushing for greater familiarity with religious Jewish practice acknowledge the core goal of inculcating a positive Humanistic Judaism (see Daniel Friedman, "Recovering Our Stories," chapter 9).

At the 1990 International Federation of Secular Humanistic Jews conference on the future of the Jewish people, Ruth Duskin Feldman (1934–2015) addressed what Humanistic Jewish education should look like. The editor of the Society for Humanistic Judaism's journal *Humanistic Judaism* for thirty-two years, Feldman was also an active member and Sunday school teacher at the Chicago-area Humanistic Congregation Beth Or. One of the first graduates of the International Institute for Secular Humanistic Judaism's *Madrikha*/Leader Program as an adult learner, she spoke forthrightly about principled challenges inherent in building Humanistic Jewish literacy in future generations.

Ruth Duskin Feldman, "Jewish Education and the Future" (1991)

We have, in our national organizations and local communities, begun the vital task of defining and organizing a Secular Humanistic Jewish educational program. We need to share our successes and failures, our problems and products. . . .

I warned that we, who have rejected the authoritarian religion of our ancestors, must avoid the twin pitfalls of abdication (setting no goals for our children) and neo-authoritarianism (establishing humanism as a new creed to be inculcated). I stressed that students must be free to choose their own values and beliefs. And they must be given opportunities to act on their principles.

Effective freedom depends on knowledge; Adam was free to make choices after he ate of the tree of knowledge, not before. Thus, I argued, we must help students gain a clear enough understanding of their history and heritage so they can make informed choices. And, I said, our most crucial and perhaps most challenging task is to awaken our children to the rewards and responsibility of thinking for themselves.

The goals adopted for the Beth Or school were twofold. The first was to help children develop the ability to formulate a philosophy of life, based on a study of human and, particularly, Jewish experience. The second was to help children develop a realistic, positive Jewish identity and to express that identity through holiday celebrations and other activities. In order to achieve these dual objectives, our school sought to provide "a spiritually free and intellectually honest environment" in which children can pursue their natural quest for answers that make life meaningful and satisfying. . . .

What may be lacking is depth of Jewish background. My daughter Laurie was bat mitsva and confirmed at Beth Or, later taught in the Sunday school, and now tutors our Hebrew students. Two years ago, in a keynote address at the annual meeting of the Society for Humanistic Judaism . . . she described her experience as a second-generation Humanistic Jew.

Unlike her parents, who had made an informed choice to be Humanistic Jews, Laurie had grown up largely unfamiliar with customs and ceremonies of mainstream Judaism. When she went to Hebrew University in Jerusalem for her junior year in college, she felt like an "ignorant stranger" with an impoverished background. She did not like being a "foreigner" among Jews. More importantly, she felt she could not meaningfully reject a tradition of which she knew so little.

As she began to fill in the gaps, she found richness, warmth, and a link to history. She found the Bible and the Talmud intellectually challenging. She found value in learning respectfully about the origins of Jewish laws and customs and the teachings of the sages, even if she then made an informed choice not to follow them. . . .

I am not saying that we should have our children recite the Sh'ma. I am saying that they should know what the Sh'ma is and what it meant historically to our martyred people who went to their deaths with those words on their lips. We might even wish to substitute a humanistic version of the Sh'ma, expressing the same beautiful concept of unity in a similar poetic cadence. . . .

We, too, have a Jewish tradition, a proud tradition that is not limited to Tanakh and Talmud. It includes rebels, freethinkers, and doers of every age: Abraham challenging God's injustice in destroying the innocent with the guilty; the Baal Shem Tov throwing off the hidebound yoke of formal prayer to commune joyfully with nature; Y.L. Peretz and Sholem Aleichem exposing the hypocrisy of a society that gave obeisance to symbols rather than substance; the voices that rose from the flames of the Holocaust, echoing Abraham's challenge in anguished awareness that there was no one to answer; the Zionist pioneers who made the desert bloom and built a state against overwhelming odds. We need to make our tradition available to our children.

Today many people, including secular humanists, are seeking something they call spirituality. Spirituality—a soul-satisfying sense of self-transcendence in the face of mortality—tends to arise from an experience that has resonance because it taps deep wells of memory, of knowledge, and, therefore, of feeling: people respond spiritually to events, words, and images that evoke early learnings and deep-seated yearnings. Thus, we deprive our children if we give them no more than a smattering of knowledge of Jewish history, traditions, law, and literature. We need to do this, of course, from a secular humanist perspective—not blindly accepting but constantly evaluating, critiquing, sifting.[2]

Torah as Human Creation

Humanistic Judaism ascribes to the Torah a place of importance in historical Jewish culture as the oldest Jewish book, but does not look to the Torah for definitive guidance on how to live as a Jew or to be a good person. Humanistic Jews do not claim that their values derive from or depend upon a human-authored book from centuries ago. They are empowered to agree or disagree with its specific laws and values. It serves as one source of teaching and learning among many (alongside rabbinic literature, philosophy, human experience, and individual insight). Parallels between contemporary values and Torah teachings can sometimes be found and are appreciated for their cultural resonance and ancient insight into the human condition.

In this passage from his key work *Judaism beyond God*, Humanistic Judaism founder Rabbi Sherwin Wine (see chapter 1) affirms that familiarity with the stories, rhetoric, and values of the Torah and TANAKH is a key element of Jewish literacy.

Wine walked his talk. He led regular Hebrew Bible study on Shabbat mornings for over a decade before his death. But the Torah did not define the Shabbat and High Holiday messages he delivered. In the congregation he founded, the Torah was kept in the congregational library, as it is today, and there was and is no ark in the congregation's ceremonial meeting room. In its stead, a sculptural representation of the Hebrew word *adam*, "humanity," is installed on the front wall. The architectural messages therein—the importance of humanity and the proper place of the Torah as an important book among other human-authored books—continue to represent Humanistic Judaism.

Sherwin Wine, "The Torah" (1985)

What is the place of the Torah in the educational and ceremonial life of the humanistic Jew?

Whatever answer we give to this question, it must be consistent with the basic affirmations of a humanistic approach to Judaism: the irrelevance of God, a rational ethic which derives its authority from human need, a lifestyle consistent with reason and personal dignity, a naturalistic view of Jewish history, the rejection of all idols. It is not our job to fit these beliefs into the Torah. It is our job to fit the Torah into these commitments.

First, let us describe how *not* to deal with the Torah.

We do not need to rescue the Torah. We do not need to make the Torah do more for us than it can. The Torah is the supreme document of priestly Judaism. It is a skillful expression of a theocratic view of the world and society. . . . No matter what interpretive genius we bring to the text, the Torah cannot be turned into a humanistic constitution—not even a shabby version of one. A document, two thirds of the contents of which are humanistically embarrassing, cannot—without dishonesty—be made to serve as the foundation code of a secular approach to Jewish identity.

We must not mock the Torah. It deserves its own dignity. It rightfully belongs to the traditional Jews who live by its prescriptions. Texts deserve their own integrity. They mean what their authors intended them to mean. They do not mean what desperate liberals want to make them mean. The writer of Genesis 1 believed in a flat earth and a flat heaven. He did not believe in galaxies and evolution. If he had endorsed these convictions, he would have said so. The writer of Exodus 19 believed in supernatural intrusion and divine voices. He did not believe in Moses the philosopher engaging in philosophic introspection on top of a mountain. The author of Leviticus 19 believed in divine dictatorship and priestly government. He did not embrace personal freedom and egalitarian democracy. There is a right of original intent, a moral claim to let texts mean what they say and what their authors meant them to say....

We must not misrepresent ourselves. We must not use false advertising. We must not imitate Reform Judaism and pretend that Zadokite priests were the precursors of the Enlightenment. The Torah is an appropriate emblem for rabbinic Jews. It fits their aspirations and the lifestyle they are promoting. But for humanistic Jews, it is a lie. It points to the wrong tradition. Humanistic Judaism is not the child of the official documents of priestly and rabbinic Judaism. It is the child of Jewish experience, of twenty-five centuries of human ingenuity in the face of cruel and unkind fates. Jewish history was different from the way the priests and rabbis saw it. The Jewish personality is the product of Jewish history, not the product of the Torah.

If this is the reality of our roots, how then *should* we use the Torah?

A humanistic Judaism should use the Torah as an important historical document, a resource book for the study of the ancient history of the Jewish people. Although it seems to focus on the lives of Abraham, Isaac, Jacob, Joseph, and Moses, it actually describes the power struggles and ambitions of priests and Jews who lived many centuries after the death of Moses. The Torah is less a description of the life of the Hebrews in the nomadic period and more a revelation of the beliefs and anxieties of the Jews before and after the Chaldean conquest. The editors of the Torah put their sixth-century laws and convictions into the mouths of the patriarchs and Moses.

The Torah is a book of clues. If it is studied scientifically (not piously), it will lead us to the real events that lie behind the mythology. Abraham, Isaac, and Jacob may turn out to be symbols of three Amorite invasions of Palestine. Joseph may be transformed into a Semitic occupation of Egypt. And Joshua may end up living three hundred years before Moses. The authors of the Torah saw the past through their own political and theological convictions. Jewish history is not necessarily what the priestly writers say it was. It is a collection of events that lie behind the descriptions. And the Torah is a collection of clues that lead us to the events.

The Torah is also a book about past and present beliefs. Even if all the historical statements of the Torah were false, even if all the laws of the Torah were ethically invalid, they are still assertions in which many of our ancestors fervently believed and which guided their behavior.... Much of establishment Jewish behavior comes from ideas that are to be found in the Torah and its commentaries. The study of these ideas is part of the study of Jewish history, just as the study of the conditions that undermined these ideas is part of the study of Jewish history.

The Torah is a book of shared conclusions. The priestly writers often reached ethical conclusions that humanistic Jews have also reached. The priests came to these moral precepts with the reasoning of an authoritarian God. Humanistic Jews come to these rules with a commonsensical testing of their consequences. Rabbinic Jews come to these commandments with the knowledge that the Torah gives them validity. Humanistic Jews approach them with the awareness that human experience makes them worthwhile (even if the Torah never existed). Millions of people in dozens of cultures have discovered that honoring parents and telling the truth are morally important, even though they have never seen a Torah. Ethics do not come from a book. They come from human needs and human experience. . . .

All literature is of human creation, designed to appeal to human audiences and filled with human imperfection. Books are never holy. They may be useful and inspirational. But they are never all true and all perfect. And they bear no guarantee of eternal validity.

The Torah belongs in the library. As a scroll, it deserves a place of special honor in the museum of famous Jewish books. Let students study it and evaluate it. Let teachers talk about it and explain its historic power. But let no humanist worship it or imagine that Jewish identity and ethical living depend on it.[3]

Self-Selected Torah Study

Humanistic Jewish communities are not bound by the conventional Torah portion of the week for their events on the Jewish liturgical calendar. Their Shabbat services, study sessions, and b mitzvah (gender-neutral term for bar/bat/b'nai mitzvah) celebrations can draw from the entire range of the Jewish experience and Jewish culture. When that includes Torah (see chapter 13), Humanistic Jews study Torah in their own way, with their own values, approaches, and understandings.

In her *derash* (interpretation) on the story of the Golden Calf in Exodus, Rabbi Denise Handlarski (see chapter 4) applies the Torah portion's lesson to today's world by treating the Golden Calf not as a historical event or a warning against worshiping idols, but rather as a symbolic motif for greed and misplaced priorities. While this general approach to Torah commentary is not unusual among liberal Jews, Humanistic Judaism's distinct understanding of the text as human-authored and myth rather than history influences the results.

Denise Handlarski, "The Torah, the Ten Commandments and Us" (2019)

This week's Torah portion [Ki Tissa', Exod. 30:11–34:35] is . . . a familiar story: Moses ascends the mountain and while he's gone, the people build a Golden Calf. Moses comes down with the Ten Commandments and is so angry that he smashes the tablets.

There are lots of interpretations for what the Golden Calf might symbolize. For many today, we see it as money or stuff—the true idolatry of our day is that we as a society worship things. The goldenness of the calf fits nicely with that drash/interpretation. The Golden Calf is, of course, symbolic of any form of idolatry for, as we see when we get the decalogue [ten commandments], the first commandment is all about having only one God.

Years ago when I studied in Israel as part of my rabbinic training, I attended a great class at the non-denominational Pardes Institute for Jewish Studies. In the week of Ki Tissa, this biblical portion, the instructor posted a question I had never thought of: how did this group of Israelites wandering around the desert have the gold to make the calf? She suggested we look earlier in the Exodus narrative. Sure enough, just before the Israelites are leaving Egypt and about to cross the Red Sea, they ask their Egyptian neighbours for stuff to take on their journey.

So, according to the story (and, yes, I believe this is a story, not history), the Egyptians helped the Israelites with items of value, including gold, and the Israelites used all that to build a golden calf instead of building a better life.

What's the lesson? Well, firstly, we are told many times in the Bible to "love the stranger, for you (we) were strangers in the land of Egypt." It's worth remembering that the Egyptian folks in the story weren't uniformly bad—they tried to help us out, even after the plagues! And that the Israelites in the story weren't uniformly good—they mess up too.

I loved thinking of the golden calf in these terms because it's a reminder that we as humans have the potential to build amazing things, particularly when we share and cooperate, and yet so much of what we do with our resources amounts to nothing but garbage.

Whatever you have been given and are carrying with you, my hope is that you use it towards good. The golden calf provided false hope for a desperate people. Our job is to avoid succumbing to such false hope, to meet our own desperation or fear or despair or yearning with bravery and courage, and to build something more beautiful.[4]

Principles of Humanistic Jewish Youth Education

In Humanistic Judaism, each member community considers it a personal responsibility to educate its own young people. The national umbrella organization, Society for Humanistic Judaism (see chapter 7), has not issued a national youth curriculum, but provides its approximately thirty member communities with resources and guidance for administering both youth and adult educational programs.

Because Humanistic youth education is designed to train young people to participate in adult community, the content of an individual community's curriculum reflects that community's priorities and principles. Many communities prioritize hiring members who agree with the movement's philosophy as teachers lest non-Humanistic approaches to Jewish identity and culture be taught as normative by those outside the movement.

At the same time, the Society for Humanistic Judaism does call upon member congregations to uphold shared Humanistic Jewish values and objectives in educating Humanistic Jews at every age. The following statement articulating the consensus philosophy of Humanistic Jewish children's education reflects the basic values of learning programs for any age.

Society for Humanistic Judaism, Curriculum for Children's Education, "Philosophy" (2013)

1. Our curriculum should enable students to learn the history, cultures, customs, holidays and beliefs of the Jewish people and to feel a personal connection to the Jewish community.
2. Completing a Humanistic Jewish education program should allow students to make ongoing informed decisions about their Jewish identity with full knowledge of the Humanistic Jewish perspective.
3. We strive to make the entire educational experience enjoyable and relevant for our students, an experience that encourages a positive relationship to Judaism.
4. Our education curriculum includes goals in the cognitive, attitudinal and affective domains. We strive to instill critical thinking skills based on reason and science. We seek to promote a love of learning, an appreciation and desire for ethical behavior, and a healthy respect for and attachment to Jewish identity.
5. Our curriculum is human-centered rather than God-centered. We are humanistic and non-theistic; we direct the course of our own lives independent of a supernatural being. We recognize that the concept and literary character of God play an important role in historical Judaism as well as in other branches of current Judaism. We teach our students to be familiar with this tradition even as we differentiate our beliefs from it.
6. We teach ethics based on essential humanistic values such as integrity, justice, truth, dignity, respect for diversity, compassion and civic responsibility.
7. A student completing our curriculum should be able to describe the fundamental beliefs of Humanistic Judaism.
8. We believe that part of our students' education should include learning about the practices of the other branches of Judaism, as well as the practices and beliefs of other religions.

9. The Hebrew Bible is an essential source of Jewish tradition, legend and history. It and other traditional Jewish texts are human documents that reflect the interests and concerns of those who composed them. Our students should be familiar with the Bible's contents and development. We do not view the Bible as divinely revealed, but we do view it as important in understanding Judaism. We agree with the founder of Humanistic Judaism, Rabbi Sherwin Wine, who held that the Bible is an important part of Jewish literature, but we value many other books as well.
10. Our Jewish heritage includes strong ties to Hebrew and other Jewish languages that evolved throughout Jewish history. While we do not expect fluency in these languages as a result of our program, we do expect that students will know the Hebrew alphabet and some basic words, phrases and expressions in these languages.
11. We recognize the significance of the existence of Israel as a Jewish state and historical homeland while respecting the rights of other peoples in the region.
12. We recognize the importance of literature, music, art and other aspects of Jewish culture.
13. We recognize that many of the children in our affiliate programs come from intercultural families. Our role is to present a Jewish education to the children and to be sensitive to the fact that other religious and cultural traditions may be observed in these families.[5]

Afterword

Choosing to Live as a Secular Humanistic Jew: Declaration of Eighth Biennial Conference of the International Federation of Secular Humanistic Jews, 2000

We live in a pluralistic world that is increasingly secular. There is a growing conviction that human problems need human solutions, that justice is a human creation, that ethics is the child of human need. ...

In a free society Jewish identity is no longer just a matter of birth and social hostility. It has now become a matter of choice. Jews can choose to make their Jewish identity significant. Or they can choose to be absorbed into the larger community. In a free world a meaningful Jewish identity is a free choice.

One of the important options in contemporary Jewish life is choosing to live as a secular and humanistic Jew. For Jews who identify with the history and culture of the Jewish people and who no longer believe in the theology of theistic Judaism, this option is a choice of integrity, passion, and courage.

Secular Humanistic Jews who make this choice build our Jewish lives through the following commitments:

Dignity: We strive to become the masters of our own lives and to achieve our own dignity.

Reason: We pursue the truth about ourselves and the world around us through the light of reason, always willing to live with uncertainty where evidence provides no answer.

Justice: We accept ultimate responsibility to work for justice in the world and strive to guarantee freedom and equality for all people.

Study: We study the history, literature and experience of the Jewish people, finding inspiration for our own struggle to achieve personal dignity and social justice.

Celebration: We celebrate the major events of Jewish history, the great moments of personal development, and the seasons of nature through the holidays of the Jewish tradition, infusing these celebrations with our own convictions.

Jewish Culture: We fill our lives with the flavor and substance of Jewish culture, cultivating Jewish languages, literature, music, art, and symbols.

Spirituality: We connect with experiences of beauty and self-transcendence, which give meaning to our lives and become the foundation of our own naturalistic spirituality.

Pluralism: We work together with other Jews to guarantee equality of all Jews, traditional or non-traditional, religious and non-religious, and demonstrate by our action that diversity in Jewish life is a strength, not a weakness.

Openness: We open ourselves to wisdom and beauty from other cultures and have adopted universal standards of tolerance, pluralism, democracy, equality of status for men and women, and the pursuit of peace.

Creativity: We use creativity of the Jewish past whenever it addresses our needs and convictions, always understanding that the creativity of the Jewish present may speak with equal or greater authority.

In a world filled with injustice, pain and inequality, it takes an act of courage to live a life without guarantees and without reliance on supernatural power. This approach to life has deep roots in Jewish history. In defense of dignity through human determination, our ancestors passionately lived lives of integrity. Now, choosing to live as Secular Humanistic Jews, we continue that tradition which has long been part of the Jewish experience.[1]

Go Forth and Learn

A famous talmudic story describes Rabbi Hillel welcoming a potential convert by encapsulating the Torah in the phrase "What is hurtful to you, do not do to your fellow" and then adding, "Now, go forth and learn."[1]

Traditional Jewish study considers the Torah and Talmud and their commentaries to be a bottomless library. The open canon of contemporary Humanistic Judaism is even wider; it includes the Torah and Talmud and also encompasses critical Jewish history and archaeology, artistic Jewish culture, Jewish food, Jewish music and movies, and much more.

The following "Go Forth and Learn" recommendations for each chapter of this volume suggest avenues for future exploration of this open canon beyond sources listed in the bibliography. You will find works that influence secular Jewish thought, including scholarship and literature relevant to Humanistic Jews, as well as general Jewish cultural works such as art, music, and film. Where possible, more recent and accessible sources have been selected. Since this list itself could be endless—consider the hundreds of television episodes that touch on Jewish identity—we hope it inspires further exploration.

Introduction
Written Material

Cohn-Sherbok, Dan, Harry Cook, and Marilyn Rowens, eds. *A Life of Courage: Sherwin Wine and Humanistic Judaism*. Farmington Hills MI: International Institute for Secular Humanistic Judaism, 2003.

Kogel, Renee, and Zev Katz, eds. *Judaism in a Secular Age*. Farmington Hills MI: International Institute for Secular Humanistic Judaism, 1995.

1. The Jewish Experience
Written Material

Biale, David. *Not in the Heavens: The Tradition of Secular Jewish Thought*. Princeton NJ: Princeton University Press, 2011.

Finkelstein, Israel, and Neal Silberman. *The Bible Unearthed*. New York: Free Press, 2001.

Seltzer, Robert. *Jewish People, Jewish Thought: The Jewish Experience in History*. Upper Saddle NJ: Pearson College Div., 1980.

Wine, Sherwin. *A Provocative People: A Secular History of the Jews*. Farmington Hills MI: International Institute for Secular Humanistic Judaism, 2012.

Television

The Story of the Jews. Season 1, episodes 1–5—"In the Beginning," "Among Believers," "A Leap of Faith," "Over the Rainbow," "Return"—written by Simon Schama, directed by Tim Kirby, aired March and April 2014 on PBS.

2. The God Question
Written Material

Book of Job and book of Ecclesiastes. In *JPS TANAKH*. Philadelphia: The Jewish Publication Society, 1985.

Goldstein, Rebecca. *36 Arguments for the Existence of God*. New York: Pantheon Books, 2009.

Hecht, Jennifer Michael. *Doubt: A History—The Great Doubters and Their Legacy of Innovation from Socrates and Jesus to Thomas Jefferson and Emily Dickinson*. San Francisco: HarperSanFrancisco, 2003.

Magee, Brian. "Atheists Do Got Songs: Lots of 'Em." *The Humanist*, September 13, 2012. https://thehumanist.com/arts_entertainment/culture/atheists-do-got-songslots-of-em/.

Rubenstein, Richard. *After Auschwitz: History, Theology, and Contemporary Judaism*. Baltimore: Johns Hopkins University Press, 1992.

Steinberg, Milton. *As a Driven Leaf*. New York: Behrman House, 1939.

Art

Bak, Samuel. *Creation of Wartimes II*. 1999. https://www.kunst-archive.net/en/wvz/samuel_bak/works/creation_of_war_time_ii_creation_of_wartimes_ii/type/all.

Film

Gervais, Ricky, and Matthew Robinson. *The Invention of Lying*. 2009. Warner Brothers, 1 hr., 40 min.

Zemeckis, Robert. *Contact*. 1997. Warner Brothers, 2 hrs., 30 min.

Music

Cohen, Leonard. "You Want It Darker." On *You Want It Darker*, 2016.

Martin, Steve, and the Steep Canyon Rangers. "Atheists Don't Got No Songs." On *Rare Bird Alert*, 2011.

3. Positive Humanism

Written Material

American Humanist Association. "Humanism and Its Aspirations: Humanist Manifesto III." 2003. https://americanhumanist.org/what-is-humanism/manifesto3/.

Aronson, Ron. *Living without God: New Directions for Atheists, Agnostics, Secularists, and the Undecided*. New York: Counterpoint, 2008.

Bakewell, Sarah. *Humanly Possible: Seven Hundred Years of Humanist Freethinking, Inquiry and Hope*. Toronto: Alfred A. Knopf Canada, 2023.

Berlinerblau, Jacques. *How to Be Secular: A Call to Arms for Religious Freedom*. Boston: Houghton Mifflin Harcourt, 2012.

Jacoby, Susan. *Freethinkers: A History of American Secularism*. New York: Henry Holt, 2004.

Music

Bedingfield, Natasha. "Unwritten." On *Unwritten*, 2004.

4. Ethics

Written Material

Grayling, A. C. *Meditations for the Humanist: Ethics for a Secular Age*. Oxford: Oxford University Press, 2002.

Zuckerman, Phil. *What It Means to Be Moral: Why Religion Is Not Necessary for Living an Ethical Life*. Berkeley CA: Counterpoint, 2019.

Television

The Good Place. 2016–20, NBC.

Music

Gevatron. "Mi HaIsh" ("Who Is the Person"). On *The Israeli Jewish Folk Singers*, 1979.

5. Spirituality

Written Material

Batchelor, Stephen. *Buddhism without Beliefs: A Contemporary Guide to Awakening.* New York: Riverhead Books, 1997.

Comte-Spoonville, André. *The Little Book of Atheist Spirituality.* New York: Viking, 2007.

Harris, Sam. *Waking Up: A Guide to Spirituality without Religion.* New York: Simon and Schuster, 2015.

Humanistic Judaism magazine. "Secular Spirituality: Our Capacity for Awe." Summer 2023 (full issue).

Kopitz, Barbara. *Morning Meditations: Daily Meditations for Spiritual Humanists.* Farmington Hills MI: International Institute for Secular Humanistic Judaism, 1999.

Lamott, Anne. *Help Thanks Wow.* New York: Riverhead Books, 2012.

"Secular Spirituality: Passionate Search for a Rational Judaism." Colloquium 2001 hosted by the International Institute for Secular Humanistic Judaism, video and publication of selected proceedings.

Music

Minchin, Tim. "White Wine in the Sun." On *Ready for This*, 2009.

Film

Marshall, Penny. *Awakenings.* 1990. Columbia Pictures, 2 hr., 1 min.

6. Jewish Self-Definition

Written Material

CCAR Responsum NYP 5759.3, "Who Is a Rabbi?" https://www.ccarnet.org/ccar-responsa/nyp-no-5759-3/.

Humanistic Judaism magazine. "Many People, Many Hats: Jewish Pluralism Means Making Space for Secular Jews." Winter 2022 (full issue).

Stein, Abby. *Becoming Eve.* New York: Seal Press, 2019.

Video

International Institute for Secular Humanistic Judaism Colloquia: "Half Jewish? The Heirs of Intermarriage" (2012) and "The Future of Jewish Peoplehood" (2013). https://www.youtube.com/user/IISHJvid/playlists.

Film

Shlain, Tiffany. *The Tribe.* 2005. Moxie Institute, 18 min.

7. Welcoming and Inclusion

Written Material

Handlarski, Denise. *The A–Z of Intermarriage.* Toronto: University of Toronto Press, 2020.

Katz Miller, Susan. *Being Both: Embracing Two Religions in One Interfaith Family.* Boston: Beacon Press, 2013.

Kaye/Kantrowitz, Melanie. *The Colors of Jews: Racial Politics and Radical Diasporism.* Bloomington IN: University of Indiana Press, 2007.

Video

McGinity, Keren. "The Gendered Reality of Intermarriage in America." Presented at the International Institute for Secular Humanistic Judaism's Colloquium 2014 "Evolution or Revolution? Intermarriage, Jewish Culture, and the Future of Jewish Community." https://youtu.be/9iLPATp6SsA?si=jmiyIxPC7syZzYdX. Also printed in *Humanistic Judaism* 36, no. 1 (2017): 18–27.

Film

Norton, Edward. *Keeping the Faith.* 2000. Touchstone Pictures, 2 hr., 9 min.

Television

The Rehearsal. Season 1, episode 5, "Apocalypto," written by Nathan Fielder, Carrie Kemper, and Eric Notarnicola, directed by Nathan Fielder, aired August 12, 2022, Blow Out Productions, HBO, 29 min.

8. Israel/Zionism and Diaspora

Written Material

Boyarin, Daniel. *A Traveling Homeland: The Babylonian Talmud as Diaspora.* Philadelphia: University of Pennsylvania Press, 2015.

Rabinyan, Dorit. *All the Rivers.* New York: Random House, 2014.

Shapira, Anita. *Israel: A History.* Waltham MA: Brandeis University Press, 2012.

Waxman, Dov. *Trouble in the Tribe: The American Jewish Conflict over Israel.* Princeton NJ: Princeton University Press, 2016.

Yishai-Levi, Sarit. *The Beauty Queen of Jerusalem.* New York: St. Martin's Press, 2013. Also television show of the same name (2021–).

Music

Rotblit, Yaakov, and Yair Rosenblum. "Shir LaShalom/A Song for Peace." On *In the Nahal Settlements in the Sinai,* 1969.

9. Cultural Judaism

Written Material

Biale, David, ed. *Cultures of the Jews: A New History*. New York: Schocken Books, 2002.

Gross, Rachel. *Beyond the Synagogue: Jewish Nostalgia as Ritual Practice*. New York: New York University Press, 2021.

Kaplan, Mordecai. *Judaism as a Civilization*. Philadelphia: The Jewish Publication Society of America, 1934.

Solomon, Alisa. *Wonder of Wonders: A Cultural History of Fiddler on the Roof*. New York: Metropolitan Books, 2013.

Whitfield, Stephen J. *In Search of American Jewish Culture*. Hanover, NH: University Press of New England, 1999.

Television

Broadway Musicals: A Jewish Legacy. Written and directed by Michael Kantor, aired January 1, 2013, WNET, Albert M. Tapper Production, 90 min.

10. A Cultural Jewish Canon

Written Material

Bialik, H. N., and Y. Ravnitzky. *Sefer Ha-Aggadah/The Book of Legends*. Translated by W. Braude. New York: Schocken Books, 1911/1992.

Calderon, Ruth. *A Bride for One Night: Talmud Tales*. Philadelphia: The Jewish Publication Society, 2014.

Gitlitz, David M. *A Drizzle of Honey: The Lives and Recipes of Spain's Secret Jews*. New York: St. Martin's Press, 1999.

Kirsch, Adam. *The Blessing and the Curse: The Jewish People and Their Books in the Twentieth Century*. New York: W. W. Norton, 2020.

Nathan, Joan. *King Solomon's Table: A Culinary Exploration of Jewish Cooking from Around the World: A Cookbook*. New York: Alfred A. Knopf, 2017.

Richler, Mordecai. *The Apprenticeship of Duddy Kravitz*. Boston: Little, Brown, 1959. Also see the film adaptation, 1974.

Seidman, Naomi. *The Marriage Plot Or, How Jews Fell in Love with Love and with Literature*. Stanford CA: Stanford University Press, 2016.

Wisse, Ruth. *The Modern Jewish Canon: A Journey through Language and Culture*. Chicago: University of Chicago Press, 2000.

Film

Coen, Joel, and Ethan Coen. *A Serious Man*. 2009. Focus Features, 1 hr., 46 min.

11. Living Humanistic Judaism
Written Material

Humanistic Judaism magazine. Society for Humanistic Judaism, 2017–present. https://shj.org/meaning-learning/humanistic-judaism-magazine/magazine-archive/.

"Living Humanistic Judaism." Society for Humanistic Judaism, 2022. shj.org/living-humanistic-judaism/.

12. Liturgy
Written Material

Auslander, Shalom. "It Ain't Easy Bein' Supremey." In *Beware of God: Stories*. New York: Simon and Schuster, 2006.

Bloch, Chana, and Stephen Mitchell, eds. *Selected Poetry of Yehuda Amichai*. Berkeley CA: University of California Press, 1996.

Falk, Marcia. *The Days Between: Blessings, Poems, and Directions of the Heart for the Jewish High Holiday Season*. Waltham MA: Brandeis University Press, 2014.

Gales, Julie, and Pat Martz, eds. *Apples and Honey: Music and Readings for a Secular Humanistic Observance of the Jewish New Year Festival*. Southfield MI: Congress of Secular Jewish Organizations, 1995.

Yoreh, Tzemah. *The Skeptical Siddur*. Self-published by Tzemah Yoreh, 2022.

Music

Cohen, Leonard. "Who by Fire." On *New Skin for the Old Ceremony*, 1974.

Kol Hadash Humanistic Congregation. "Kol Hadash Music YouTube Playlist." https://www.youtube.com/@kolhadashhumanisticcongreg7534/playlists.

Yarrow, Peter. "Don't Let the Light Go Out." On *A Holiday Celebration*, 1988.

13. Life Cycle
Written Material

Didion, Joan. *The Year of Magical Thinking*. New York: Alfred A. Knopf, 2005.

Keshet. *Celebrating the Age of Mitzvah: A Guide for All Genders*. https://www.keshetonline.org/celebrating-the-age-of-mitzvah-a-guide-for-all-genders/.

Marcus, Ivan. *The Jewish Life Cycle: Rites of Passage from Biblical to Modern Times*. Seattle: University of Washington Press, 2004.

Rojstaczer, Stuart. *The Mathematician's Shiva*. New York: Penguin Books, 2014.

Willson, Jane Wynne. *Funerals without God: A Practical Guide to Non-Religious Funerals*. Amherst NY: Prometheus Books, 1989.

Art

Chagall, Marc. *Birth*. 1910. Art Institute Chicago. https://www.artic.edu/artworks/76258/birth.

Chagall, Marc. *The Cemetery Gates*. https://www.marcchagall.net/cemetery-gate.jsp.

Obican, Jovian. *Chuppah Wedding*. 1995. https://www.artnet.com/artists/jovan-obican/chuppah-wedding-bmZtqmRACuh2fojxivVqcQ2.

Oppenheim, Moritz. *The Bar Mitzvah Discourse*. 1869. The Jewish Museum (NYC). https://thejewishmuseum.org/collection/27128-the-bar-mitzvah-discourse-bar-mizwa-vortag.

Film

Cohen, Sammi. *You Are So Not Invited to My Bat Mitzvah*. 2023. Netflix Studios, 1 hr., 43 min.

Davis, Tamra. *13, The Musical*. 2022. Zadan/Meron Productions, Netflix, 94 min.

Levy, Shawn. *This Is Where I Leave You*. 2014. Warner Brothers, 1 hr., 43 min.

Seligman, Emma. *Shiva Baby*. 2021. Dimbo Pictures, 78 min.

Television

The Wonder Years (original). Season 2, episode 13, "Birthday Boy," directed by Steve Miner, written by David M. Stern, aired April 11, 1989, ABC, 23 min.

The Wonder Years (reboot). Season 1, episode 11, "Brad Mitzvah," directed by Fred Savage, written by Yael Galena, aired January 12, 2022, Disney+, 21 min.

14. Education

Written Material

Chalom, Adam. "The Challenge and Promise of Secular Jewish Education." *Humanistic Judaism*, Autumn 2011/Winter 2012.

Humanistic Judaism magazine. "Education for Humanistic Jews." Summer/Autumn 1994 (full issue).

Malkin, Yaakov. *Humanism and Nationality: Humanistic Education in Judaism as Culture*. New York: Center for Cultural Judaism, 2002.

McGowan, Dale, Molleen Matsumura, Amanda Metskas, and Jan Devor. *Raising Freethinkers: A Practical Guide for Parenting beyond Belief*. New York: AMACOM Books, 2009.

Video

Chalom, Adam. "Introduction to Secular Humanistic Judaism: Jewish History, Jewish Culture, Philosophy of Secular Humanistic Judaism." On International Institute for Secular Humanistic Judaism YouTube channel. www.youtube.com/@IISHJvid/playlists.

Source Acknowledgments

1.1 Sherwin Wine, "Jewish History—Our Humanist Perspective." *Humanistic Judaism* 13, no. 3 (Autumn 1985): 49–53. With permission of the Society for Humanistic Judaism.

2.1 Sherwin Wine, "Judaism without God," *Humanistic Judaism* 11, no. 4 (Winter 1983): 26–31. With permission of the Society for Humanistic Judaism.

2.2 Yaakov Malkin, "God as a Literary Figure," in Yaacov Malkin, *Judaism without God? Judaism as Culture and Bible as Literature* (Jerusalem: Library of Secular Judaism 2007), 216–20. With permission of Sivan Malkin Maas, daughter o/b/o estate.

3.1 Sherwin Wine, "Believing Is Better Than Non-Believing," *Humanistic Judaism* 13, no. 1 (Spring 1986): 7–11. With permission of the Society for Humanistic Judaism.

3.3 Peter Schweitzer, "Purpose," in *Contemplation: Humanistic Reflections by Members of The City Congregation*, edited by Carol Sternhell and Ernie Rubinstein (New York: The City Congregation of New York, 2021), 89–90. With permission of Peter Schweitzer.

4.1 Daniel Friedman, "After Halakha, What?," *Humanistic Judaism* 24, no. 1–2 (Winter/Spring 1996): 6–7. With permission of the Society for Humanistic Judaism.

4.2 Adam Chalom, "Are There Jewish Values?," *Humanistic Judaism* 37, no. 1–2 (Winter/Spring 2009): 10–13. With permission of the Society for Humanistic Judaism.

4.3 Amos Oz, "Jews Argue with God," from Amos Oz, "A Full Cart or an Empty One?," in *Secular Jewish Culture*, edited by Yaakov Malkin, 17–32 (Jerusalem: Library of Secular Judaism, 2017). With permission of Sivan Malkin Maas, daughter o/b/o estate.

4.4 Denise Handlarski, "Truth and Reconciliation on Race," *Humanistic Judaism* 45, no. 2 (2016): 38–39. With permission of the Society for Humanistic Judaism.

5.1 Yaakov Malkin, "What Makes the Secular Need Spirituality," in *Secular Spirituality: Passionate Journey to a Rational Judaism*, edited by Bonnie Cousens, 161–76 (Farmington Hills MI: International Institute for Secular Humanistic Judaism, 2003). With permission of the International Institute for Secular Humanistic Judaism.

5.2 Judith Seid, "A Secular Spirituality," in *God-Optional Judaism: Alternatives for Cultural Jews Who Love Their History, Heritage, & Community* (Farmington Hills MI: International Institute for Secular Humanistic Judaism, 2018), loc. 860–94, Kindle. With permission of the International Institute for Secular Humanistic Judaism.

5.3 Terry Toll, "Lighting Candles," *Humanistic Judaism* (Spring 1994): 24. With permission of the Society for Humanistic Judaism.

5.4 "Humanistic Judaism Facebook Discussion on Ritual Practice" (2020), from William Thompson et al., post to "Humanistic Judaism Discussion" Facebook group and comments, January 19, 2020. With permission of the commentators whose comments are included in the selection: Adam Chalom, Paul Golin, Courtney Harrison, Jeremy Kridel, Sivan Maas, Jen Naparstek Klein, Joshua Silberstein-Bamford, William Thompson.

6.1 Sherwin Wine, "Kinship," in *Judaism beyond God: A Radical New Way to Be Jewish* (Farmington Hills, MI: Society for Humanistic Judaism, 1985), 99–101. With permission of the International Institute for Secular Humanistic Judaism as the heir to the literary estate of Sherwin Wine.

6.2 International Federation of Secular Humanistic Jews, "Who Is a Jew?," October 1988, https://www.ifshj.net/1988-position-statements-full. With permission of the International Institute for Secular Humanistic Judaism, which runs ifshj.net as a successor organization to IFSHJ.

6.3 Association of Humanistic Rabbis, "Statement on Conversion/Adoption," June 2005, https://www.humanisticrabbis.org/conversion-adoption. With permission of the Association of Humanistic Rabbis.

6.4 Karen Levy, "Changing Perceptions, Changing Realities," *Humanistic Judaism* (Winter 2002): 14–16. With permission of the Society for Humanistic Judaism.

7.1 Tamara Kolton, "Healing the Jewish People through Pluralism," *Humanistic Judaism* 33, no.1 (Winter 2005): 40–41. With permission of the Society for Humanistic Judaism.

7.2 Jeffrey Falick, "Dancing at Two Weddings," *Humanistic Judaism* 42, no. 3–4

(Summer/Autumn 2014): 3–10. With permission of the Society for Humanistic Judaism.

7.3 Miriam Jerris, "Gate Openers: Reaching Out to the Next Generation of Children from Intermarriage," *Humanistic Judaism* 46, no. 1 (2017): 28–35. With permission of the Society for Humanistic Judaism.

7.4 Society for Humanistic Judaism, "Radical Inclusion," 2021, https://shj.org/living-humanistic-judaism/radical-inclusion/. With permission of the Society for Humanistic Judaism.

8.1 Sherwin Wine, "Being a Secular Humanistic Jew in the Diaspora," *Humanistic Judaism* (Spring 1993): 3–6. With permission of the Society for Humanistic Judaism.

8.2 Shulamit Aloni, "One Hundred Years of Zionism, Fifty Years of Statehood," *Humanistic Judaism* 28, no. 4 / 29, no. 1 (Winter/Spring 2000): 37–39. With permission of the Society for Humanistic Judaism.

8.3 Tzemah Yoreh, "Constructive Conversations about Israel," April 2019, https://youtu.be/BI0sEZ6rbGQ. With permission of Tzemah Yoreh.

9.3 Daniel Friedman, "Recovering Our Stories," *Humanistic Judaism* 23, no. 2 (Spring 1995): 12–13. With permission of the Society for Humanistic Judaism.

9.4 Sivan Malkin Maas, "Cultural Zionism: Reclaiming Convention," transcribed from presentation at the International Institute for Secular Humanistic Judaism's Colloquium 2009, "Challenging Convention: Secular and Humanist and Jew," presentation October 25, 2009, video published December 15, 2014, https://youtu.be/b2BT9V46eEs. With permission of the International Institute for Secular Humanistic Judaism.

10.1 Julian Levinson, "People of the (Secular) Book: Literary Anthologies and the Making of Jewish Identity in Postwar America," in *Religion or Ethnicity: Jewish Identities in Transition*, edited by Zvi Gitelman, (New Brunswick NJ: Rutgers University Press, 2009), 131–46. With permission of Rutgers University Press.

10.2 Jodi Kornfeld, "Of Course There's Jewish Art!" (2022), adapted for this volume from Jodi Kornfeld, "Jewish Art as Polemic," doctoral project, Spertus Institute for Jewish Learning and Leadership, 2015. With permission of the author.

10.3 Jonathan L. Friedmann, "Music by, for, as Humanistic Jews," written for this volume 2023 by Jonathan L. Friedmann, "Humanistic Jewish Music." With permission of the author.

11.2 Society for Humanistic Judaism, "Statement of Values," August 2021, https://shj.org/about-shj/mission-and-vision/. With permission of the Society for Humanistic Judaism.

12.2 Adam Chalom, "Our Quarterback, Our King: Two Problems with Liberal Theology," *Humanistic Judaism* 21, no. III—IV (Summer/Autumn 2007): 12–14. With permission of the Society for Humanistic Judaism.

12.3 Adam Chalom, Jodi Kornfeld, Jeremy Kridel, Peter Schweitzer, Frank Tamburello, "Liturgical Readings," in *Here Is Our Light*, edited by Miriam Jerris and Sheila Malcolm (Farmington Hills MI: Society for Humanistic Judaism 2019), 11–12, 30, 34, 40–41, 99, 117. With permission of the Society for Humanistic Judaism.

12.4 Yehuda Amichai, "A Man Doesn't Have Time" (1986). With permission of the Amichai Estate in cooperation with The Deborah Harris Agency.

12.5 Yehuda Amichai, "The Waters Cannot Return in Repentance" (1986). With permission of the Amichai Estate in cooperation with The Deborah Harris Agency.

12.6 Peter Schweitzer, "The Passover Symbols," in *The Liberated Haggadah: A Passover Celebration for Cultural, Secular and Humanistic Jews* (New York: Center for Cultural Judaism, 2003), 24–27. With permission of the author.

13.1 Leadership Conference of Secular and Humanistic Jews, "Circumcision and Jewish Identity," April 2002, https://iishj.org/lcshj/lcshj-resolutions/. With permission of the International Institute for Secular Humanistic Judaism as the sponsor organization of LCSHJ and host of the text.

13.2 Camila Grunberg, "Rosh Hashana 2016: The Meaning of Life," in *Contemplation: Humanistic Reflections by Members of The City Congregation*, edited by Carol Sternhell and Ernie Rubinstein (New York: The City Congregation for Humanistic Judaism, 2021), 98–101. With permission of the author.

13.3 Association of Humanistic Rabbis, "Wedding *Ketubah* Texts" (1999). With permission of the Association of Humanistic Rabbis.

13.4 Sherwin Wine, "Response," *Humanistic Judaism* (Summer 1992): 63–64. With permission of the Society for Humanistic Judaism.

14.2 Ruth Duskin Feldman, "Jewish Education and the Future," *Humanistic Judaism* 19, no. 1 (Winter 1991): 52–56. With permission of the Society for Humanistic Judaism.

14.3 Sherwin Wine, "The Torah," in *Judaism beyond God: A Radical New Way to Be Jewish*, 199–203. (Farmington Hills MI: Society for Humanistic Judaism, 1985). With permission of the International Institute for Secular Humanistic Judaism as the heir to the literary estate of Sherwin Wine.

14.4 Denise Handlarski, "The Torah, the Ten Commandments and Us," March 5, 2019, https://www.denisehandlarski.com/blog/2019/3/5/the-torah-the-ten-commandments-and-us. With permission of the author.

14.5 Society for Humanistic Judaism, "Philosophy," in *SHJ Recommended Topical Curriculum for Children's Education Programs* (Farmington Hills MI: 2013), 3. With permission of the Society for Humanistic Judaism.
15.1 International Federation of Secular Humanistic Jews, "Choosing to Live as a Secular Humanistic Jew," 2000. https://www.ifshj.net/statement-of-principles. With permission of the International Institute for Secular Humanistic Judaism as the sponsor organization of IFSHJ and host of the text.

Appendix

American Jews' Identity and Beliefs

The majority of American Jews view Jewish identity as cultural. When the Pew Research Center asked a random sample of American Jews to complete the sentence, "To you personally, is being Jewish mainly a matter of..." with "religion," "ancestry," "culture," or "some combination" as options, 53 percent of the "Jewish Americans in 2020" survey participants said "ancestry," "culture," or "ancestry and culture"—not "religion," and not even "religion" in combination with "ancestry" or "culture."

American Jews with non-Jewish spouses (68 percent) and those who do not identify with a particular branch of Judaism (79 percent) are even more likely to identify non-religiously than the general Jewish population. Even among religiously identified Jews, a plurality (43 percent) believe that Jewish identity is based on "ancestry," "culture," or "ancestry and culture" and not "religion" alone or in combination. The cultural and "kinship" Jewish identity of Humanistic Judaism (see part 2) reflects these results.

TABLE 1. Jewish identity

	Ancestry	Culture	Ancestry and culture	Religion and ancestry and/or culture	Religion	Other/no answer
Net Jewish	21	22	10	25	11	10 = 100
Jews by religion	14	21	8	29	14	11
Jews of no religion	41	25	15	11	3	5
Orthodox	16	4	3	29	40	9
Reform	14	27	9	29	10	12
No particular branch	37	25	17	12	4	6
Married, Jewish spouse	14	18	8	33	15	12
Married, not Jewish spouse	26	26	16	18	7	6

Source: Pew Research Center, "Jewish Americans in 2020," May 11, 2021, https://www.pewresearch.org/religion/wp-content/uploads/sites/7/2021/04/PF_05.11.21.Jewish_Survey_Topline.pdf.

The Pew study also demonstrates Jewish secularization in theological belief. Respondents were first asked, "Do you believe in God or not?" and then asked to clarify if the God they did or did not believe in was "God as described in the Bible" or "some other higher power or spiritual force in the universe." The vast majority of American Jews (about 72 percent) did *not* express belief in the God of the Bible, differing greatly from the belief patterns of most American adults, the majority of whom (56 percent) *do* believe in such a God. Indeed, Reform Jews' beliefs corresponded closely to those of American adults with no religious affiliation, while an extremely small share of Jews of no religion (7 percent) expressed belief in the God of the Bible—and nearly half (44 percent) do not believe in any spiritual power at all. As with Jewish identity, Humanistic Judaism's nontheistic philosophy reflects the beliefs of a substantial proportion of American Jews.

TABLE 2. Belief in God

	Believe in God of the Bible	Believe in other higher power / spiritual force	Don't believe in either	Unclear
Net Jewish	26	50	22	2 = 100
Jews by religion	33	51	14	3
Jews of no religion	7	48	44	1
Orthodox	93	6	1	<1
Reform	18	59	21	2
No particular branch	12	52	35	1
U.S. adults	56	33	10	<1
Christian	80	18	1	<1
Unaffiliated	18	54	27	1

Source: Pew Research Center, "Jewish Americans in 2020," May 11, 2021, https://www.pewresearch.org/religion/wp-content/uploads/sites/7/2021/04/PF_05.11.21.Jewish_Survey_Topline.pdf.

Readers of this volume might consider how they would answer these survey questions and what implications those answers might have for their Jewish identities and expressions.

Notes

Introduction

1. Reflecting this view that there is no God in the sense of a divine force (or being or spirit), but that the biblical deity is a character within the TANAKH, Humanistic Jews often use the term "god" (in lowercase letters) instead of "God." Accordingly, in this volume the editors use "god" when discussing Humanistic Jewish views on this concept and "God" when invoking views in traditional Jewish sources or other contemporary denominations (including Conservative, Orthodox, Reconstructionist, and Reform forms of Judaism).
2. The framing of Jewish identity as "belonging, behaving, and believing" is conventionally attributed to rabbi Mordecai Kaplan, the founding thinker of Reconstructionist (now Reconstructing) Judaism.
3. Pew Research Center, "Jewish Americans in 2020," May 11, 2021, https://www.pewforum.org/2021/05/11/jewish-americans-in-2020/. The Pew researchers had asked a random sample of American Jews, "What is your present religion, if any?" Those who said "Jewish" were counted as "Jewish by religion." Those who said they were not religious were then asked, "Aside from religion, do you consider yourself to be Jewish in any way (for example ethnically, culturally or because of your family's background)?" Pew then identified 27 percent of American Jews—and 40 percent of those aged eighteen to twenty-nine—as "Jews of no religion."
4. Pew Research Center, "Jewish Americans in 2020."
5. Pew Research Center, "Israel's Religiously Divided Society," March 8, 2016, https://www.pewforum.org/2016/03/08/religious-commitment/.
6. Pew Research Center, "Jewish Americans in 2020."
7. Michael Lipka, "A Closer Look at America's Rapidly Growing Religious 'Nones,'" Pew Research Center, May 13, 2015, https://www.pewresearch.org

/fact-tank/2015/05/13/a-closer-look-at-americas-rapidly-growing-religious-nones/.

8. As one example, see Noah Berlatsky, "Yom Kippur 2019," NBC News, October 9, 2019, https://www.nbcnews.com/think/opinion/yom-kippur-2019-best-thing-about-judaism-according-jewish-atheist-ncna1063986.

9. Figures cited in Fishman, "Yiddish Schools," 72, are based on surveys by the Workmen's Circle and the Jewish Education Association of New York City. These schools and associated summer camps are discussed in depth in Friedenreich, *Passionate Pioneers*.

10. April Rosenblum, "Offers We Couldn't Refuse: What Happened to Secular Jewish Identity?," *Jewish Currents* 63, no. 3 (May–June 2009): 11–12.

11. Mendes-Flohr and Reinharz, "The Beginnings of Secular Yiddish Schools (1918–1920)," in *Jew in the Modern World*, 503–4.

12. Will Herberg's 1955 study *Protestant, Catholic, Jew: An Essay in American Religious Sociology* placed Jewish identity in the same category as Christianity, rather than comparing Jewishness to being Italian or Irish.

13. See, for example, Secular Synagogue, "Welcome to Secular Synagogue," www.secularsynagogue.com; or the Spinoza Havurah, Spiritual Humanistic Judaism, https://spinozahavurah.wordpress.com/.

14. Over the decades, many organizations have changed their names. The Birmingham Temple (founded in Birmingham MI, but currently located in Farmington Hills MI) is now Congregation for Humanistic Judaism of Metro Detroit. The Conference on Secular Jewish Education became the Congress of Secular Jewish Organizations and is today the Cultural and Secular Jewish Organization. Additionally, for a time the International Federation of Secular Humanistic Jews operated as the International Federation for Secular and Humanistic Judaism. This book uses the organizational names contemporary to the events being described.

15. Goren, "Birthing of Humanistic Judaism," 174–75.

16. Goren "Birthing of Humanistic Judaism," 175.

17. Ritual Committee of The Birmingham Temple, *Sabbath Services in the spirit of a humanistic Judaism* (Birmingham MI: The Birmingham Temple, n.d.), 7.

18. Ritual Committee of The Birmingham Temple, *Sabbath Services*, 3.

19. Ritual Committee of The Birmingham Temple, *Holiday Services in the spirit of a humanistic Judaism* (Birmingham MI: The Birmingham Temple, n.d.), 3.

20. Wine, "Birmingham Temple's First Quarter Century," 8.

21. Secular Jewish creativity is not unique to Humanistic Judaism. Secular Israelis have also significantly revised traditional Jewish holiday and life-cycle

celebrations. See, for example, the Chagim Center, "Festivals and Ceremonies Map," https://www.eng.chagim.org.il/ (based on the archives at Kibbutz Beit Ha-Shita); and Lilker, *Kibbutz Judaism*. Likewise, Reconstructing Judaism, the *havurah* movement, and Jewish feminism all celebrate ritual and liturgical creativity to reflect new nontraditional, yet Jewish values. As feminist liturgist Marcia Falk explains in her innovative *The Book of Blessings: New Jewish Prayers for Daily Life, the Sabbath and the New Moon Festival* (263), "The rabbis said, 'Turn it, turn it, for all is contained in it.' We turn and we turn—but *not* all is in it. We find we have more to add. We cannot read all our truths into a place where they have never been. So we invent and inscribe, and we ask: 'Can new texts, too, become sacred? Can our own voices become Torah?'"

22. Wine, "Birmingham Temple's First Quarter Century," 8.
23. "Judaism: The Atheist Rabbi," *Time*, January 29, 1965, https://content.time.com/time/subscriber/article/0,33009,839200,00.html.
24. For more on the architectural ideology of The Birmingham Temple, see Adam Chalom, "To Have and to Hold: Torah Scrolls in Humanistic Judaism," *Humanistic Judaism* magazine, Summer 2022, 10–11.
25. Other online options for Humanistic Jews include Secular Synagogue, "Welcome to Secular Synagogue," www.secularsynagogue.com (founded by IISHJ-ordained Rabbi Denise Handlarski); the Spinoza Havurah: Spiritual Humanistic Judaism, https://spinozahavurah.org; and Our Jewish Community, an online initiative of the unaffiliated Humanistic Congregation Beth Adam in Cincinnati, https://www.ourjewishcommunity.org/.
26. Wine, "Jewish History—Our Humanistic Perspective," 53.
27. John Keats, "Lamia" (1820), https://www.bartleby.com/126/37.html.
28. A total of 439 temple members responded to the survey conducted by APB Associates in Southfield MI. This question asked: "In what denomination were you raised? Conservative, Humanistic or secular, Orthodox, Reform, 'Just Jewish' (no denomination), other Jewish (SPECIFY), non-Jewish."
29. However, some Israeli-Americans are not convinced that Jews should change traditional Jewish texts and practices ("The synagogue I don't go to is Orthodox"). Israelis also tend to want more Hebrew language than Humanistic Jewish congregations provide, another major reason why they are not represented in the movement in greater numbers.
30. This usage of "rooted cosmopolitan" is similar but not identical to its usage in Appiah's *The Ethics of Identity*. Its relationship to Humanistic Judaism is

explored in Chalom, "Why Be Anything?" See also Jonathan Freedman, "'The Ethics of Identity': A Rooted Cosmopolitan," *New York Times*, June 12, 2005.
31. *Mishnah Pirkei Avot (Ethics of the Fathers)* 5:26.
32. Wine, "Reflections," 310.

Part 1. Introduction
1. Wine, "What Could Be More Humanistic," 9.

1. The Jewish Experience
1. Wine, "Jewish History—Our Humanistic Perspective," 53.

2. The God Question
1. Pew Research Center, "Jewish Americans in 2020: Jewish Identity and Belief," May 11, 2021, https://www.pewresearch.org/religion/2021/05/11/jewish-identity-and-belief/.
2. Teutsch, *Kol Haneshamah*, "Lighting Shabbat Candles," 4; Frishman, *Mishkan T'filah*, "Morning Blessings," 24.
3. See Kaplan, *Meaning of God*; Kushner, *When Bad Things*; Plaskow, *Standing Again at Sinai*; Central Conference of American Rabbis, "A Statement of Principles for Reform Judaism," May 1999, https://www.ccarnet.org/rabbinic-voice/platforms/article-statement-principles-reform-judaism/.
4. "Judaism, The Atheist Rabbi," *Time*, January 29, 1965, https://content.time.com/time/subscriber/article/0,33009,839200,00.html.
5. Wine, "Judaism without God," 26–31.
6. Malkin, *Judaism without God?*, 216–20.

3. Positive Humanism
1. For the talmudic narratives concerning Elisha ben Abuya/*Acher*, see the collected sources in Bialik and Ravnitzky, *Sefer ha-Aggadah/The Book of Legends*. For Saadiya Gaon's medieval refutations of Hiwi al-Balkhi's challenges to biblical claims, see Kaufmann Kohler and Max Schloessinger, "Hiwi al-Balkhi," *Jewish Encyclopedia*, https://www.jewishencyclopedia.com/articles/7777-hiwi-al-balkhi. For early modern examples Uriel da Costa and Baruch Spinoza, see Bodian, "Crypto-Jewish Criticism," 38; and Nadler, "Spinoza," 59.
2. For the complete text and list of signatories with affiliations, see the 1933 Humanist Manifesto, https://en.wikipedia.org/wiki/Humanist_Manifesto_I.
3. American Ethical Union, "Mission and Values," https://aeu.org/who-we-are/mission-vision/.

4. The founding date of Humanistic Judaism is open to interpretation. The founding congregation The Birmingham Temple in suburban Detroit was started in November 1963, but as a Reform congregation. It evolved into a Humanistic congregation in its practice by mid-1964. The national Society for Humanistic Judaism was founded in 1969. Conventionally the movement has claimed 1963 as a starting date.
5. Wine, "Believing Is Better Than Non-Believing," 7–11.
6. Hobbes, *Leviathan*, 97.
7. Epstein, *Good without God*, loc. 114–147.
8. For more on Schweitzer's personal theological journey, see Schweitzer, "Rabbi's Journey," 2–3.
9. Shakespeare, *Macbeth*, act V, scene 5.
10. Jason Mraz, "What Would Love Do Now," https://www.youtube.com/watch?v=lIP5RzH-8Ns, April 20, 2011.
11. Schweitzer, "Purpose," 89.

4. Ethics

1. Pew Research Center, "Worldwide, Many See Belief in God as Essential to Morality," March 13, 2014, https://www.pewresearch.org/global/2014/03/13/worldwide-many-see-belief-in-god-as-essential-to-morality/.
2. See Lydia Saad, "Socialism and Atheism Still US Political Liabilities," *Gallup*, February 11, 2020, https://news.gallup.com/poll/285563/socialism-atheism-political-liabilities.aspx.
3. Friedman, "After Halakha," 6–7.
4. Wine, "Yom Kippur—Peoplehood" (unpublished High Holiday service), 10.
5. *Mishnah Sanhedrin* 8:1ff.
6. Wine, *Humanistic Judaism*, 57.
7. Luke 6:31 or Matt. 7:12, slightly variant.
8. Babylonian Talmud, *Shabbat* 31a.
9. Tsu, *Tao Te Ching*, 15.
10. Lao-Tse [Lao Zi], *The Analects Attributed to Confucius [Kongfuzi]*, 551–479 BCE, trans. James Legge (1815–97), https://china.usc.edu/confucius-analects-15.
11. Kant, *Grounding for the Metaphysics of Morals*, 30.
12. Wine, "Yom Kippur," 10.
13. Chalom, "Are There 'Jewish Values'?," 10–13.
14. For a survey of the phenomenon, see Laytner, *Arguing with God*. For examples specifically from talmudic and later rabbinic literature, see Weiss, *Pious Irreverence*.

15. Hayim Nachman Bialik (1873–1943), Berl Katznelson (1887–1944), A. D. Gordon (1856–1922), and Yosef Haim Brenner (1881–1921) were all early creators and defenders of the secular Jewish culture of the early Zionist movement: Bialik through poetry, Brenner through essays and fiction, Katznelson and Gordon through Labor Zionist ideology.
16. Oz, "Full Cart," 17–19, 32.
17. See, for example, Shlain, 24/6; or Ruttenberg, *On Repentance and Repair*.
18. Handlarski, "Truth and Reconciliation on Race," 38–39.

5. Spirituality

1. Comte-Spoonville, *Little Book of Atheist Spirituality*, 1593.
2. Keats, "Lamia" (1820), https://www.bartleby.com/126/37.html.
3. Malkin, "What Makes the Secular Need Spirituality," 161–62, 167–68, 170–72, 175.
4. Seid, *God-Optional Judaism*, loc. 860–894.
5. Toll, "Lighting Candles," 24.
6. Society for Humanistic Judaism, *Guide to Humanistic Judaism*, 75–76.
7. William Thompson et al., post to "Humanistic Judaism Discussion" Facebook group and comments, January 19, 2020. Changes have been made to ensure editorial consistency.

6. Jewish Self-Definition

1. Central Conference of American Rabbis, "Declaration of Principles: 1885 Pittsburgh Conference," https://www.ccarnet.org/rabbinic-voice/platforms/article-declaration-principles/.
2. Herzl, *The Jewish State*, 76.
3. Wine, *Judaism beyond God*, 99.
4. Wine, *Judaism beyond God*, 99–101.
5. International Federation of Secular Humanistic Jews, "Who Is a Jew?," October 1988, https://www.ifshj.net/1988-position-statements-full.
6. The last sentence of the certificate shown here is excerpted from Ruth 1:16, as the certificate itself explains.
7. Association of Humanistic Rabbis, "Statement on Conversion/Adoption," June 2005, https://www.humanisticrabbis.org/conversion-adoption.
8. Levy, "Changing Perceptions," 14.
9. Levy, "Changing Perceptions," 14–16.

7. Welcoming and Inclusion

1. Kolton, "Healing the Jewish People," 40–41.

2. Falick, "Dancing at Two Weddings," 3, 9–10.
3. "In 1909, and again in 1947 and in 1973, the Central Conference of American Rabbis declared its opposition to the performance of mixed marriages by its members. Mindful of these prior resolutions, we now call special attention to the most flagrant form of mixed marriages—co-officiating with non-Jewish clergy—and publicly repudiate that practice." Central Conference of American Rabbis, "Ecumenical Wedding Ceremonies: Co-Officiation with Clergy of Other Faiths," June/July 1982, https://www.ccarnet.org/ccar-resolutions/ecumenical-wedding-ceremonies-co-officiation-with-clergy-of-other-faiths-1982/.
4. Cheryl Jacobs, "The Heirs of Intermarriage," *Oy!Chicago*, May 22, 2012, http://www.oychicago.com/article.aspx?id=21252&blogid=132.
5. Jerris, "Gate-Openers," 28–29.
6. Society for Humanistic Judaism, "Radical Inclusion," 2021, https://shj.org/living-humanistic-judaism/radical-inclusion/.

8. Israel/Zionism and Diaspora

1. Pew Research Center, "Jewish Americans in 2020: U.S. Jews' Connections with and Attitudes toward Israel," May 11, 2021, https://www.pewresearch.org/religion/2021/05/11/u-s-jews-connections-with-and-attitudes-toward-israel/.
2. "Israeli culture" is not synonymous with "Israeli Jewish culture," since a substantial proportion of the Israeli population is Arab, Druze, or something else.
3. For more on the indeterminacy of "diaspora" and "homeland" in the twenty-first century, see Aviv and Shneer, *New Jews*.
4. Wine, "Being a Secular Humanistic Jew in the Diaspora," 3–6.
5. Mendes-Flohr and Reinharz, *Jew in the Modern World*, 420.
6. Aloni, "One Hundred Years of Zionism," 37–39.
7. Society for Humanistic Judaism, "SHJ Stands with Israel," July 21, 2014, https://shj.org/organize/social-justice-issues-and-resolutions/shj-stands-with-israel/.
8. Tzemah Yoreh, "Constructive Conversations on Israel," Society for Humanistic Judaism, April 2019, https://youtu.be/BI0sEZ6rbGQ.

Part 3. Introduction

1. Pew Research Center, "Jewish Americans in 2020: Jewish Identity and Belief," May 11, 2021, https://www.pewresearch.org/religion/2021/05/11/jewish-identity-and-belief/.

2. Taio Cruz, "Dynamite," https://www.youtube.com/watch?v=VUjdiDeJ0xg; the Maccabeats, "Candlelight," https://www.youtube.com/watch?v=qSJCSR4MuhU. The Maccabeats' video was based on an earlier a capella adaptation of the Cruz song by Mike Thompson, https://www.youtube.com/watch?v=qjCLQaTFXx0.

9. Cultural Judaism

1. Oz, *Dear Zealots*, 92–93.
2. Oz, *In the Land of Israel*, 135–138.
3. Bauer, introduction to *Judaism in a Secular Age*, xiv.
4. Andrew Greeley, "Why Do Catholics Stay in the Church? Because of the Stories," *New York Times Magazine*, July 10, 1994.
5. Friedman, "Recovering Our Stories," 12–13.
6. Lovers of Zion, a nineteenth-century Zionist organization.
7. Transcribed from Sivan Malkin Maas's "Cultural Zionism: Reclaiming Convention" presentation delivered on October 25, 2009 at the International Institute for Secular Humanistic Judaism's "Colloquium 2009." Video published December 15, 2014: https://youtu.be/b2BT9V46eEs.

10. A Cultural Jewish Canon

1. See Yerushalmi, *Zakhor*.
2. Seidman, *Marriage Plot*, 263 n. 22.
3. Levinson, "People of the (Secular) Book," 131–34, 145.
4. "Jacques Lipchitz," *World Over* 34, no. 1 (October 6, 1972): 2.
5. Rosen, "Imagining Jewish Art," 8.
6. Adapted by Kornfeld from Kornfeld, "Jewish Art as Polemic," 9–16, 52–60, 68–69, 80–97.
7. Longfellow, *Prose Work of Henry Wadsworth Longfellow*, 4.
8. Idelsohn, *Jewish Music in Its Historical Development*, 24.
9. Englander, *What We Talk About When We Talk About Anne Frank*, 4–5, 21–22.
10. Keret, *Seven Good Years*, 80, 82–85.
11. Krauss, *Forest Dark*, 74–76, 84–85.

11. Living Humanistic Judaism

1. The emphases are rendered in bold in the original text.
2. Goldfinger, *Basic Ideas of Secular Humanistic Judaism*, 58–59.
3. Society for Humanistic Judaism, Mission and Vision, "Values," August 2021, https://shj.org/about-shj/mission-and-vision/.

12. Liturgy

1. Jerris and Malcolm, *Here Is Our Light*, 9.
2. "[Mordecai] Kaplan believed the traditional image of the Jews as God's chosen people was theologically untenable and morally undesirable. The siddur must therefore be divested of all references to Jewish chosenness" (Caplan, *From Ideology to Liturgy*, 64).
3. Teutsch, *Kol Haneshamah*, 90.
4. Falk, *Book of Blessings*, 261–63.
5. Deut. 26:8: "And YHVH brought us out of Egypt with a mighty hand, and with an outstretched arm, and with great awesomeness, and with signs, and with wonders."
6. Lev. 26:3–12: "If you walk in my statutes, and keep my commandments, and do them . . . I will give peace in the land, and you shall lie down, and none shall make you afraid; and I will remove evil beasts from the land, nor shall the sword go through your land. And you shall chase your enemies, and they shall fall before you by the sword. . . . For I will turn myself to you, and make you fruitful, and multiply you, and establish my covenant with you. . . . And I will walk among you, and will be your God, and you shall be my people."
7. Lev. 26:15–17: "And if you shall despise my statutes, . . . so that you will not do all my commandments, but that you break my covenant; I also will do this to you; I will appoint over you terror, consumption, and fever, that shall consume the eyes, and cause sorrow of heart; and you shall sow your seed in vain, for your enemies shall eat it. And I will set my face against you, and you shall be slain before your enemies; they who hate you shall reign over you; and you shall flee when none pursues you."
8. The punishment of being "cut off" (*karet*) from the people of Israel for breaking specific ritual commandments appears at least thirteen times in the book of Leviticus alone.
9. Judg. 10:6–7: "And the people of Israel did evil again in the sight of YHVH, . . . and forsook YHVH, and did not serve him. And the anger of YHVH was kindled against Israel, and he sold them into the hands of the Philistines, and into the hands of the sons of Ammon."
10. Exod. 15:6–7.
11. Central Conference of American Rabbis, "Commentary on the Principles for Reform Judaism," October 27, 2004, https://www.ccarnet.org/rabbinic-voice/platforms/article-commentary-principles-reform-judaism/.

12. Union for Reform Judaism, "Daily Blessings: Birkat HaMazon (Grace after Meals)—Long Version," https://reformjudaism.org/beliefs-practices/prayers-blessings/daily-blessings-birkat-hamazon-grace-after-meals-long-version. Note that the Hebrew text that appears on that website maintains the traditional *melekh* (king) language, which has been "softened" in translation to "sovereign."
13. Well-known from Handel's *Messiah*, originally in the New Testament, Rev. 19:16.
14. Aleph—Alliance for Jewish Renewal, "Four Worlds Judaism," https://aleph.org/four-worlds-judaism/.
15. Abraham Lincoln's "Gettysburg Address."
16. Chalom, "Our Quarterback, Our King," 12–14.
17. Babylonian Talmud, *Bava Metzi'a* 49a.
18. Jerris and Malcolm, *Here Is Our Light*, 11–12.
19. Chalom, "Rosh Hashanah Morning Reading," 30.
20. Kridel, "A Tashlikh Meditation," 34.
21. Tamburello, "A Humanist Al Chet," 40–41.
22. Kornfeld, "Readings before Torah," 99.
23. Schweitzer, "Modern Kaddish / Glory of Life," 117.
24. Maron L. Waxman, "A Passover Haggadah: Go Forth and Learn," September 13, 2011, https://www.jewishbookcouncil.org/book/a-passover-haggadah-go-forth-and-learn.
25. The offering of multiple meanings for the same symbol is a reflection of both the Rabbinic *davar acher* (another interpretation) and postmodern reading. See Stern, *Midrash and Theory*.
26. Schweitzer, "Symbols," 24–27.

13. Life Cycle

1. The Leadership Conference of Secular and Humanistic Jews formed in 1982 to facilitate communication and cooperation among leaders in Secular and Humanistic Jewish organizations.
2. Leadership Conference of Secular and Humanistic Jews, "Circumcision," April 2002, https://iishj.org/lcshj/lcshj-resolutions/.
3. "What My Bar Mitzvah or Bat Mitzvah Means to Me," https://humanisticbarandbatmitzvahs.wordpress.com/students-comment-on-the-experience/.
4. Grunberg, "Meaning of Life," 98–101.

5. "Secular Humanist 1" and "Secular Humanist 2," https://ketubah.com/shop/products/ketubah-text/secular-humanist/.
6. For example, instead of praising *"sh'mei raba*—the great name" (i.e., God), a Humanistic *Kaddish* may praise "peace in the world—*shlama b'alma*" or speak about the importance of comforting mourners. Some Humanistic *Kaddish* texts are largely in English (see chapter 12, "Liturgy"), while others are in two languages, as is "A Humanistic Kaddish" written by Sherwin Wine in the late 1990s, https://sherwinwine.com/a-humanistic-kaddish/.
7. While the movement's journal *Humanistic Judaism* published articles titled "Responsa" in the 1980s and 1990s, these are generally very different from conventional rabbinic *responsa* (answers to questions of Jewish law) in other Jewish movements. When answering questions of Jewish practice, the Humanistic texts do not thoroughly review what biblical, rabbinic, medieval, and/or modern Jewish sources have to say on the subject; instead, they summarize the traditional perspective and then describe a Humanistic approach.
8. Wine, "Response," 63–64.

14. Education

1. Silver, *Respecting the Wicked Child*, 13–14, 23–24, 171–72.
2. Feldman, "Jewish Education," 52–56.
3. Wine, *Judaism beyond God*, 199–203.
4. Denise Handlarski, "The Torah, the Ten Commandments and Us," March 5, 2019, https://www.denisehandlarski.com/blog/2019/3/5/the-torah-the-ten-commandments-and-us.
5. Society for Humanistic Judaism, "Philosophy," in SHJ *Recommended Topical Curriculum*, 3.

Afterword

1. International Federation for Secular and Humanistic Judaism, "Choosing to Live as a Secular Humanist Jew," Eighth Biennial Conference, New York, 2000, https://www.ifshj.net/2000-position-statements-full.

Go Forth and Learn

1. Babylonian Talmud, *Shabbat* 31a.

Bibliography

Aloni, Shulamit. "One Hundred Years of Zionism, Fifty Years of Statehood." *Humanistic Judaism* 28, no. 4 / 29, no. 1 (Winter/Spring 2000 double issue): 37–39.

Appiah, Kwame Anthony. *The Ethics of Identity*. Princeton NJ: Princeton University Press, 2005.

Aviv, Caryn, and David Shneer. *New Jews: The End of Diaspora*. New York: New York University Press, 2005.

Bauer, Yehuda. Introduction to *Judaism in a Secular Age: An Anthology of Secular Humanistic Jewish Thought*, edited by Renee Kogel and Zev Katz, xiv. Farmington Hills MI: International Institute for Secular Humanistic Judaism, 1995.

Bialik, H. N., and Y. Ravnitzky. *Sefer ha-Aggadah/The Book of Legends*. Translated by W. Braude. New York: Schocken Books, 1992.

Bodian, Miriam. "Crypto-Jewish Criticism of Tradition and Its Echoes in Jewish Communities." In *Religion or Ethnicity: Jewish Identities in Transition*, edited by Zvi Gitelman, 38–58. New Brunswick NJ: Rutgers University Press, 2009.

Caplan, Eric. *From Ideology to Liturgy, Reconstructionist Worship and American Liberal Judaism*. Cincinnati: Hebrew Union College Press, 2002.

Chalom, Adam. "Are There 'Jewish Values'?" *Humanistic Judaism* 37, no. 1–2 (Winter/Spring, 2009): 10–13.

———. "Our Quarterback, Our King: Two Problems with Liberal Theology." *Humanistic Judaism* 21, no. 3–4 (Summer/Autumn 2007): 12–14.

———. "Rosh Hashanah Morning Reading." In *Here Is Our Light: Humanistic Jewish Holiday and Life-Cycle Liturgy for Inspiration and Reflection*, edited by Miriam Jerris and Sheila Malcolm, 30. Teaneck NJ: Ben Yehuda Press, 2019.

———. "Why Be Anything? And Why Be Jewish?" *Humanistic Judaism* 46, no. 1 (2017): 3–10.

Comte-Spoonville, André. *The Little Book of Atheist Spirituality*. New York: Viking, 2007.

Englander, Nathan. *What We Talk About When We Talk About Anne Frank*. New York: Alfred A. Knopf, 2012.

Epstein, Greg. *Good without God: What a Billion Nonreligious People Do Believe*. New York: HarperCollins E-Books, 2009.

Falick, Jeffrey. "Dancing at Two Weddings." *Humanistic Judaism* 42, no. 3–4 (Summer/Autumn 2014): 3–10.

Falk, Marcia. *The Book of Blessings: New Jewish Prayers for Daily Life, the Sabbath, and the New Moon Festival*. Boston: Beacon Press, 1996.

Feldman, Ruth Duskin. "Jewish Education and the Future." *Humanistic Judaism* 19, no. 1 (Winter 1991): 52–56.

Fishman, Michael. "Yiddish Schools in America and the Problem of Secular Jewish Identity." In *Religion or Ethnicity: Jewish Identity in Evolution*, edited by Zvi Gitelman, 69–89. New Brunswick NJ: Rutgers University Press, 2009.

Friedenreich, Fradle Pomerantz. *Passionate Pioneers: The Story of Yiddish Secular Education in North America*. Teaneck NJ: Holmes & Meier, 2010.

Friedman, Daniel. "After Halakha, What?" *Humanistic Judaism* 24, no. 1–2 (Winter-Spring 1996): 6–7.

———. "Recovering Our Stories." *Humanistic Judaism* 23, no. 2 (Spring 1995): 12–13.

Frishman, Elyse, ed. *Mishkan T'filah: A Reform Siddur*. New York: Central Conference of American Rabbis, 2007.

Goldfinger, Eva. *Basic Ideas of Secular Humanistic Judaism*. Farmington Hills MI: International Institute for Secular Humanistic Judaism, 1995.

Goren, Judith. "The Birthing of Humanistic Judaism." In *A Life of Courage: Sherwin Wine and Humanistic Judaism*, edited by Dan Cohn-Sherbok, Harry Cook, and Marilyn Rowens, 174–75. Farmington Hills MI: International Institute for Secular Humanistic Judaism, 2003.

Grunberg, Camila. "Rosh Hashana 2016: The Meaning of Life." In *Contemplation: Humanistic Reflections by Members of The City Congregation*, edited by Carol Sternhell and Ernie Rubinstein, 98. New York: The City Congregation for Humanistic Judaism, 2021.

Handlarski, Denise. "Truth and Reconciliation on Race." *Humanistic Judaism* 45, no. 2 (2016): 38–39.

Herberg, Will. *Protestant, Catholic, Jew: An Essay in American Religious Sociology*. Garden City NY: Doubleday, 1955.

Herzl, Theodor. *The Jewish State*. New York: Dover Publications, 1988.

Hobbes, Thomas. *Leviathan*. Oxford: Oxford University Press, 1909.

Idelsohn, Abraham Z. *Jewish Music in Its Historical Development.* New York: Henry Holt, 1929.

Jerris, Miriam. "Gate Openers: Reaching Out to the Next Generation of Children from Intermarriage." *Humanistic Judaism* 46, no. 1 (2017): 28–35.

Jerris, Miriam, and Sheila Malcolm, eds. *Here Is Our Light: Humanistic Jewish Holiday and Life-Cycle Liturgy for Inspiration and Reflection.* Teaneck NJ: Ben Yehuda Press, 2019.

JPS TANAKH. Philadelphia: The Jewish Publication Society, 1985.

Kant, Immanuel. *Grounding for the Metaphysics of Morals.* Translated by James Ellington. Indianapolis: Hackett, 1981.

Kaplan, Mordecai. *Judaism as a Civilization.* New York: Macmillan, 1934.

———. *The Meaning of God in Modern Jewish Religion.* Detroit: Wayne State University Press, 1995.

Keret, Etgar. *The Seven Good Years: A Memoir.* New York: Riverhead Books, 2016.

Kolton, Tamara, "Healing the Jewish People through Pluralism." *Humanistic Judaism* 33, no. 1 (Winter 2005): 40–41.

Kornfeld, Jodi. "Jewish Art as Polemic." Doctoral project, Spertus Institute for Jewish Learning and Leadership, 2015 (updated for this volume).

———. "Readings before Torah (Version 1)." In *Here Is Our Light: Humanistic Jewish Holiday and Life-Cycle Liturgy for Inspiration and Reflection,* edited by Miriam Jerris and Sheila Malcolm, 99. Teaneck NJ: Ben Yehuda Press, 2019.

Krauss, Nicole. *Forest Dark.* New York: HarperCollins, 2017.

Kridel, Jeremy. "A Tashlikh Meditation." In *Here Is Our Light: Humanistic Jewish Holiday and Life-Cycle Liturgy for Inspiration and Reflection,* edited by Miriam Jerris and Sheila Malcolm, 34. Teaneck NJ: Ben Yehuda Press, 2019.

Kushner, Harold. *When Bad Things Happen to Good People.* New York: Schocken Books, 1981.

Laytner, Anson. *Arguing with God: A Jewish Tradition.* Lanham MD: Jason Aronson, 1998.

Levinson, Julian. "People of the (Secular) Book: Literary Anthologies and the Making of Jewish Identity in Postwar America." In *Religion or Ethnicity: Jewish Identities in Transition,* edited by Zvi Gitelman, 131–46. New Brunswick NJ: Rutgers University Press, 2009.

Levy, Karen. "Changing Perceptions, Changing Realities." *Humanistic Judaism* 30, no. 4 (Winter 2002): 14–16.

Lilker, Shalom. *Kibbutz Judaism: A New Tradition in the Making.* East Brunswick NJ: Cornwall Books, 1982.

Longfellow, Henry Wadsworth. *The Prose Work of Henry Wadsworth Longfellow*. London: David Bogue, 1851.

Malkin, Yaakov. *Judaism without God? Judaism as Culture and Bible as Literature*. Jerusalem: Library of Secular Judaism, 2007.

———. "What Makes the Secular Need Spirituality." In *Secular Spirituality: Passionate Journey to a Rational Judaism*, edited by Bonnie Cousens, 161–76. Farmington Hills MI: International Institute for Secular Humanistic Judaism, 2003.

Mendes-Flohr, Paul, and Jehuda Reinharz, eds. *The Jew in the Modern World: A Documentary History*, 2nd ed. New York: Oxford University Press, 1995.

Nadler, Steven. "Spinoza and the Origins of Jewish Secularism." In *Religion or Ethnicity? Jewish Identities in Evolution*, edited by Zvi Gitelman, 59–66. New Brunswick NJ: Rutgers University Press, 2009.

Oz, Amos. *Dear Zealots: Letters from a Divided Land*. Translated by Jessica Cohen. New York: Houghton Mifflin Harcourt, 2018.

———. "A Full Cart or an Empty One?" In *Secular Jewish Culture*, edited by Yaakov Malkin, 17–32. Jerusalem: Library of Secular Judaism, 2017.

———. *In the Land of Israel*. Orlando FL: Harcourt Brace Jovanovich, 1983.

Plaskow, Judith. *Standing Again at Sinai*. New York: HarperCollins, 1990.

Rosen, Aaron. *Imagining Jewish Art: Encounters with the Masters: Chagall, Guston, and Kitaj*. London: Modern Humanities Research Association and Maney Publishing, 2009.

Rubenstein, Richard. *After Auschwitz: Radical Theology and Contemporary Judaism*. Ann Arbor: University of Michigan Press, 1966.

Ruttenberg, Danya. *On Repentance and Repair: Making Amends in an Unapologetic World*. Boston: Beacon Press, 2022.

Schweitzer, Peter. "Modern Kaddish / Glory of Life." In *Here Is Our Light: Humanistic Jewish Holiday and Life-Cycle Liturgy for Inspiration and Reflection*, edited by Miriam Jerris and Sheila Malcolm, 17. Teaneck NJ: Ben Yehuda Press, 2019.

———. "Purpose." In *Contemplation: Humanistic Reflections by Members of The City Congregation*, edited by Carol Sternhell and Ernie Rubinstein, 89–90. New York: The City Congregation for Humanistic Judaism, 2021.

———. "A Rabbi's Journey to Humanistic Judaism." *Sh'ma: A Journal of Jewish Responsibility* 31, no. 573 (June 2000): 2–3.

———. "Symbols." In *The Liberated Haggadah: A Passover Celebration for Cultural, Secular and Humanistic Jews*, 24–27. New York: Center for Cultural Judaism, 2003.

Seid, Judith. *God-Optional Judaism: Alternatives for Cultural Jews Who Love Their History, Heritage, & Community*. Farmington Hills MI: International Institute for Secular Humanistic Judaism, 2018.

Seidman, Naomi. *The Marriage Plot Or, How Jews Fell in Love with Love and with Literature*. Stanford CA: Stanford University Press, 2016.

Shakespeare, William, *Macbeth*. New York: Simon and Schuster, 1992.

Shlain, Tiffany. *24/6: The Power of Unplugging One Day a Week*. New York: Gallery Books, 2019.

Silver, Mitchell. *Respecting the Wicked Child: A Philosophy of Secular Jewish Identity and Education*. Amherst: University of Massachusetts Press, 1998.

Society for Humanistic Judaism. *The Guide to Humanistic Judaism*. Farmington Hills MI: Society for Humanistic Judaism, 2017.

———. *SHJ Recommended Topical Curriculum for Children's Education Programs*. Farmington Hills MI: Society for Humanistic Judaism, 2013.

Stern, David. *Midrash and Theory: Ancient Jewish Exegesis and Contemporary Literary Studies*. Evanston IL: Northwestern University Press, 1998.

Tamburello, Frank. "A Humanist Al Chet (Version 1)." In *Here Is Our Light: Humanistic Jewish Holiday and Life-Cycle Liturgy for Inspiration and Reflection*, edited by Miriam Jerris and Sheila Malcolm, 40–41. Teaneck NJ: Ben Yehuda Press, 2019.

Teutsch, David, ed. *Kol Haneshamah: Shabbat Vehagim*. Elkins Park PA: Reconstructionist Press, 1994.

Toll, Terry. "Lighting Candles." *Humanistic Judaism* 22, no. 2 (Spring 1994): 24.

Tsu, Lao. *Tao Te Ching*. Translated by Gia-Fu Feng and Jane English. New York: Vintage Books, 1972.

Weiss, Dov. *Pious Irreverence: Confronting God in Rabbinic Judaism*. Philadelphia: University of Pennsylvania Press, 2017.

Wine, Sherwin. "Being a Secular Humanistic Jew in the Diaspora." *Humanistic Judaism* 21, no. 2 (Spring 1993): 3–6.

———. "Believing Is Better Than Non-Believing." *Humanistic Judaism* 14, no. 1 (Spring 1986): 7–11.

———. "The Birmingham Temple's First Quarter Century." *Humanistic Judaism* 16, no. 4 (Autumn 1988): 7–8.

———. *Celebration: A Ceremonial and Philosophic Guide for Humanists and Humanistic Jews*. Buffalo NY: Prometheus Books, 1988.

———. *Humanistic Judaism*. Buffalo NY: Prometheus Books, 1978.

———. "Jewish History—Our Humanist Perspective." *Humanistic Judaism* 13, no. 3 (Autumn 1985): 49–53.

———. *Judaism beyond God: A Radical New Way to Be Jewish*. Farmington Hills MI: Society for Humanistic Judaism, 1985.

———. "Judaism without God." *Humanistic Judaism* 11, no. 4 (Winter 1983): 26–31.

———. "Reflections." In *A Life of Courage: Sherwin Wine and Humanistic Judaism*, edited by Dan Cohn-Sherbok, Harry Cook, and Marilyn Rowens, 310. Farmington Hills MI: International Institute for Secular Humanistic Judaism, 2003.

———. "Response." *Humanistic Judaism* 20, no. 3 (Summer 1992): 63–64.

———. "What Could Be More Humanistic than Jewish Humor?" *Humanistic Judaism* 19, no. 3 (Spring 1991): 7–9.

Yerushalmi, Yosef Hayim. *Zakhor: Jewish History and Jewish Memory*. Seattle: University of Washington Press, 1982.

Index

Abraham/Abram, 20, 32, 42, 68, 71, 73, 74, 111, 204, 207
"Abraham and Isaac: In Memory of May 4, 1970 Kent State" (Segal), 118, 144
Adler, Felix, xix, 23
adoption. *See* conversion
Agnon, S. Y., 124
agnostics/agnosticism, 19, 20, 24
Ahad Ha-Am, 130–31
AHR. *See* Association of Humanistic Rabbis (AHR)
Akedah (the Binding of Isaac), 118, 135, 144
aliyah (move to Israel), xx, 99
Aloni, Shulamit: background of, 106; "One Hundred Years of Zionism, Fifty Years of Statehood," 106–10
American Jews, xviii, 10, 69, 73, 99–100, 117, 198–200, 229–31
Amichai, Yehuda, 121, 124, 180–81; background of, 180; "A Man Doesn't Have Time," 180; "The Waters Cannot Return in Repentance," 181
ancestry, xviii, 67–69, 71, 74, 77, 229
Ansky, S., 144

anti-authoritarianism, 8, 17, 25, 76, 83, 202, 208
antisemitism, 45, 61, 75
arguing with religious authority, xxx, 20, 31–32, 41–44
Aristotle, 30
art and artistic creativity, 140–44
Ashkenazic Jews, xxi, 102, 119, 122, 145
Association of Humanistic Rabbis (AHR), xxvii, 188, 192–95; background of, 79; "Statement on Conversion/Adoption," 79–80; "Wedding *Ketubah* Texts," 193–94
atheists/atheism, xxvi, 12–14, 19, 20, 22, 72, 118
authority: challenging of, 31–32, 41–44; God as, xxviii, 208; and king imagery, 174–75; to make ethical decisions, 31–36. *See also* anti-authoritarianism
autonomy, 31–36, 191
Ayfo Oree ("Where Is My Light") (Wine), 147, 167

Babylonian Talmud, 22, 122
baby-welcoming/baby-naming ceremonies, 185, 188

251

Bamford, Joshua Silberstein, 58–59, 61
bar mitzvah/bat mitzvah. *See* b mitzvah
Bauer, Yehuda, 123; background of, 126; "Judaism Is . . . ," 126
belief in God, xxix, 230–31
belonging, xviii, 25, 46, 49, 51, 68, 164, 233n2
Ben-Gurion, David, 105, 123–24
Bialik, Hayim Nachman, 43, 124, 238n15
Bible as literature, 17–21, 123, 132–33, 139
biblical narratives, 126–29, 132–33
Birkat ha-Mazon (grace after meal), 173–74, 242n12
The Birmingham Temple, xxi–xxiv, xxvi, xxxi, 3–4, 7–8, 234n14, 237n4
blessings, 174–79; and Humanistic Judaism, 157–59, 166, 168, 171; and traditional Jewish liturgy, xxii, xxiii, xxvii, xxix, 166, 242n12
b mitzvah, xxvi, xxxiv, 63–64, 178–79, 186, 187–88, 189–92, 208
The Book of Blessings (Falk), 169–70, 235n21
Brenner, Yosef Haim, 43–44, 238n15
The Bund. *See* Jewish Labor Bund

candle lights, 55–57
Central Conference of American Rabbis, 12, 239n3
Chagall, Marc, 141–44
Chalom, Rabbi Adam: "Are There Jewish Values?," 37–41; background of, 36–37, 171; and the Humanistic Judaism Facebook Discussion on Ritual Practice, 59, 61–64; "Our Quarterback, Our King," 168, 172–75; "Rosh Hashana Morning Reading," 177
Chanukah. *See* Hanukkah
chosenness, xxii, 8–9, 87, 169, 241n2
Christians/Christianity, 44, 74, 75, 97, 118, 119, 231, 234n12
circumcision, 185, 187–89
citizenship, 107–8, 175
The City Congregation for Humanistic Judaism, 190–92
Colloquia of the International Institute for Secular Humanistic Judaism, 49, 94, 96–97, 106, 130, 169, 180
commandments. *See* mitzvot (commandments)
Communist ideology, xx–xxi, 198–99
community, xxviii, 164–65; of culture, 51–52; and membership, 51; and practice, boundaries for, 58, 164
Comte-Sponville, André, 47
Conference on Secular Jewish Education. *See* CSJO (Congress of Secular Jewish Organizations)
Confucius, 40
Congregation for Humanistic Judaism of Metro Detroit, xxvii, 234n14. *See also* The Birmingham Temple
consequentialism/consequentialist, 5, 32
contemporary Judaism/Jews, xxv, xxxiii, 38, 68, 163
continuity/discontinuity, xxii, xxxiv, 36, 129, 159, 161, 162–63, 171–72, 176, 185, 193
conversion, 67–69, 70, 72, 74, 78–80, 97, 108
courage, xxxv, 88–90, 213–14

covenant with God, xvii, 67, 188, 189
creativity, xxxiv, 100, 117, 121–23, 140–44, 157–58, 175, 201, 214, 234–35n21
critical thinking, 121, 165, 211
CSJO (Congress of Secular Jewish Organizations), xxvii, 4, 80, 234n14
Cultural and Secular Jewish Organization. *See* CSJO (Congress of Secular Jewish Organizations)
cultural appropriation, 76
cultural heritage, 6, 11, 31, 51–52, 122, 129, 141, 193
cultural Jewish canon, 117–20; as alternative to the traditional religious canon, 122–23; art and artistic creativity, 140–44; and defining Jewish literature, 135–40; and Jewish literature as a mirror, 148–50; and the Jewish writer as interpreter, 152–54; and living Humanistic Judaism, 157; and music, 144–48
cultural Jewish identity, 4, 101, 106, 123, 137, 167, 198–200
cultural Jews/Judaism, xiii, 53, 72, 84, 90, 117, 120, 121–23, 129–31

deism/deists, 10, 19–20
Detroit Jewish News (newspaper), 86–87
Diaspora, 69, 70, 73, 99, 101–5, 109, 119, 148. *See also* Israel; Zionism
dignity, xxx, xxxv, 5, 9, 16–17, 32, 69, 89, 98, 112, 164–65, 191, 213–14
discontinuity. *See* continuity/discontinuity
discrimination, 25, 38, 45, 108–9
Di Shvue (Ansky), 144

diversity, 87, 88, 97, 98, 102, 121–23, 164, 192, 211, 214
divinity, 7, 10, 12–14, 19, 47, 169–70

Ecclesiastes, 20, 180
education: and a community of culture, 51–52; and Humanistic Jewish education, xxxiv, 159–60; and Jewish identity, 75; and Jewish literacy, 200–204; and Jewish values, 37–40; and principles of Humanistic Jewish youth education, 210–12; and the Torah as human creation, 204–8; and transmitting a cultural Jewish identity, 198–200; and Yiddish schools, xviii–xx
Einstein, Albert, 19, 105
Elisha ben Abuya, Rabbi, 122, 236n1
Englander, Nathan, 135; background of, 148; "What We Talk About When We Talk About Anne Frank," 148–50
Enlightenment, xix, 30, 34, 103, 143. *See also* Haskalah (Jewish Enlightenment)
Epicurus, 30
Epstein, Rabbi Greg: background of, 26–27; "What is Humanism?," 27
equality, xxxiii, 45–46, 98, 107, 109, 192–93, 214
Ethical Culture, xix, 23
ethics: application of to lived experience, 44–46; and arguing with religious authority, 31–32, 41–44; and autonomy, 32–36; and consequentialism, 5; and education, 211; human-centered approach to, 5, 30–31, 208; and the Jewish

ethics (*continued*)
  experience, 31, 41, 105; and Jewish values, 36–41; and nonreligious ethics, 30; traditional Jewish approach to, 5–6, 13, 30; and the Zionist ideal, 107
ethno-religion, 67–69

Facebook Humanistic Judaism Discussion Group, 58–64
Falick, Rabbi Jeffrey: background of, 90–91; "Dancing at Two Weddings," 91–92
Falk, Marcia, 168, 182, 235n21; background of, 169–70; *The Book of Blessings*, 169–70, 235n21; "Honoring Torah," 170–71; *Night of Beginnings*, 182
Feldman, Ruth Duskin: background of, 202; "Jewish Education and the Future," 202–4
food, 117–20
freedom, xxx, 9, 32–36, 52, 127, 165, 183, 184, 191, 214
Friedman, Rabbi Daniel, 4, 61; "After Halakha, What?," 33–36; background of, 32–33, 127; "Recovering Our Stories," 123, 127–29
Friedmann, Jonathan L., 135; background of, 145; "Music by, for, as Humanistic Jews," 145–48
funerals. *See* memorial

gender equality, 39, 187, 189
God/god, 233n1; and agnosticism, 24; and American Jews' belief in, 230–31; arguing with, xxx, 20, 31–32, 42–44, 204; awe before, 59–60; and consistency between belief and liturgy, 171–75; and contemporary liturgy, 169; covenant with, xvii, 67, 68, 188, 241n6, 241n7; and halakha (Jewish religious law), 34; and Humanistic Jewish education, 211; in Humanistic Jewish thought, xxviii–xxxi; and Jewish history, 8, 9, 13, 14, 24; and king imagery, 174–75; as literary character, 17–21, 233n1; and nonreligious ethics, 30, 34; redefinitions of, xxii, 5, 10–15, 172–74; and shivah mourning rituals, 194–95
God language, xxii, xxviii, 157–59, 169
God of the Bible, xvii–xviii, 10–12, 230–31
Golden Calf, 208–10
Goldfinger, Rabbi Eva, xxxiii; background of, 162; "Is Judaism Worth Preserving?," 162–63
Golin, Paul, 59, 62–63, 96
Gordon, A. D., 43, 238n15
Goren, Judith, xxii–xxiii
Greeley, Andrew, 127–29
Grunberg, Camila: background of, 190; "The Meaning of Life," 190–92
Guide to Humanistic Judaism, xxxi, 58–64

Haggadah/Haggadot, 132, 140, 143, 158, 182–84
halakha/halakhah (Jewish religious law), xxv, 19, 33–36, 108, 124
Handlarski, Rabbi Denise: background of, 44–45, 208–9; "The Torah, the Ten Commandments and Us," 209–10; "Truth and Reconciliation on Race," 45–46
Hanukkah, xx, xxiv, 119, 145, 167

Haroset, 183–84
Harrison, Courtney, 58–59, 60
Haskalah (Jewish Enlightenment), 3, 135
Hatikvah (Imber), 144
Hava Nagila (Idelsohn), 144
Hebrew, xix–xxi, 73, 100, 132, 158, 171, 175, 186, 190, 197, 212, 235n29. *See also* Jewish languages
Hebrew Bible, xxii, xxxiv, 5, 17, 126–29, 134–35, 212
Hebrew literature, xxvi, 135–36, 153, 186, 190
Hebrews, 16, 172, 207
Herzl, Theodor, 71, 105
High Holidays, 29, 167–68. *See also* Rosh Hashanah; Yom Kippur
Hillel, Rabbi, 40, 215
Holocaust, 9, 13–14, 75, 77, 136, 149
human condition, xxviii, 11, 17, 23, 42, 127, 198, 205
humanism, 72, 85, 91; in Humanistic Jewish thought, xxviii–xxx; and the Jewish experience, 7–9, 41; and Judaism, 90, 92, 105; and positive humanism, 5, 22–29, 52, 121; and religious humanism, 23, 81–82; and the Zionist ideal, 107
Humanistic Judaism, xvii–xviii, 3–6, 117–20, 157–60; and biblical narratives, 126–29, 132, 208–10; and The Birmingham Temple, xxii–xxiv, xxvi, xxxi–xxxii; and b mitzvahs, 189–92; and candle lights, 55–57; and circumcision, 188–89; and the conversion/adoption process, 78–80; as cosmopolitan and particular, 45, 90–92, 235n30; creation of, xxi–xxvi, 237n4; and cultural Judaism, 121–23; and Diaspora, 100–105; and diversity, 52–55, 97–98; and education, xxxiv, 159, 197–212; and ethics, 30–46; and evolution of Humanistic Jewish practice, 57–64; and intermarriage, 77, 92–98, 186; and Israel/Palestine, 99, 105–13; and Jewish identity, xxviii–xxix, xxxii–xxxiii, 11, 68–70, 72–80, 136–37; and Jewish literacy, 159, 199, 200–204, 205; and life-cycle celebrations and rituals, 185–96; and liturgy, xxiv, 175–79; and music, 144–48; as a organized movement, xxvi–xxviii; and positive humanism, 22–29; religion label for, 80–85; and rituals, 55–64; and shivah mourning rituals, 194–96; and spirituality, 47–64, 204; and symbols, 59–64, 182–84; and the Torah, xvii, xix, xxxiv, 31, 38, 60–63, 131, 139, 170–71, 204–10; welcoming and inclusion in, 86–98; and Zionism, 70, 99–113, 130–33. *See also* Society for Humanistic Judaism (SHJ)
Humanistic Judaism (journal), 8, 12–13, 32, 36–37, 44–45, 87, 88, 97, 171, 195
Humanistic rabbis, 57–58, 81, 95, 168, 192–95
Humanist Manifesto (1933), 22–23
human rights, xxix, 8, 11, 31, 69, 99, 107, 164–65

Idelsohn, Abraham Zvi, 144, 148
idolatry, 140–41, 209
IFSHJ. *See* International Federation of Secular Humanistic Jews (IFSHJ)

ignosticism, 12
IISHJ. *See* International Institute for Secular Humanistic Judaism (IISHJ)
illuminated manuscripts, 143
Imber, Naftali, 144
inclusion, 86–98, 121–22
individualism, 32–36, 103
inspiration, 47–48, 53, 56, 148, 180
integrity, xi, xxii, 3, 70, 77, 135, 158, 166, 168, 172, 175, 185, 194, 199, 206, 211, 213–14
interfaith and intercultural families. *See* intermarriage
intermarriage, xxxii–xxxiii, 77, 86–88, 92–97, 103, 186
International Federation of Secular Humanistic Jews (IFSHJ), xxvii, 101, 202–4, 234n14; background of, 76; "Choosing to Live as a Secular Humanistic Jew," 213–14; "Who is a Jew," 77–78
International Institute for Secular Humanistic Judaism (IISHJ), xxvii, 4, 7, 49, 80, 87, 95, 96–97, 169, 188
International Worker's Order, xx
Islam/Muslims, 44, 75
Israel, xvii–xviii, xix, 99–113; and American Jews, 99–100; and Humanistic Judaism, 99–100; and Israeli Jews, xviii, 68, 100; as a Jewish and democratic state, 105–10; and Jewish identity, 67–70, 73, 77; and Palestine, 110–13; and a world people, 101–4

Jeremiah, 20
Jerris, Rabbi Miriam: background of, 93–94; "Gate Openers: Reaching Out to the Next Generation of Children from Intermarriage," 94–97
Jesus, 29, 39
Jewish art and artists, 140–44
Jewish civilization, 105, 124–25, 126, 163, 199
Jewish continuity, xxii, 36, 159, 161–63, 171, 176, 185, 193
Jewish cultural literacy, 127–29, 159, 199, 200–204, 205
Jewish culture, xxxiii–xxxiv, 100, 117–20, 121–23, 131; and education, 197–212; as human creation, xxv, 161, 204–8; and Jewish art and artists, 140–44; and Jewish identity, xxxiv, 69, 76, 134–35, 157, 164, 214; and literature, 135–40, 148–54; and music, 144–48; and religion, 124–25, 126. *See also* Jewish identity
Jewish experience, 7–9, 40–41, 104–5, 118, 141
Jewish feminism, 158, 169, 182, 235n21
Jewish history, xxv–xxvi, 213–14; and continuity, 162–63; and the Diaspora, 102–5; and Jewish cultural context, 8–9; and Jewish values, 40–41; and Judaism without God, 13–14; message of, xxx, 9, 41; and secular Jewish education, 200, 211; and the Torah, 205–8, 209, 212
Jewish holidays, xx–xxi, xxiv–xxv, 81, 118, 158, 167–68
Jewish identity, xxi–xxvi, xxviii–xxix, xxxii–xxxiii, 67–70, 117–20, 234n12; and American Jews' identity and beliefs, xiii, xviii, 117, 229–31, 233n3; and baby-welcoming ceremonies,

256 Index

185; and Bible stories, 127–28, 206–8; and boundaries, xvii, xxxii, 68, 70; and circumcision, 188–89; as cultural inheritance, 124–25, 175; in the Diaspora, 102–5; and Humanistic Jewish education, 199–200, 203, 211; and intermarriage, 77, 95–97; and Jewish culture, 121–23, 134–35; and Jewish literature, 135–40, 148; and secular and orthodox in one family, 150–52; and self-definition, 71–85

Jewish inheritance, xxxi, xxxiii–xxxiv, 42–44, 118, 123–25, 127, 129–31, 157

Jewish Labor Bund, xx, 106, 144

Jewish languages, xxv, 73, 135–36, 158, 212, 214. *See also* Hebrew; Ladino; Yiddish

Jewish literature, xvii, 25, 118, 134–40, 148–54

Jewish liturgical poetry, 179–81

Jewishness, xxxiii, 234n12; and ancestry, 68–69; and assumption that Jewishness may be ethnic, xix; and the conversion/adoption process, 78; ethno-religious consensus of, xxiv, 67, 71; and Jewish identity, xviii, xxix, 77, 150; and Jewish literature, 136, 139–40; and Jewish peoplehood, 72–73

Jewish peoplehood, xxviii, xxx, xxxii, 55, 70, 72–75, 76, 100

Jewish socialists, xx–xxi, 99, 106, 198–99

The Jewish State (Herzl), 71

Jewish tradition, xxv; of argument, 31–32, 41–42; and cultural Judaism, 121–23, 130–33; of god-redefinition,

xxii, 5, 10–15; Jewish choice as, 129–33; and rituals, 55–56; and shivah mourning rituals, 194–95; values in, 37–39; and weddings, 119, 192–93

Jews by Choice. *See* conversion

Jews by religion, 100, 230–31, 233n3

Jews of no religion, xviii, 100, 230–31, 233n3

Job, 17, 20, 42–43, 128, 134

Judaism, 126, 164; and biblical narratives, 127–28; beyond God, Torah, and Israel, xvii–xviii; and humanism, 90–92, 105; and modernity, 34, 70, 123, 134; preservation of, 162–63; as a religion of memory, 75, 134

Judaism beyond God (Wine), 12, 73–75, 205–8

Judaism without God, 11, 12, 18

justice, xxx, 31, 43, 131, 191, 211, 214

Kaddish memorial prayer, xxiii, 11, 159, 179, 194, 201, 243n6

Kafka, Franz, 136, 139

Kant, Immanuel, 30, 40

Kaplan, Rabbi Mordecai, xxii, 12, 104, 169, 233n2, 241n2

Katznelson, Berl, 43, 238n15

Keret, Etgar, 135; background of, 150; "My Lamented Sister," 150–52

keriah (ritual tearing of clothing), 187

Kerlitz, Rabbi Avraham Yeshayahu, 124

ketubah/ketubot, 188, 192–94

kibbutz movement Judaism, 100, 157, 234–35n21

kinship, 73–75, 229–31

kippah/kippot (skullcaps), xxxi, 58, 60–62

Klausner, Amos. *See* Oz, Amos
Klein, Jen Naparstek, 59, 63
Kol Haneshamah prayer book, 11
Kol Nidrei, 22, 158
Kolton, Rabbi Tamara: background of, 88; "Healing the Jewish People through Pluralism," 89–90
Kornfeld, Rabbi Jodi, 135; background of, 140, 176; "B Mitzvah: Reading Before the Torah," 177; "Of Course There's Jewish Art!," 141–44
Krauss, Nicole, 135; "Adding to the Jewish Story," 152–54; background of, 152
Kridel, Rabbi Jeremy, 59, 63, 176–78
Kushner, Rabbi Harold, 12, 14

Labor Zionist Farband, xix–xx
Labor Zionist ideology, 198–99
Ladino, 101, 105, 122, 136, 158. *See also* Jewish languages
Lao Tsu, 40
Leadership Conference of Secular and Humanistic Jews (LCSHJ), xxvii, 7, 242n1; background on, 188; "Statement on Circumcision and Jewish Identity," 189
Levinson, Julian, 135; background of, 136–37; "People of the (Secular) Book," 137–40
Levy, Rabbi Karen: background of, 81–82; "Changing Perceptions, Changing Realities," 82–85
LGBTQ, xxix, 68, 98, 122, 182
liberal Judaism(s), xxxiii, 10–11, 31, 69, 73, 93, 110, 162, 169, 171. *See also* Reconstructionist (Reconstructing) Judaism; Reform Judaism; Renewal Judaism
liberal theology, 172–75
The Liberated Haggadah (Schweitzer), 182
life-cycle celebrations and rituals, xxxiv, 157–59, 185–96, 214; and b mitzvahs, 63–64, 178–79, 186, 189–92; and candle lighting, 55–57; and circumcision, 185, 188–89; and funerals, 159, 179, 187; and *ketubot*, 192–94; and poetry, 179, 185–87; and shivah mourning rituals, 187, 194–96; and weddings, 119, 159, 186
Lipchitz, Jacques, 141–42
The Little Book of Atheist Spirituality (Comte-Spoonville), 47
liturgy, xxiv, 157–60; and The Birmingham Temple, xxii–xxiv; God language in, xxii, xxviii, 11, 171–75; and Jewish holidays, 167–68; and liberal theology, 172–75; and liturgical integrity, 166; and poetry as secular liturgy, 120, 179–82; and Reconstructionist (Reconstructing) Judaism, xxii, 11, 166, 169; and Reform Judaism, xxv, 11, 166, 173; and secular Jewish identity, xviii–xix; and service structure, xxiii, 166–67
Lubavitcher *Rebbe*, 14

Maas, Rabbi Sivan Malkin, 59, 123; background of, 129–30; "Cultural Zionism: Reclaiming Convention," 130–33
Madrikh/Vegvayzer/Leader Program, 188

Malkin, Yaakov, xxviii, 11–12, 42, 64; background of, 17; "God as a Literary Figure," 18–21; "What Makes the Secular Need Spirituality," 49–52
Margolin, Anna, 136
Maror, 118, 183
marriage. *See* weddings
matrilineal descent, 68–69, 72, 76
Matzah/Matzoh, 60, 61, 118, 183
meaning and purpose, xxxiii, 28–29, 59
melekh (king), 11, 171, 174, 176, 242n12
memorial, 179, 187, 194
memory, 75, 134
Michigan Board of Rabbis, 87, 95
Mill, John Stuart, 30
Mishkan T'filah, 11
Mishnah, 38
mitzvot (commandments), xxix–xxxi, 5, 16, 19, 30–31, 48, 55, 60–61, 67, 201, 208–10
mixed marriages, 93, 239n3. *See also* intermarriage
Mizrahi (Jews from the Orient) Jews, 36, 119
modernity, 34, 70, 123, 134
modern Jewish writers, 152–54
Modigliani, Amadeo, 143
Molodowsky, Kayla, 136
morality/moral values, xxiv, 13–21, 30, 34–35, 107
Mr. Mani (Yehoshua), 134–35
music, 54, 118–19, 144–48

naming ceremonies, 185, 188, 189
nationalism, 67, 69, 106, 108
Nevelson, Louise, 143

"new Jew," 22
Night of Beginnings (Falk), 182
Nizkor/Yizkor, 158
non-believers. *See* unbelievers
non-Jews, xxix, 39, 49, 143, 146
non-Orthodox Judaism, xviii, 68, 93, 162
non-theism/non-theistic, 81, 106, 211
nostalgia, 146, 171
novels, 137–39, 152

Oppenheim, Moritz, 142–43
orange on seder plate, 184
Orthodox Jews/Judaism, xxxii, 25, 35, 39, 68, 92, 148, 150–52, 230, 231
Oz, Amos, xxx, xxxiii; background of, 41–42, 124; "A Full Cart or an Empty One? Thoughts on Jewish Culture," 124–25; "Jews Argue With God," 42–44

Palestine/Palestinians, 99, 110–13
pantheists, 19–20
particularism, xix, xxxiii, 87, 90–92
Passover, xx, xxv, 73, 118, 119, 168, 182, 199
Passover Haggadah. *See Haggadah/Haggadot*
Peretz, Y. L., 204
personal God, xxii, xxviii–xxix, 3, 15, 17, 111, 129, 157–59, 169, 171
Pesach, 182–83
Pew survey of American Jews, xiii, xviii, 100, 117, 229–31, 233n3
philosophy, 8, 30, 48; and consistency, 49, 171–72; and humanism, xxviii, 7, 72, 90–92; and Humanistic Jewish

philosophy (*continued*)
  education, 210–12; and Humanistic Judaism, xxi, xxiv, xxxiii, 4, 23, 31, 64, 167, 201
Pissarro, Camille, 142
Pittsburgh Platform of Reform Judaism, 61, 71
Plaskow, Judith, 12
Plato, 20–21
pluralism, 87–90, 214
poetry, 120, 179–81
popular culture, 69, 75, 145
positive humanism, 5, 22–29, 52, 121
priests, 8, 9, 163, 184, 206–8
prophets, 8, 9, 42, 109, 163

Rabbinic Judaism, 34, 71, 163, 195–96, 206–8
rabbinic literature, xxxiv, 5, 10, 134, 136
race/racism, 45, 46, 67, 74, 108, 164, 165
Rachel the poetess, 124
radical inclusion, xxxiii, 98, 122
reason, 24–25, 30, 34, 41, 46, 50, 103, 165, 205, 213
Reconstructionist (Reconstructing) Judaism, xxii, xxiv, 61–62, 87, 158, 169, 179, 235n21
redefining God, xxii, 5, 10–15
Reform Judaism, xxv, 3–4, 67, 86–87, 99, 158, 168–69, 173–74, 179, 206, 230–31. *See also* Pittsburgh Platform of Reform Judaism
religious humanism, 23, 81–82
Rembrandt, 142
Renewal Judaism, 49, 174–75
ritual(s), 58–64. *See also* life-cycle celebrations and rituals

Ritual Committee of The Birmingham Temple, xxii–xxiv
rooted cosmopolitanism, xxxiii, 235–36n30
Rosenblum, April, xx
Rosenfeld, Max, 53–54
Rosh Hashanah, xxi, xxiv, 167, 177–78, 180
Rothko, Mark, 143
Rowens, Marilyn, 54
Rubenstein, Richard, 14

Sabbath. *See* Shabbat
Sabbath Services in the spirit of a humanistic Judaism, xxii–xxiv
same-sex marriages, 93. *See also* LGBTQ
Santayana, George, 54
Sarah, 68, 71, 74
Schweitzer, Rabbi Peter: background of, 28; "Funeral: Modern Kaddish," 179; "Passover Symbols," 182–84; "Purpose," 28–29
Second Commandment, 140, 141
secular approach, xx, xxvi, 22, 204, 206
secular Humanistic Judaism, xxvii, 17, 80–85, 96, 102–5, 163, 213–14
secular humanists, 49–52, 55, 64
secularism, xx, 102–3, 124, 199
secular Israelis, xxxii, 69, 100, 130, 135
secularization, xviii, xix, 30–31, 134, 230
secular Jewish culture, 18–19, 25, 101–5, 120, 122–23, 137–40, 148, 200, 238n15
secular Jews/Judaism, xviii–xxi, xxiv, xxxii, 121–23; in the Diaspora, 104–5; and early leaders in Humanistic Judaism, 86; and Jewish identity, 69; and Jewish inheritance,

xviii, 123–24; and negative self-definition, 23, 121; and Orthodox Jews/Judaism, 150; and secular Jewish education, 198–204; and secular Jewish schools/organizations, xx, xxi, xxvii, 76; and spirituality, 49–52. *See also* Humanistic Judaism

secular spirituality, 48–52

Segal, George, 118, 143–44

Seid, Rabbi Judith: background of, 52–53; "A Secular Spirituality," 53–55

self-actualization, 32, 167

self-definition, 68–69, 71–85, 136–37, 152

self-determination, xxix, 13, 31, 76

self-identification. *See* self-definition

"Self-Portrait with Seven Fingers" (Chagall), 144

Sephardic Jews, 119

Shabbat, 7–8, 25, 167, 176–77

Shakespeare, William, 128

Shapira, Tzvi Herman, 130–31

Shavuot, 127, 168

shivah mourning rituals, 187, 188, 194–96

SHJ. *See* Society for Humanistic Judaism (SHJ)

Sholem Aleichem (Shalom Rabinowitz), 134, 136

Sholem Aleichem Folk Institute, xix

siddur (prayer book), xxii, 158, 166–67, 175, 179, 241n2

Silver, Mitchell, xxxiv; background of, 199; "Treasures of the Legacy," 199–200

Simchat Torah, xxvi, 167

skepticism, 24–25, 83, 101

slavery, xxix, 38–39, 183

social justice, xx, 164, 165, 191, 214

Society for Humanistic Judaism (SHJ), xxvii–xxviii; background of, 4, 97, 237n4; and conversion/adoption, 79; Curriculum for Children's Education, "Philosophy," 210–12; and the Facebook Humanistic Judaism Discussion Group, 58–64; and Humanistic Jewish youth education, 210–12; and Rabbi Sherwin Wine, 7; "Radical Inclusion," xxxiii, 98; "SHJ Stands With Israel," 110; "Statement of Values," 164–65

Song of Songs, 139

Spinoza, Baruch, 19, 105, 122

spirituality, 47–64, 84, 204, 214; diversity in, 48–55; and the human need for inspiration, xxx, 6, 48–52; and the reframing of traditional rituals, 55–57

study, 78, 186, 214

Sukkot, 167

symbols, 56, 59–64, 118, 182–84, 187, 209

tallit/tallis, 59–63, 118, 187

Talmud, 40, 118, 122, 126, 139, 203, 204

Tamburello, Frank, 176, 178–79

TANAKH. *See* Hebrew Bible

Thompson, William, 58, 59–60

tikkun olam (repair of the world), xxx, 45–46, 198

Tmura-IISHJ, xxvii, 4, 17–18

Toll, Terry, xxxi; background of, 56; "Lighting Candles," 56–57

Torah, xvii, xix, xxxiv, 31, 38, 60–63, 131, 139, 170–71, 204–10

Index 261

Torah scroll, xxvi, 62, 190, 208
traditional Judaism, 23, 52, 58, 92, 162, 172, 198, 201–2

unbelievers, 22–26, 121
Unitarian Universalism, 23
universalism, xxxiii, 87, 90–92, 143; and human identity and needs, xix, 26, 166; and human lessons and experiences, 128–29, 164–65

values, 22, 31–32, 69–70, 157–60, 161–62, 164–65; and creation of Humanistic Judaism, xxv–xxvi; and cultural Judaism, 121–22; and cultural Zionism, 131–33; and diversity, 87, 97–98, 121, 211; and humanism, 27, 41, 211; and Humanistic Jewish youth education, 210–12; and *ketubot*, 192–94; and life-cycle celebrations and rituals, 185; and liturgy of Humanistic Judaism, 166; and the Torah, 204–5; and the Zionist ideal, 107, 109

weddings, 86–87, 93, 186
welcoming. *See* radical inclusion
"Who is a Jew?" question, 68, 76–78, 86, 95
Wine, Rabbi Sherwin, xxi–xxvi, xxx, 3–4, 7–9; *Ayfo Oree* ("Where Is My Light"), 147, 167; background of, xxi–xxii, 7; "Being a Secular Humanistic Jew in the Diaspora," 101–5; "Believing Is Better Than Non-Believing," 23–26; *Celebration*, 175; and courage, xxxv, 88; and interfaith weddings and families, 87; "Jewish History—Our Humanist Perspective," 8–9; and Jewish peoplehood, 72–75; and Jewish values, 37, 39, 41; *Judaism beyond God*, 12, 73–75, 205–8; "Judaism without God," xxviii, 13–17; "Kinship," 73–75; "Sitting Shiva," 195–96; in *Time* magazine, xxvi; "The Torah," 205–8
Workmen's Circle/Arbeter Ring, xx

Yahveh/Yahweh/YHVH/YHWH, 11, 13, 17, 18, 20–21, 128, 172, 176
Yehoshua, A. B., 134–35
Yiddish: language and culture, xviii–xxi, 3, 101–2, 158; literature, 134–35; schools and camps, xix–xx, xxvii, 198–99; theater, 134; and Yiddishism, 67. *See also* Jewish languages
Yom Kippur, xxi, xxiv, xxvi, 22, 52, 117, 121, 158, 167, 178, 180
Yoreh, Rabbi Tzemah: background of, 110–11; "Constructive Conversations about Israel," 111–12

Zionism: and anti-Zionists, 110; and cultural Zionism, 130–33; and the Humanistic Jewish identification with Israel, 105–10; and Israel/Palestine, 110–13; and Jewish identity, 67–68; and positive commitment to a global Jewish identity, 101–5

In the JPS Anthologies of Jewish Thought Series

Exile and the Jews: Literature, History, and Identity
Edited by Nancy E. Berg
and Marc Saperstein

Modern Responsa: An Anthology of Jewish Ethical and Ritual Decisions
Pamela Barmash

Contemporary Humanistic Judaism: Beliefs, Values, Practices
Edited by Adam Chalom
and Jodi Kornfeld

Modern Musar: Contested Virtues in Jewish Thought
Geoffrey D. Claussen

Modern Conservative Judaism: Thought and Practice
Elliot N. Dorff
Foreword by Julie Schonfeld

Modern Orthodox Judaism: A Documentary History
Zev Eleff
Foreword by Jacob J. Schacter

A Kabbalah and Jewish Mysticism Reader
Daniel M. Horwitz

Modern Jewish Theology: The First One Hundred Years, 1835–1935
Edited by Samuel J. Kessler
and George Y. Kohler

The Growth of Reform Judaism: American and European Sources
W. Gunther Plaut
Foreword by Jacob K. Shankman
New introduction by
Howard A. Berman
New epilogue by David Ellenson
With select documents, 1975–2008

The Rise of Reform Judaism: A Sourcebook of Its European Origins
W. Gunther Plaut
Foreword by Solomon B. Freehof
New introduction by
Howard A. Berman

The Zionist Ideas: Visions for the Jewish Homeland—Then, Now, Tomorrow
Gil Troy

To order or obtain more information on these or other Jewish Publication Society titles, visit jps.org.

Works by Adam Chalom

Introduction to Secular Humanistic Judaism: Part I—Jewish History (International Institute for Secular Humanistic Judaism, 2002)

Introduction to Secular Humanistic Judaism: Part II—Jewish Culture (International Institute for Secular Humanistic Judaism, 2007)

Introduction to Secular Humanistic Judaism: Part III—Philosophy of Secular Humanistic Judaism (International Institute for Secular Humanistic Judaism, 2009)

Jews and the Muslim World: Solving the Puzzle (International Institute for Secular Humanistic Judaism, 2010) (editor)

www.ingramcontent.com/pod-product-compliance
Lightning Source LLC
Chambersburg PA
CBHW021820300426
44114CB00009BA/250